TROPHIES
AND SCARS

TROPHIES AND SCARS

RAY EVERNHAM

AS TOLD TO JOE GARNER

FOREWORDS BY
JEFF GORDON, RICK HENDRICK, AND ROGER PENSKE

Octane Press, Edition 1.0, March 2024
Copyright © 2024 by Ray Evernham Enterprises LLC

On the cover: Ray Evernham. *Nigel Kinrade*

On the front endpapers: My first feature win was in
June 1976. I was eighteen years old and sporting
some sideburns. *Ray Evernham Enterprises Archives*

On the back endpapers: Competing at Pikes Peak was the most
incredible thing I've ever done in a race car. *Larry Chen*

Hardcover ISBN: 978-1-64234-146-1
Softcover ISBN: 978-1-64234-177-5
ePub ISBN: 978-1-64234-149-2

Library of Congress Control Number: 2023949049

Copyedited by Faith Garcia
Designed by Tom Heffron
Proofread by Dana Henricks

octanepress.com

Octane Press is based in Austin, Texas

Printed in China

This book is dedicated to all of those who picked me
up and told me I could when I thought I couldn't.

CONTENTS

Contents

TOUCH THE SKY

By Jeff Gordon

I've been very fortunate throughout both my personal and professional life to have had two guys at my side. They are among the smartest, hardest-working, most disciplined, most honest, reliable, principled, and trustworthy people I've ever known.

One is my stepfather, John Bickford.

The other I consider my older brother and one of my best friends, Ray Evernham. Without a doubt, I wouldn't be where I am today if either hadn't shown up in my life.

John put me in the car when I was five. He also nurtured and coached me through every stage of my early racing career, from quarter midgets to sprints to stock cars. John, along with my mom, Carol, selflessly sacrificed in ways only the most loving and supportive parents do in order to get me to the threshold of my NASCAR racing career with Hendrick Motorsports.

Then, through a chance meeting, they passed the baton to Ray, whose unmatched ingenuity, inspiring leadership, and relentless work ethic helped further unleash my talent as a NASCAR Cup driver. Together we reached heights neither of us ever imagined possible.

Believe me, if I hadn't lived it, I'd have thought it was fiction.

I was thrilled when Ray told me he'd decided to share his story. Now you'll have the chance to get to know him like few of us do.

When most people think of Ray Evernham, they think aggressively intense and beyond demanding.

While most of that's accurate, or at least it was back when we raced the No. 24, it's an unfair characterization and out of context. When we raced, we adopted the slogan "Refuse to Lose." (You can only transform that from catchphrase to championship if you take it seriously and don't allow any-thing—or anyone—to distract your focus.) Also, as the expression goes, Ray did not suffer fools gladly—either in the No. 24 shop or in the pits.

Oh, and you can add laziness and excuse makers to that list.

Yet his intensity, innate boundary-pushing mechanical skill, and inspiring team-building style forever changed our sport, as well as the record books, as evidenced by our shelves full of trophies, honors, and championships.

It's funny. He reminded me recently how he'd never been a crew chief until he became mine. Well, the fact is, I'd never been a Cup driver until I became his Cup driver.

The other thing we share, which again, I only recently discovered, is both of us were motivated to do our jobs to the very best of our abilities due to a deep desire not to disappoint the other. We each respected how hard we knew the other worked and how determined we were to win every race. There was no way either of us would allow ourselves to be the weak link.

But nobody worked harder than Ray.

While he had high expectations for our team, Ray possessed even higher expectations for himself. He also took full responsibility for any mistake made by the team.

I realize now Ray was not just knowledgeable about race car mechanics, he was also a savvy leader. He studied leadership. Ray knew how to motivate and guide our team. I admired those qualities because I didn't have such natural ability. I'm confident I can lead when required, but I struggled with setting goals and planning the team's objectives. Ray had a clear plan and vision, and everyone on the team respected him for it.

I knew I could learn a lot from Ray. When we first connected, I trusted he'd always put me in the best race car. Ray was unbeatable when it came to delivering the finest race car and race team, especially with the resources Rick provided us. And he had the same level of trust in me. I knew when I told him what was going on with the car he would listen to every word and do whatever it took to fix it. And if he gave me advice on how to approach a race or a pit stop, I had absolute faith in him.

The only time I ever questioned Ray's decision was when it came to adjusting the track bar. After a few years of working together and having some success, I became sensitive to any changes made to this component.

Ray would even joke about it. "Jeff, I only lowered it a quarter of an inch. It couldn't have made that big of a difference."

Still, I knew when the track bar went up, I didn't like how it felt. When Ray put it back down, I swear it was better.

I used to tell him, "Hey buddy. My butt doesn't lie."

Our 1998 season was the epitome of our career together. It's still one of the most successful seasons of any team in NASCAR history. We dominated in laps led, wins, and top fives, and we clinched the championship prior to the last race under the old points system. That season was a game changer for NASCAR. Literally.

Our success changed the sport.

However, it was also the peak of our career. Heading into the 1999 season, we asked ourselves, "Where do we go from here?"

We'd accomplished one of the greatest seasons in NASCAR history, and we had to maintain our competitive edge. Ray believed the only way we could do that was by finding new areas of the car to engineer. He believed our competitors were going to catch up to us mechanically. We had to maintain that competitive gap.

Unfortunately, we started having failures and problems, and our relationship also suffered. As for me, I would have been fine holding back a little if it meant giving us a chance at winning more races and championships. Ray had a different philosophy in mind, and that led to our relationship deteriorating. We were victims of our own success.

But that wasn't the only reason.

We had each allowed certain people and influences into our respective lives, and our magic dimmed. If we had been able to see it, I'm convinced there would have been many more trophies for Ray, me, and the No. 24 team. Because of our bond, we could have worked through our differences, maybe with one of Rick Hendrick's famous "milk and cookie" sit-downs.

Instead, we went our separate ways.

In the end, it worked out well for both of us, and we have a great relationship today. Ray and I spend more time together, and have more fun now, than we ever did when we worked together. And we have more in common than I realized.

Though we're older, our confidence and competitiveness haven't diminished one bit. That was clear to all who watched us race in the Porsche Cup Series at Indianapolis over Labor Day weekend, September 2022. It didn't take for the spark to be triggered—as if we were right back to the good old days. We proved we still had it.

And who knows, maybe more races to come.

Ray and I share a relentless competitive nature. We used to have a basketball arcade game in the No. 24 shop. I played it every time I was there. I know it sounds obsessive, but I had to earn the high score. It really used to bug the hell out of me if anyone ever topped it. But it annoyed Ray even more, since I refused to meet with him until I put the high score back on the board.

Ray and I also share a love of sprint car racing, and we try to get to Knoxville Raceway whenever we can. Across from the track, since 1956, is a cool little self-described dive bar called Dingus. In addition to the tasty food and cold beers, they have some fun bar games. One night after the races, Ray and I went in for a burger and beer. Not surprisingly, we got into a beanbag toss battle with a couple of other guys. We played until they kicked us out late in the evening.

We weren't leaving until we'd beat them—mercilessly.

With few exceptions, when Ray and I were racing, our relationship was pretty much all business. If we were together, it was because we were either testing, racing, or in the shop figuring out how to make the car go faster. Now I love being around him because we get to relax, enjoy his special cocktail concoction, the "Lima Rita," tell stories, smile. These days when I'm around Ray, I just smile and laugh a lot.

Moreover, I think we both have gotten to a place in our lives where we can enjoy our success. As Ray has gotten older, he's become humbler and more sensitive. He focuses on being a good husband to his wife Erin, and a good father to his son Ray J. and his daughter Cate.

Sometimes we have a certain view of someone based on what we see on TV or how we've interacted with them. Yet, when you dive into someone's story and really get into the details, you get to know them in a whole new way. On a human level, there's not a whole lot that separates us.

As the title of this book suggests, Ray's story is about more than winning races and trophies. It's about facing life's many challenges and disappointments, and finding opportunity even in failure. The "scars," as he puts it. Most of which he shares with unbridled honesty.

You may be surprised to learn Ray is just an everyday guy, one with a unique ability to work on another level. He's humble and appreciative, and you'll love hearing how he worked in the gray area to achieve success.

Ray's story will inspire you to chase your own dreams relentlessly. It will also remind you that with hard work, determination, and perseverance, anything is possible. So go ahead and immerse yourself in Ray's journey. Let it fuel your own passion in life.

THE RAY I KNOW

By Rick Hendrick

I want to begin by sharing one of my favorite memories of Ray Evernham. It was the moment I realized I'd hired an innovator who would go on to revolutionize NASCAR. Shortly after Ray came on board, I was driving down the road that leads into Hendrick Motorsports where there was a large open field. A group of guys were running wind sprints and doing calisthenics. I was thinking to myself, who are these people, and what are they doing on my property?

It wasn't a football team that got their practice location wrong—it was the pit crew Ray was building and training, the Rainbow Warriors. These were genuine athletes. Before Ray came along, you'd sometimes see crew members smoking cigarettes after they changed a tire. Today, you only see the type of competitors Ray introduced to the sport. That's just one example of how he changed NASCAR, but it's always stuck with me.

When Ray takes on any project or challenge, he gives 100 percent. He never does anything halfway. When we were racing, Ray was like a general going to war. He laid out a battle plan and then executed it better than anyone else. It's an awe-inspiring thing to witness, especially when he's on your side.

Ray's a perfectionist and a forward thinker. Of course, I didn't know that when I hired him, I just knew what my gut was telling me. I knew that Jeff Gordon believed in him, and Ray believed in Jeff. Although Ray may have been leery of taking the crew chief job in the beginning, I could see he had a natural instinct for what it took to synchronize the car, Jeff, and the team. Add in his take-no-prisoners competitive nature and it's little wonder we had such incredible success for all those years.

From the beginning of his time with Hendrick Motorsports, Ray did things differently. I don't mind admitting I learned a few things about management from him. Instead of just taking someone and sticking them into a role that needed to be filled, Ray would create a detailed job description and then find the right person to fit that role. He surrounded himself with people who had the same enthusiasm and goals he had. If you weren't in all the way, then you didn't fit the team. Before long I looked at his group as SEAL Team Six. They were the elite of the racing world, and they reminded me of an old saying, "You carry the wounded and shoot the stragglers."

Ray was so far out in front of other people. He never took his foot off the gas, which meant competitors simply couldn't catch up—at least not without help. NASCAR had to regulate our team to bring them back to the field. One of the best examples was the car called T-Rex. Although Ray shares the whole story in this book, in short, our Hendrick Motorsports team designed that car for the No. 24 team and Ray got NASCAR's approval to race it. But after a single race and dominant win, NASCAR changed its tune and banned the car. It knew the other teams were spending a fortune trying to catch up, which wasn't happening, so it started inventing rules to slow Ray and Jeff down.

I sometimes wonder if Ray missed his calling and should have been a lawyer. He used to find every single gray area in the NASCAR rulebook. If you look at the current rules, many come from trying to close loopholes Ray exploited. He started this tradition and handed it down to Chad Knaus, who he raised in the sport. Chad went down the same road and finally NASCAR had to design a car you couldn't build yourself.

Ray approached stock car racing with a completely fresh mindset. Instead of sticking to the usual ways of doing things, he focused on imagining what could be possible. He set new standards in everything he did, from managing a pit crew to calling a race. People then copied him—from the way he worked in the garage to the type of people he hired. He did amazing things with Jeff at Hendrick Motorsports, but eventually it was time for a split.

When the opportunity came to be an owner and work with Dodge to build his own dream team, there was no way he could pass that up. Almost every crew chief out there wants to be an owner, but very few ever get the opportunity. Ray did, and he was a success right out of the gate. He got an unbelievable once-in-a-lifetime opportunity and he took it—I don't blame him.

When Ray was with Hendrick Motorsports, racing was his life and being the best in the world was his goal. He accomplished that. Now other things pique his interest. He gives back to worthy charities and loves his family deeply. Of course, he loved his family back in those early days too, but he is clearly a man who has reflected on how to balance the sport and his personal life. He's a happy guy and he's still building things. It brings me joy to see him so comfortable in his own skin these days.

Ray's philosophy is simple; if you want to be successful, have a plan and stay committed to seeing it through. You do not have to come from privilege or have an Ivy League degree to be successful in life—Ray had neither. I hope young folks read this book and ask themselves, "Am I as committed to what I'm doing as Ray Evernham was?" If the answer is no, look to Ray's work ethic and attention to detail for inspiration.

I've always believed that to achieve success, you have to do three things: you have to show up, you have to show up on time, and you have to show up on time with your game face on. Ray did that every day of his career. Now, to readers young and old: It is your turn.

ONE OF OUR SPORT'S TRUE INNOVATORS

By Roger Penske

From the moment I first started working with Ray Evernham, two things became pretty clear. Ray shared my passion for racing, and he had all the tools to become a great leader. I knew that Ray had the vision and the drive to make an impact in motorsports. I'm not sure anyone would have guessed he would become one of the greatest crew chiefs in NASCAR history and one of our sport's true innovators when he began working with us in the early 1980s, but we knew Ray was someone very special.

As a young aspiring driver coming up in New Jersey, Ray earned a reputation as a hard-nosed racer who always found a way to Victory Circle. From the modified races at Flemington Speedway to his memorable victories at Wall Stadium Speedway, where he earned Modern Stock Rookie of the Year honors in 1977, Ray learned some valuable lessons that he would carry with him throughout his career.

When Jay Signore brought Ray on board to help revive our International Race of Champions (IROC) operations in 1983, we quickly realized that he had a very bright future on the technical side of our sport. It didn't matter if the drivers were from NASCAR, IndyCar, or sports car racing, the IROC racers were all impressed by how Ray would take their input and make the right adjustments to improve the car's performance.

The technical prowess that he showed in IROC helped Ray develop a reputation as a chassis specialist in NASCAR, and from there his star began to shine—brightly. After he was paired with a promising young driver named Jeff Gordon in the early nineties, Ray redefined the role of a modern-day NASCAR crew chief. Once Ray joined Hendrick Motorsports as crew chief of the No. 24 Chevrolet team at the end of the 1992 season, the Gordon/Evernham combination became virtually unstoppable. Producing nearly fifty victories and three NASCAR Cup Series Championships over six-plus seasons, Ray helped establish a standard of excellence at Hendrick Motorsports that continues to this day.

Ray also became a pit road pioneer. As the driving force behind the Rainbow Warriors crew, Ray helped revolutionize pit stops with a commitment to athletic training, analysis, and world-class precision that transformed pit road service into an art form.

Always ready for a new challenge, Ray welcomed the opportunity to become a team owner while successfully leading Dodge's return to NASCAR competition in 2001. Whether it was breaking ground as a team owner or entertaining fans with his analysis as a race broadcaster, Ray has always helped take our sport in new directions. Honoring his many accomplishments and overall impact, Ray proudly took his place in the NASCAR Hall of Fame in 2018.

He has continued to open new doors in racing, working with motorsports trailblazer Tony Stewart to form the entertaining Superstar Racing Experience (SRX) Series in 2021.

Ray's story is one of determination, innovation, and achievement. As someone who has watched Ray grow, lead, and usher racing into a new era, I hope you enjoy the ride as much as he has.

RUSTY TROPHIES AND OPEN DOORS

By Ray Evernham

"If it's not going to kill you, you might as well do it."

I was at Mario Andretti's house, and he was showing me all his trophies. I remember seeing the sterling plates from Formula One wins and the Indy rings and just . . . wow. He's freaking Mario Andretti, right? And in the middle of this beautiful trophy case, there's a little midget trophy from a race in Pine Brook, New Jersey. A rusty old trophy from a tiny three-quarter midget track—just a tenth of a mile.

And I said, "Wow, Pine Brook, New Jersey, you won there?"

"Yeah, I did."

"And you know why that trophy is in there with all these?" Mario said. "Because it's just as important as any of them."

I think he was trying to tell me that we have to remember our roots. Had he not won that race, he might not have been invited to the next one. That win was part of his journey to world championships, IndyCar wins—all the things that make Mario racing royalty.

I'm not an Andretti or Foyt, but that hit home for me. When I won my first race in 1976 at Wall Stadium, it was something that no one could take away from me. I wanted to win more, but there was no guarantee. Every time you win, you don't know if it will be your last. Every victory has meaning.

As I looked back on my life while making this book, I came to understand that every story, every win, every lesson that I learned prepared me for the next stage, or it sent me in a direction where a door was going to open for me.

Working hard and walking through those open doors left me with a lot of trophies and scars that remind me what I won and what I lost. Some would say I'm lucky, others would say I'm smart. I guess there is some truth to both. I like to think of myself as the Forrest Gump of motorsports.

I started racing cars in 1975. After a lot of laps and learning as a driver, my career took a turn and I became a crew chief and team manager. My claim to fame was my stint as the crew chief for NASCAR superstar Jeff Gordon and his team the Rainbow Warriors, but that's just a small part of my story.

I wrote this book because I believe it's time to share my roller-coaster ride of a life in racing. I also think documenting my story—my connections to our history and all the people who became part of my DNA along the way—can give something back to the sport that gave so much to me.

I'm going to be truthful. I'm not going to be easy on myself. And I hope my example helps people understand that life is a journey full of challenges and opportunities; if you want the opportunities that produce the trophies you have to be willing to accept the scars from the challenges.

I lived by the mantra that you jump out of the plane and build a parachute on the way down. I hope you take away the idea that, "Hey, if it's not going to kill you, you might as well do it." And you might just find yourself, like me, in places you never expected to be.

My time as a crew chief with Jeff Gordon and the No. 24 was one of those. I mean, it's not like I was the first great crew chief. I didn't know a lot of crew chiefing things in NASCAR, so I studied the guys who did the job before me. But things worked in our favor, and Jeff and I, along with Rick Hendrick, had a big influence on the direction the sport took in the late '90s and early 2000s.

When Jeff Gordon came in, I came in with him. We were both relatively unknown, we were close, and we were always together. Jeff and I came in and found success together, and I think that people started to notice some of the things that I did.

At that time, TV was looking for stuff to talk about. They found stories in the pit box with some of the strategy in the cars. And the radios were being used a lot so that they had access to scanners and they could hear me coaching Jeff, calling pit stops, and directing race strategy.

So I think the evolution of television and the fact that press had access to people behind the scenes made the timing right for a crew chief to step into the light. And I feel like people started to look at crew chiefs differently because of the media attention that I got.

I'm proud of my career, but I also want to acknowledge that my success was because of more than just hard work. I've worked to keep my pride in check and to take those hard looks at myself in order to evolve and improve. And if I give myself credit, I'll give it for the fact that no matter how good I do, I always look at what I could have done better.

Yeah, we had a lot of success, but I also learned lessons that I didn't know I was learning. And now I'm getting more keys to that equation. I can be a better mentor, a better storyteller, because I do understand more. I look back at that and I can explain why. And I hope that that explains to my family who I am. I want people to know who I am, what I was thinking, and whether it was right or wrong. And again, how much some of it was just dumb luck.

Books have been very important in my life because I sucked as a student. I didn't study much, but I did like to read. Reading stuck with me, especially once I realized I had to go back and learn everything that I'd screwed off and could have learned in high school. I now have a huge collection of books about history, racing, sports . . . everything.

The Winner Within by Pat Riley became the building block for the No. 24 team. That book taught me about sports and management. I got very much into the whole psyche of sports and the psyche of people.

Another book that meant a lot to me was Al Unser Jr.'s book. It hit me hard because he is a friend, and his words were very personal, honest, and open. So that's had an influence on me wanting to be truthful about my life in this book.

I want you to pick up my book, read it, and say, "You know what? He was trying to be a better person, trying to be a good guy." And maybe that can counter those who like to say good guys finish last. At least in my experience, good guys may not finish first every week, but they certainly don't finish last.

I wasn't always perfect, but I had a purpose: to be better tomorrow than I was today.

So that's it and that's me. I hope you enjoy the book. See you at the end.

ON THE LINE AT 9,000 FEET

Sunday, June 24, 2018

It's a clear sunny day, not a cloud in the sky, seventy-eight degrees at 1:00 p.m. Central Time. I am tightly buckled into the best race car I've ever driven, staged just a few feet from the starting box at 9,000 feet above sea level on the fabled mountain that is Pike's Peak, Colorado.

Looking through the four-inch-by-eight-inch opening of a Bell race helmet, I have the same field of vision that I had the very first time I ever drove a race car. Of course, this helmet fits much better and smells a lot nicer than the one I wore that day. For this race, my hands are covered by real fireproof driving gloves and I'm gripping a nicely covered purpose-built racing steering wheel.

I'm checking my gauges, which are displayed on a computer screen instead of the old black-faced Stewart Warner mechanical gauges that were the standard when I started racing in 1975. I am looking through a Lexan windshield instead of a screen, but I'm in a race car just the same.

My foot isn't shaking on the clutch pedal like it did for my first race, but I am still filled with emotion. Like that first race, this race will be a defining moment in my career . . . or maybe the end of it.

The starting box is lined on both sides by spectators and photographers standing three deep. As I roll forward into my position with cameras flashing, a smile is hidden under my helmet, and I know that in eleven minutes or less I will have the answers to the questions I have asked myself for many years. I envision myself as a small boy on a plastic go-kart, and as I think about the journey that brought him here my smile starts to grow.

Maybe I ought to take some time to tell you that story before I pop the clutch and "send it," as they say.

PART I

FOUNDATION

1957–1991

Me and Willie in
1964. *Ray Evernham
Enterprises Archives*

CHAPTER 1

SIDEWAYS IN JERSEY

Childhood Years

"You'll never take Jersey out of the boy."

My life and career may have led this boy out of Jersey, but it never took Jersey out of the boy.

When I was growing up, New Jersey, particularly the Bayshore area, was truly a melting pot. The whole culture—the people, the cars, the music—helped shape me into the man I am today.

My dad, Ray Sr., was born in 1931, my mom, Mary Lou, in 1939. At seventeen or eighteen years old, my dad went off to fight in the Korean War. As soon as he was back stateside, they got married. Their dream was to have a nice house, a job, a couple of kids, and Sundays off. (They wound up with three of us!)

My life began in the small Bayshore fishing town of Port Monmouth. We lived there until I was four and a half. The only memory I have of our life there is the rancid smell of the nearby fish factory. It stunk to high heaven.

My mom and dad had been renting houses. When they finally scraped enough money together to get their first shot at homeownership, Mom, Dad, my sister Luann, and I moved four miles inland to the small town of Hazlet. They bought a two story, two bedroom on Union Avenue that sat on just over an acre of property. It seemed huge back then. Little did any of us know that that big yard is where I would launch my racing career.

When my little brother Willie was born, my folks built on another bedroom. That was the Evernham family home until I moved my parents to Charlotte, North Carolina, forty years later.

Hazlet was a great place to grow up. Union Avenue was a connector between Route 35 and Route 36, running four miles in total. Route 35 went through an industrial area that included car dealerships and one of the area's biggest employers, a Lily-Tulip Cup Corporation factory. It's where they made the cardboard coffee cups with the little fold-out handles.

Meanwhile, Route 36 ran down to the more touristy area of the shore. There you'd find ice cream stands, little restaurants, and the boardwalk. Bell Laboratories was in Holmdel, the next town over. One of the first space satellites was built there in the early 1960s. Then, a little further inland were the farmers. Southern Jersey is famous for its pines and blueberry farms.

On the other hand, people at the nearby beach made their living from fishing. So, in our part of Jersey, between fishermen, factory workers, and Bell technicians, it was a real mix of blue- and white-collar folks. Then you had the people freshly moved in from New York and Staten Island.

Jersey is also famous for our entertainers. It was home to Frank Sinatra and Jack Nicholson, and, of course, "The Boss" Bruce Springsteen and Jon Bon Jovi. All and all, some really cool people have come out of Jersey.

New York City is only a forty-mile drive on the parkway and just five miles across the water by ferry boat. But it might as well have been on the other side of the country. While it's a place with tons of opportunities that people with big dreams flock to, it never really interested me.

I grew up in a simple family that had been around the Jersey Shore their whole lives. People called folks like us clamdiggers. There was rarely talk of chasing goals or pursuing dreams.

You got a job here or there, but seldom a career. You made enough to put food on the table, keep a roof over your head, and pay some bills. You went to the shore, had fun with family and friends, and enjoyed being Jersey Shore folks. You hung out—lived your life. No expectations.

No matter the current financial situation, we always had pretty damn good Christmases. The one thing I've been obsessed with since childhood is cars. It's always been cars. I can't recall anything else that captured my imagination more. To this day I remember a Christmas gift I got when I was about five: a plastic, battery-powered go-kart called a Marx-a-Kart. It had a red seat and manifold, a yellow roll bar, and black plastic wheels.

It was the coolest thing I'd ever seen.

There was a sidewalk next to the house that ran about twenty feet, from the front porch to the back. I remember just riding the shit out of that thing. I was driving EV before it was cool! I'd go up and back and up and back—for hours and hours. I drove it until I wore out the plastic wheels.

But I'd put some miles on that thing before it finally broke.

————

My dad was a fantastic athlete, a hell of a baseball player. He even had a shot to try out for the New York Yankees farm club. But he'd injured his arm in a pickup baseball game and for some reason just didn't feel he should follow through with the tryout. I wish he'd had someone who would have pushed him a little to do it. Who knows what could have happened. It seemed common for him, and guys like him, not to allow themselves to think they could ever get out of Jersey.

Mom and Dad both worked. Mom was a nurse and Dad was a jack-of-all-trades. He served as a mechanic at the gas station for his buddy Jack Stoddard, as a pastry chef at one of the local inns, and as a mason, building cinder block walls.

He had an "I can do that" attitude. He would just do whatever it took. I don't remember my dad ever not having a job.

Because my parents both worked, our grandparents would babysit us. Mom and Dad's families could not be more different. Mom's was more traditional. Dad's was more the clamdigger type.

Dad and his brothers were masons, and good ones. As a kid, I'd sometimes get to help them. My job was mixing mortar in the wheelbarrow. They'd use strings to establish a straight line and level. Then they'd lay the blocks and slap in the mixed mortar. It was all so impressive how fast they could build a wall.

When they weren't building cinder block walls, they would fish and catch muskrats. They'd skin the muskrats and sell the pelts. They also caught eels and crabs and sold them by the pound. In the winter, they'd cut holes in the ice with an ax, stab the eels with these long forks, and pull them out of the water as fast as they could. They're like giant snakes. Then they'd sell them to the fresh fish stands along Route 36.

As for my grandparents, they'd buy stuff at estate and yard sales. What they could repair and refurbish they would resell at the Englishtown Flea Market on Saturdays. They had a little booth where they'd sell their latest pickings. I used to love going with them. If my grandparents were around today, they'd be selling stuff on eBay or Facebook Marketplace.

One Saturday I was walking through the flea market and spotted a go-kart for sale. I swear I heard a chorus of angels singing.

But the go-kart came with a twenty-five-dollar price tag.

It was definitely used, with flat tires and everything. But it was a thing of beauty. I had to have it. I told my dad about it, and we went back the next week, but it was gone.

I was devastated.

Turned out, it was gone because my dad had bought it to surprise me. He got it running, but again, my dad had his own way of doing things. He didn't see the need to add an on-off switch when you can just reach back and pull the spark plug wire off. But I'll tell you, it'd shock the shit out of me every time.

I soon made a track out of our big side yard. My poor parents never had grass on their lawn after that. I ran that thing around and around for hours. I'd run it until it ran out of gas.

In those days, we used to go to Nazareth to watch dirt track racing. When Mario Andretti would round a corner, he worked the steering wheel in one direction, then another.

I would go around every corner in my go-kart, working the wheel just like Mario. I was going to be the greatest driver in the world. I remember in the summertime I would run so many laps in a row that the kart would get so hot it would just stop, and I'd have to let it cool off.

One time I was screwing around and came flying off the grass onto the gravel driveway. I'd slid the kart sideways trying to thrill everybody. Instead, I smashed right into the front of my aunt's '65 Chevy Impala. I hit it so hard, it knocked the motor sideways and put a big dent in the lower grille. I also thought I broke my shoulder. But what hurt even worse? Having the go-kart taken away for a while.

———

My dad's parents were also the odd couple. My grandmother was a big woman, six feet tall and bulky. She would wear muumuus, those big ole house dresses. She was a very loving, good woman. Especially with us kids.

My grandfather was a short, thin guy. He was at least two or three inches shorter than Grandma and probably fifty pounds lighter. Although he didn't say much, I'm told in his day, he was quite a hell-raiser. But his hell-raising days were long over by the time I was born, and Grandma pretty much ran that house.

One of my favorite memories of her is from a wedding we all attended.

I can't for the life of me recall whose it was. But in typical small-town fashion, I remember the reception was held at the local VFW Hall.

The band was whaling on some loud bluesy tune. The place was rockin'. Next thing I knew, my grandmother got out of her seat, jumped on the stage, grabbed the microphone, and started belting out the song.

My jaw hit the table. She was like a real blues singer, and she looked like a movie star. Apparently, singing was something she'd done years before. I was so impressed she was my grandma. I've never forgotten that. In fact, I credit her for my interest in music.

Unfortunately, she passed away fairly young, in her early sixties. My grandfather lived into his mid-eighties.

My father had two brothers and two sisters. One brother, Alfred, was just a total derelict. As the saying goes, "You can't pick your family." Good or bad, sometimes there are members that teach us the person we want be, and the person we don't.

I learned both from Dad's family.

My Uncle Alfred, who everybody called "Duke," was a mean drunk. He'd been in and out of jail. Scrawny, with sort of puny, prison-yard muscles. The bad seed in the family. Since he wasn't working, he loafed around all day at my grandparents. If Grandma was watching us, he'd be around watching TV.

One afternoon, when I was five or six, I was running around the house, no doubt making a racket. I'm sure he told me to stop but I didn't.

He just freaked out and began beating me with this wire. He hit me so hard, the wire cut into my legs, and I started bleeding.

As I said, Grandma was a big lady, so she got him to stop.

I'll tell you, from that day forward, I thought, "Someday I'm gonna get that bastard." But when my father came to pick us up, I wasn't sure how much of my uncle was going to be left for me to get.

My father was a stud. He was a gunner on a destroyer in the US Navy. It took a lot of strength to load those shells.

He also boxed. He was champion on his ship, the USS *Roosevelt*. He confessed to me he had a less-than-perfect record. He'd accepted a challenge from a boxer on one of the carriers.

"I was winning the fight," he told me. "So the guy headbutted me, cutting me so badly above my eye they called the fight. I lost on a TKO," he said in an indignant tone.

I had always wondered where that scar came from.

When Dad walked into the house to get me, he saw bleeding gashes on my legs. Grandma told him what had happened, and Dad proceeded to kick the living crap out of his deadbeat, booze-soaked brother.

From behind Dad, I said, "Someday I'm gonna get you."

I never followed through with my big threat. But I did get a little revenge. After I'd become a little more affluent, he needed something from me. So I asked him, "Do you remember that time you beat the shit out of me? I do. So . . . no!"

Dad was nothing like my Uncle Alfred. I'll tell you straight up, Dad never took a dime that wasn't his.

He had a good moral code—and not a hint of racism. I'm really proud of that. Back in the 1960s, I was around a lot of racists.

Don't get me wrong. He had his wild side. His idea of getting in trouble was drinking too much and trading a few punches in some bar fight.

But as far as breaking the law, he never did.

He was also a bit of a showoff in his younger days, and it paid off for him. Eight years older than my mom, he was out riding his Harley when he happened to spot her standing on a corner with her family.

He made a move with the bike, trying to impress her. Not paying attention, a big old Buick pulled out in front of him. His motorcycle bashed into the car, sent him flying, and landed him in the street—literally right in front of her.

It was one hell of an introduction. There's got to be a better way than flying over a 1950 Buick. In this case, it worked!

―――――――

When you're a kid, it isn't easy to spot trouble in a family. As long as people are kind to you, you just assume all's right with the world. With age and hindsight comes a clearer view of how things maybe weren't what they seemed.

My mom was one of seven—four boys and three girls—raised in a strict Catholic home by her parents, Scott and Margaret Bailey. I never met my grandfather. He passed when I was two weeks old. He worked on boilers and around asbestos and coal. Cancer took him young; he was still in his fifties.

My grandma Margaret was an incredibly strong woman. She never remarried. Instead, she stayed a single mom, working at a high-end clothing store called Lerners in Red Bank, New Jersey.

Some of the boys went into the service, the US Air Force and Navy.

I thought my uncles were cool. They were car guys. They had a '49 Merc and '58 Chevy with a 327 four speed. They wore leather car coats and hung out in my grandma's yard, standing around a fire barrel singing a cappella doo-wop.

They had a neighbor friend, Joe Caprio, who had a pair of drag slicks they'd go race with at the eighth-mile Old Bridge Township Raceway.

But as we got older, things started to come out about one of my uncles. After my grandmother passed away, the lid everyone kept on the "family secret" blew off. Turns out one of her sons had molested some members of the family.

A corrosive secret like that eats away at the fabric of family. The shit hit the fan, resulting in no more interactions with Mom's side of the family—even to this day.

As of the writing of this chapter, four of Mom's six siblings have passed away, including the child molester. Only Mom and two of her brothers are left. Unfortunately, those who were victimized continued to struggle throughout their lives. I'm 100 percent convinced their struggles are a direct result of the molestation. The whole mess was difficult to process. I'd thought so much of those guys, including the uncle who turned out to be a child molester. Sadly, like so many families, ours also had its share of alcoholics and drug addicts. At one time or another, I've tried to help them all with loans and rehab treatments.

My little brother Willie struggled with alcohol. I thank God he's doing well now. For too long, he was exposed to the clamdigger mentality of "you can't go, you can't do."

He's made some mistakes in life, but he's a good person. Some days, I almost feel guilty because I think my success made things worse for him. Being "Ray's brother" saddled him with unfair comparisons and expectations. Willie had the skills; he just didn't have the opportunities.

On the other hand, while I may have gotten certain mechanical gifts, Willie got all the personality. He could have been a comedian or an actor. He's funny as shit. He could have done it. He just never had the confidence.

I'm five years older than Willie. When you're young kids, five years is a big difference. I was the big brother. He was the little one. If I was riding a 125cc motorcycle, he'd be following on a little 50cc scooter. I had a horse. Willie had a pony.

But once I was in my late teens and started racing, Willie became part of my crew, even going along to IROC with me.

We've always been close, and in some ways our closeness worked against him when he was going through his alcoholism. I went into denial. People told me he was having issues and I flat ignored them. I was like, "No, Willie's fine." I didn't want to accept that my little brother was an alcoholic.

Instead, I did the worst thing you can do.

I kept giving him money, bailing him out. I stood up for him every time he got fired. Of course, according to Willie, it was always the "other guy's" fault. So I'd become indignant right along with him.

"You're right, Willie, that's bullshit! That guy's an asshole!" I was being the big brother.

Ultimately, to his credit, it was Willie that gave me my wake-up call. He admitted he was an alcoholic. It was a crushing blow, because it wasn't somebody else telling me that Willie was screwing up. It was Willie himself finally admitting his addiction and crying out for help.

Afterward, I put him through rehab. I'm ashamed to admit that we weren't close for a long time after that. Because of me. I just didn't know how to deal with it.

I just felt so blindsided by Willie that I retreated from the whole family for a while. We weren't a warm, huggy, kissy family to begin with. Still, my parents always had a good sense of duty. They took care of us. The house was clean. There was always food on the table. They went to all the ball games. Came to all my races.

At the end of the day, I look at the things my folks did to provide for us kids, and I realize they did all they knew how to do. There weren't a lot of "I love you's" tossed back and forth. The only way they could express their affection was to work hard and give us things.

Well, this apple hasn't fallen far from the tree.

My wife Erin and daughter Cate are helping with that. Along with hours of therapy. For the record, I'm a big believer in seeking professional help, whether it's to sort out and better understand your past, or to gain clarity about your future.

I didn't do a good job with Ray Jr. when he was growing up. Yet now that I have a better understanding of what it means to be "family," I try to make sure I do the things with, and for, him and Cate that I wanted more of when I was growing up.

As I said, those close to you teach you who you want to be and who you don't. We're programmed by family, friends, and our environment. It takes a desire, life experience, or in my case, the "trophies and scars" of life to truly figure out the good and the bad.

But just because you got a trophy doesn't always mean you did a good job. Likewise, just because you have a scar, doesn't mean you did a bad job.

———

My very first race was going to watch midgets and modifieds at a place called Old Bridge Township Raceway. I went with my dad and his pal Jack Stoddard. They knew I was crazy about cars. Jack was too. He went to the Indianapolis 500 every year from 1947 into the 2000s. Just a great guy.

One of the drivers we watched was a man named Tucker Hill. He had a little convenience store and a junkyard where he kept his modified sportsman car during the week. It was white with a bright red number 888 stenciled on the doors. I used to ride my bike there to talk to him.

I remember the car and our conversation really piquing my interest. To a nine-year-old, guys like him seemed bigger than life. Wearing their fancy silk shirts embroidered with their name and number and driving those loud, fast cars made them superheroes. The local racers, who raced at Old Bridge and Wall Stadium, were my heroes.

I had heard of Richard Petty and A. J. Foyt, but Mario Andretti was my hero. We considered Mario a local since he was from Nazareth, Pennsylvania, just two hours away.

At that time, you could go up and down the Bay Shore, thirty minutes from Wall Stadium, and find lots of gas stations where guys stored their modified stock cars. I can remember riding somewhere with Mom and Dad, and I'd yell for them to pull into some random gas station just so I could go look at the car.

I must have been a pain in the ass having them stop at all those gas stations.

Most were just beat-up, old '37 Chevys and Fords. But to me, they were incredible race cars. Normally, a guy would spot me looking at his and he'd come out and talk to me. Answer my unending questions. Sometimes it would even be the guy who drove it on Saturday nights.

Then there was Bill Brice. A friend of my dad's, he actually went on to be a NASCAR inspector. We got to be friends for years. He worked at Naylors Auto Parts, which is where Dad and Jack bought their parts. Bill had a modified, and every chance I got I'd ride my bike to the parts store because I knew that car was there. It was cool—Bill even won a race with it.

Bill's business partner, Dick Bohlmer, lived in nearby Keansburg. He owned Dick's Auto Electric and he rebuilt starters and alternators.

These were just regular guys with ordinary day jobs, but they became heroes of mine because they took the time to talk to me. Even though I wasn't going to the races, Bill or Dick would always tell me about them.

Both Bill and Dick eventually became NASCAR officials, and I stayed in contact with both all the way up through my championship years with Jeff Gordon.

Sometimes a hero is not the big star who wins all the races. More often, real heroes are ordinary people who simply take time to show some interest in a kid and make a difference in his life.

———

From kindergarten to fifth grade, I attended Middle Road Elementary School. Then from sixth through eighth grade, I went to the middle school on Union Avenue. It was at Union Avenue that I met a teacher who left a lasting impression.

Her name was Ms. Cella, and she taught me in sixth and then again in eighth grade. She was one of the most compassionate, influential people in my life. She cared about kids. She held us accountable. She made us want to be good students. That helped me because my effort in a subject was dependent on the teacher. If I didn't like the person, I became lazy and didn't make the commitment to being a good student.

But that wasn't the case in Ms. Cella's class.

She taught everything from math and English to history and art. Ironically, the subject I struggled with the most was math. The one subject I counted on the most in my career.

When Ms. Cella taught, she spoke with sincerity. You didn't feel like she was just doing a job. You almost felt like you were her own child, someone she truly cared about.

She treated all of us like family. I don't recall ever hearing her raise her voice; she radiated positivity. She'd bring in cupcakes. Her attitude was, "We can do this. We're going to do it, and this is how."

For eighth grade graduation, she threw this big party at her own home. She had us all in the pool and meeting her family. I've never forgotten how she treated us. We were all kind of like brothers and sisters. I have many great memories of being in her two classes.

My high school Spanish teacher, Mrs. Fiorentino, similarly impressed me. And no surprise, I excelled in Spanish.

In hindsight, there were other subjects I could have excelled at had I applied myself: creative writing, especially. My creative writing teacher's style lacked encouragement. Yet one day she gave us an assignment that inspired me. The teacher showed our class a picture of a girl looking through the window in the lid of a coffin. Her instruction was to write an essay on our interpretation of the photo. Interestingly, around that time I'd read about the plane crash that killed Buddy Holly, the Big Bopper (J. P. Richardson), and Ritchie Valens. (Perhaps evidence that I'm close to the spectrum—I got really obsessed with the crash. I was mesmerized by it.)

I wrote this whole thing about the girl mourning the deaths of Buddy, Big Bopper, Ritchie, and rock and roll. The next day, after reading all the essays, the teacher stood up before us, my essay in her hand.

"You know, this one is amazing. But I can't believe this guy wrote it."

She was almost insinuating I'd plagiarized it. It was one of the best essays I ever wrote in her class. But the way she handled it was demoralizing, and I thought to myself, "You witch." I never wrote another thing for her.

As the quote from poet Maya Angelou goes, "People will forget what you said and what you did. But they will never forget how you made them feel."

———

My dad was a great ball player, but when I first started playing Little League I didn't have much confidence. If there were six kids, I'd get picked fourth.

I was probably eight or nine years old at the time. Back then, there was this Italian man who had five kids all playing on various teams. He was a mason by trade, and I remember seeing him at every ball game. He had a big 1965 or '66 Nova station wagon. They'd pull up to the game and I'd watch what seemed like a ton of kids pile out of that car.

I'd struck out my first two times at bat that day. I was really down. I wasn't playing well, and my teammates let me know it. The Italian man was nearby and overheard them giving me shit.

He came over, gently took my face in his calloused hands, and with a thick Italian accent said, "Don'tcha let these other guys get to you. You're just as good. Now go out there and show them how good a ball player you really are."

I was so inspired by his kind gesture and encouraging words—God, strike me dead if I'm lying—my next at bat I smacked an incredible home run. And then that year I went on to hit ten or eleven more. I even led our team in home runs after that.

I remember my dad was working at the gas station that Saturday afternoon. When he got home, he said, "I had like five people pull in to tell me you hit a ball out of the park!"

He was so happy, and I was just as proud.

I've always wondered what would have happened if I hadn't received encouragement from that kind Italian man. Would I have still hit that home run? It was a very powerful moment for me, and I've never forgotten it.

The next year, the coach moved me over to first base and made me cleanup batter. I played ball till I was thirteen.

Not too long after that, I had to make room for a bridle and saddle next to my bat and ball when Dad bought us a horse. He always loved animals. Jack Stoddard's daughter, Kathy, who was my age, kept her horse at a local stable. That's where Dad spotted ours.

It looked like he hadn't been properly cared for, and he was priced fairly at $400. He was a pretty horse, part pinto and part Appaloosa. He had what they call a bald face—half was albino—and he had one brown and one blue eye. Really, an incredible looking animal. So, Dad bought him, and because he'd been previously owned by a sea captain, Dad named him Captain Baldy.

We kept him at Jack's Horse Farm, owned and operated by a great guy named Jack Mirro. Jack had a big ole giant belly on him. But in his early years he was a competitive bodybuilder. He had all these pictures from his bodybuilding competitions on his office walls. He was funny as hell, too. In spite of his own physique, Jack was married to a beautiful woman named Ann. Me and my buddy Sal Policastro, with our adolescent hormones raging, would offer to help her walk her horse around the ring.

Since we kept Baldy at his stable, Jack hired me to work for him part-time. He paid me to muck the stalls, get hay, and take care of other people's horses. I had other jobs back then, too. Local farmers would hire me and my friends to pick corn for $10 a day.

Around then, I got interested in barrel racing competitions. I practiced and trained with Baldy, and damned if that horse didn't start to bulk up. He got really muscular and turned out to be pretty quick.

But once again, in hindsight, I know I could have done better with him if I'd been more committed. Instead, my interests drifted more toward the girls who came to the horse farm.

About that time, my uncle gave me a 1962 Chevy pickup truck. I stripped the fenders and doors off, piled friends in the back, and raced it around the horse track. That's where I learned to drive a clutch and slide around on dirt. It's a wonder somebody didn't get killed.

My folks rarely disciplined us. The only time I can remember being scolded for something was when I was fifteen.

I'd been driving a while. I had a Volkswagen dune buggy, motorcycle, and the pickup truck at the farm. One day, my friends and I were at the farm when we decided we wanted ice cream. This girl asked her mom if she'd take us.

She said no. She had things she needed to do, so I said I'd drive. She handed me her keys, assuming I was old enough. She never even asked me.

After that we took her mom's car and headed to the ice cream stand. Sure as shit, I passed my mom going in the opposite direction. As you can imagine, there was a little bit of an issue over my driving that day.

While I rarely got reprimanded, I sure did that day.

The horse competitions expanded my world a bit. We started to travel to neighboring horse shows. We'd go to the 4-H Fair, held at the Monmouth County Fair, which was a big deal. Bruce Springsteen even wrote a song about this event because it made such an impression on his life.

It's there that we'd meet kids and families from different states. These interactions opened my eyes. I discovered families didn't necessarily think and do things the way we did. I began to realize there was more out there beyond my family and the Bayshore.

I enjoyed my time with Baldy. He was good for me in many ways. To this day, I think that horse was one of my best friends. That's why I've supported my daughter Cate's interest in horse competition. She gets to have a connection with an animal and exposure to people outside her family.

By my sophomore year in high school, I had other interests and less time for horse competitions. We decided to sell Captain Baldy, but we wanted to make sure he went to a good person. I was extremely happy to learn recently that Baldy went on to have a great life, living to thirty-two years old.

———

As soon as I turned fifteen, I knew I wanted a job.

You had to be at least fifteen to get a work permit through school. In automotive mechanics class, I could work half days at Jack Stoddard's Texaco station and receive school credit for it.

No sooner had I started pumping gas at Jack's than the frigging first oil crisis hit. The price skyrocketed from the original forty cents a gallon. Soon, fuel was rationed based on odd and even license plate numbers.

People were fighting and offering me bribes. It was crazy.

Because of school, I could work only two days during the week but as much as I wanted to on the weekends. The only time it really sucked was in the summertime when I had to put gas in a buddy's car so they could all head to the beach.

Truth was, I wanted to work, and I loved working for Jack. He set an incredible example through his work ethic, the neatness and cleanliness of his shop, and not to mention his great customer service.

I was fortunate to be around a guy like him.

Everybody liked Jack. His shop was spotless. Clean uniforms. Even his trucks were washed regularly.

At first, I was just given a shirt to wear. But I'll never forget how great I felt when he presented me with my first Texaco uniform. That was a big day. The Texaco slogan was, "You can trust your car to the man who wears the star." And the star on my uniform had "Ray, Jr." embroidered above it.

At that time, Dad also worked for Jack. Dad was a "salt of the earth" kind of guy. People knew he was a great athlete.

He was also known for being brave, and he proved it one day at the station. Jack had a problem with one of the pumps. To this day, I'm not sure what happened. But it ignited, turning the workman at the flaming pump into a human fireball.

My dad ran to the guy, tackling him to the ground. He rolled around with him, ripping his flaming clothes off. Meanwhile, he's yelling to Jack to shut the pumps off.

He finally got the fire extinguished. The man was burned badly but survived.

Dad was not afraid to do what needed to be done. When we were kids, Kathy Stoddard's horse died. It got colic and its intestines became twisted. So a few of us grabbed shovels and dug a big hole for the horse's grave.

We waited until dark, when most everyone had left the stables, before we began dragging the horse's body to where we'd dug its grave.

It was raining like hell that night. Just miserable. It was like a scene out of a movie. As we pulled the horse's heavy body, our feet would slip, and we'd fall in the mud.

Worse, when it tumbled in the hole its head twisted in an awkward, uncomfortable-looking position. Despite the horse being dead, Dad said, "We can't let him go like that."

Dad jumped into the grave, filled with at least three feet of muddy water, and gently repositioned the horse's head and neck so it looked comfortable and peaceful. I never forgot that.

He was one of those guys you just knew had your back. I never heard him trash-talk people. Never heard him say unkind things, either. But you would never want to underestimate him.

If you messed with him, you were making a big mistake.

All these years later, I look at guys like Jack and my dad, and I think they both could have gone so far with different opportunities.

That said, whether they ever knew it or not, Jack and my dad positively influenced a lot of people. Me among them.

My high school years were full of long hair, motorcycles, and homemade dune buggies. *Ray Evernham Enterprises Archives*

CHAPTER 2

LESSONS ON THE STREET

High School Years

"Steve, Frank, and my '65 Chevy Malibu."

High school, finally. I was nervous as hell, yet jumping-out-of-my-skin excited all at the same time.

As we filed into Raritan High, Hazlet's only high school, everybody's eyes darted from person to person. Guys sizing each other up. Checking out all the girls we'd never seen till now.

Freshman orientation took place in the gymnasium. It was loud and packed with around five hundred of us. I didn't really know anybody, so I just grabbed the first open seat I could find.

That's when I met Steve Trimarchi.

Steve was sitting by himself, so I plopped down beside him. We started talking, and from that day on we were thick as thieves. In fact, Steve's one of my best friends to this day.

In terms of emotion, Steve and I are total opposites. He's calm, easygoing. In all the years I've known him, I don't recall hearing him raise his voice or getting into a fight.

If anyone ever said, "Hey, I found somebody that doesn't like Steve," I'd say back, "I'm afraid you must be talking about a different Steve." He's that best friend you can go have a beer with and talk about anything.

Now, back then, I didn't have many close friends from middle school, and the ones I did have, well, we drifted apart over the summer.

I was never really the stick-and-ball sports guy. I spent a lot of my time at the racetrack with my Uncle Nick, at the horse farm, or going to horse shows. I didn't hang out in the neighborhood or go to parties. I could be kind of a loner back then.

While I did know a lot of people, my circle of family and true friends was pretty small.

The cliques formed fast. I was never one of the cool kids. I wasn't a jock or one of the nerds, either. I used to hang out with this group of guys from vocational tech class.

We considered ourselves the "car kids." In truth, we were somewhere between the jocks and the nerds. We didn't wear black leather jackets or slick back our hair, but we had our own thing going on, and it suited us fine.

The core of our gang was mainly me, Steve, and this guy Frank Goglia. Because of all the crazy stuff we did with our cars, we became known as the Dukes of Hazlet, a nod to the characters and car antics in the popular TV show at the time, *The Dukes of Hazzard*.

I was from Union Avenue, and Steve and Frank came from over on Beers Street, a real Italian neighborhood with lots of folks who moved down from New York, Long Island, and Staten Island. I loved Steve's and Frank's families, and they loved me even though I was an Irish clamdigger.

Like most high schools, Raritan High was this big melting pot with kids from different neighborhoods and backgrounds. Now, I'm not going to lie. There were ethnic divides, but it wasn't in a bad way. It was mostly Italians, Jews, and Irish. We didn't have people spouting racial slurs or anything like that. It was a simpler time, and we weren't worried about everybody else's business.

In our little corner of the world, it was mostly about just hanging out and being friends, no matter where you came from, or your background.

In my freshman year, I was still into horses, going to races, riding bikes, and hitchhiking all over the place. Hitchhiking was safe back then. I hitchhiked all over Hazlet until I got my license. I'd catch rides to the beach or to hang out with Steve and Frank. It wasn't like you needed your mom and dad to take you places or get you.

As long as you had a thumb, you had freedom, you were good.

————

I was a midrange student, at best. I did just enough to get by. And I wasn't diligent about doing homework. My folks weren't on me about getting it done, either.

By the time I got into high school, my hair grew and my grades

20

failed. I flunked math once because I just didn't go. Ironically, a lot of the things I had to learn for racing, like math, geometry, writing, and history, I had to go back and relearn on my own.

Back then, schools weren't as aware as they are now of students who learn differently or had afflictions like dyslexia, which I found out later I had. I couldn't recognize certain math symbols. That made things tough, but I managed.

Given my love of cars, it's little wonder my favorite class was vocational tech. It also didn't hurt that it was taught by one of the coolest teachers I ever had, Stan Reed.

Mr. Reed epitomized cool. He looked cool. Acted cool. Dressed cool. And to top it off, he didn't drive the kind of car you'd usually see in the teacher section of the parking lot: Volvos or station wagons.

Mr. Reed drove a hot rod, a 340 Plymouth Duster, all fixed up with mag wheels, big tires, and a motor you wouldn't believe. He'd talk to us about drag racing and burnouts. He had that Big John Milner from *American Graffiti* swagger that made him the kind of guy my car buddies and I looked up to.

Coolness aside, Mr. Reed ran a tight ship.

Before we started working on cars, he made sure we knew the basics of brake hydraulics and electronics. He wasn't going to let us just start ripping cars apart. He insisted we learn fundamentals so we'd become skilled mechanics, not just a bunch of grease monkeys.

Looking back, I realized whether by divine intervention or dumb luck, I've been surrounded by quality guys like Stan Reed all my life. Starting with my dad and Jack Stoddard, then Jay Signore, Roger Penske, and Rick Hendrick.

These were people that made me want to up my game, mentors I wanted to please. Whether it was conscious or subconscious, they taught me the right way to do things.

Stan made me want to earn his respect. Even now, his opinion matters to me. I've kept in touch with him throughout my career. In fact, when I first ran a race team in New Jersey, I hired Stan to help us, and we've stayed friends since.

Once I got my license, things changed for me, Steve, and Frank. I became all about chasing girls and racing cars.

Steve and I had some crazy experiences cruising around in his old Dodge. Steve was a smoker. One time, he flicked his cigarette out the window. Unbeknownst to us, the wind had sent the still-lit cigarette boomeranging back. We realized what had happened once we saw his backseat on fire.

Not long afterward, Steve bought this really fast Ford. It had a 429 motor. Other guys knew how fast his car was and always challenged him to race.

Steve would say, "Give me a minute." Then he'd turn to me and say, "Ray, you drive." So I used to race guys with Steve's car.

When I got my race car and started out at Wall Stadium, Steve used to go with me as part of my crew. It was fun having a good friend there. If a fight broke out, he always had my back. Like Spiderman, if he even sensed trouble, he'd stand right there with me.

My street car back then was a beast.

I had a 1965 Chevy Malibu SS with a Corvette 396-cubic-inch engine. It was really fast, but it had drum brakes and no power steering, making it terrible to drive. The clutch was so stiff, it took both my legs to push it. Still, it was one of the fastest cars in the town.

It was well known around school that if you got a ride in it, you better hang on.

I had the Malibu through most of high school. Then I traded it for a 1956 Chevy. After I sold the Chevy, I bought a 1968 Camaro with a big block in it. But once I started racing, I sold the Camaro and bought a pickup truck.

Believe it or not, the Camaro was the last street car I owned until I went to work for Rick Hendrick. I always had a pickup because I needed it to tow my race cars. The first street car I got since high school was the Acura NSX I'd won in a bet from Rick Hendrick in 1994.

Steve and I loved our cars. We put thousands of miles on them just cruising, burning gas. The cost was nothing back then. You could put four dollars' worth in your car and cruise the whole night.

While it wasn't the smartest thing I've ever done, we used to street race on the highway a good bit. One night cops started chasing us. I saw their lights flashing in my rearview mirror and thought, screw this.

So we just hauled ass. My car was all black and I'd installed a taillight switch specifically for situations like this one. When I flipped the switch, my taillights went dark and we were practically invisible. We turned off the highway, sat still, and watched as the cop car sped right by. Siren blaring, lights flashing. I can still hear Steve's laugh.

He thought it was the coolest thing in the world. I was thinking, "Boy, that was really dumb."

Steve, Frank, and I loved cruising on weekends, including a street race or two. But one summer night at the start of my senior year, I learned a couple lessons that changed my whole outlook behind the wheel.

It was sometime after 9:00 p.m.

The guys and I were driving down Route 36. It ran to the shore and the Garden State Parkway. Straight as an arrow, it made the perfect route for a friendly street battle. We were looking for girls or some of our buddies as we sped past the sweet shop and drive-ins.

Whenever we stopped at lights, someone would pull up beside us. We'd each glance into the other's car to size one another up. If somebody revved their engine, it signaled a challenge. If the other car's motor revved in response, you knew the dare had been accepted.

The traffic light became the starting pole. To us, green meant race. And we'd go!

This one night we pulled into the left lane at an intersection preparing to make a left turn. To my right was this beautiful 1974 Chevelle, about ten years newer than mine. The guy driving was a great, big, former-champion wrestler from our high school who'd graduated the year before.

The guys and I were screwing around. At the exact second the light turned green, I floored it and swerved right, whipping around in front of the moving Chevelle, cutting off the wrestler. The guy slammed on his brakes. We could see he was pissed as we sped from the intersection.

At first, I thought, "Heck, he's never gonna catch me." But damned if his Chevelle wasn't barreling up behind us.

I really started leggin' it. Thank God my car was fast because I realized there was a very real possibility I was about to get my ass kicked by one of our school's friggin' one-time state champion wrestlers.

Just then, I glanced at the speedometer and was stunned to see we were approaching 140-miles-per-hour. In the distance, I watched as the traffic light was fast approaching, changing to yellow, then red.

Cars were slowing, and I could see red taillights.

We were haulin' ass and it hit me, there was no way I could stop with drum brakes, and if I did up behind that stack of cars, he'd just drag me out and punch my face in.

At the speed we were going, I had no choice. I had to find an escape route. That's when I noticed the shoulder ahead was clear. Veering to the right, I saw the curbside entrance to a liquor store on the corner.

I pulled the car back into second gear and tapped the brake, transferring the weight to the front of the car. Then I stood on the gas pedal which got the rear wheels spinning, sending me sideways clear across the parking lot.

As soon as I saw there was no oncoming traffic, I spun my steering wheel to straighten out, drove onto the cross street, and took off.

Suddenly, I thought, "Holy shit, where did that all come from?"

All those years of going to the races—watching all the crazy chases and stunts in movies—they had all registered with me. I realized I'd developed actual racing instincts. That experience gave me confidence in the thought that pursuing racing was something I should do.

Steve couldn't believe it. He just started yelling and laughing.

I said, "What the hell's the matter with you? We just damn near wrecked! This guy's gonna beat the shit outta me if he ever catches us."

"No! You don't understand," Steve said. "A guy was coming out of the liquor store carrying a case of beer just as we skidded through the parking lot. He got scared as we brushed by him, and his bottles went flying! Freakin' hilarious!"

After making it back onto the street in one piece, we headed for the local bowling alley. Once inside, I breathed a sigh of relief and challenged Steve and Frank to a pool game.

Just as I aimed my cue stick on my next shot, I glanced up to see . . . who else but the wrestler headed straight for me.

Oh my God, he's gonna pummel me in front of all these people.

To my surprise, he stopped before me and said, "That was really dumb. I wasn't chasing you down to fight. I was pissed off. Cutting me off was bad enough. But then to race down the highway and cut through the busy corner was even stupider." Then he added, "You need to wise up before you kill yourself, or worse yet, somebody else. You think you're cool, but you're gonna die."

Then he turned and walked away. I started breathing again.

He could have come in there and been a real asshole, but he wasn't. Here was a nineteen-year-old guy teaching me a lesson. It showed me a whole different perspective on how to handle my own anger.

It impressed me. I've never forgotten it.

Now, if he'd have yelled and screamed and kicked my ass, I wouldn't have blamed him, but I wouldn't have learned as much. The way he handled it had a much bigger effect.

While I learned I could handle a car at high speed, unfortunately, it was from doing something stupid. I could've killed all of us with that move.

That wrestler ended up becoming a police officer. Our conversation may have saved my life.

Truth is, street races were the cause of some horrific tragedies in our high school. You could go really fast on the highways in and around Hazlet. But the sharp turns were deadly. When I was a freshman, some seniors were killed in a horrible crash. Their car was just broken in half. That's when the faculty started preaching to us about the dangers of street racing.

About a mile as the crow flies from our house was a place called Thrill Hill. People would come from neighboring towns to race. With enough speed, their car could become airborne—it could fly over the hill.

But too often it was the scene of some crazy awful accidents. Those crashes always made the front page of the local paper. You'd see these gruesome photos of mangled cars and dead bodies covered with sheets.

Subconsciously, the thought that that might happen to me sooner or later motivated me to stop racing on the street and start racing on the track.

The last accident to occur on Thrill Hill involved a pickup truck filled with kids that came crashing down, killing four or five of them. The street department finally bulldozed the hill.

Around the same time I learned how brutal motorsports could be. But as harsh a lesson as it was, it never deterred me. About a quarter mile or so down the street from our house was Alloco Farms. It was actually a little convenience store that sold strawberries, blueberries, and fresh produce.

Joey Alloco had a little dragster he raced at Englishtown Raceway Park. He was a local hero among us race fans. One Sunday he was killed in a race. It totally blew me away. I was around fourteen or fifteen and Joey was just twenty-five years old. I was so used to seeing Mrs. Alloco and saying hello to Joey, seeing his race car and trailer parked on the street.

Then one day, the car was gone and so was Joey. I could literally feel the dark reality as it sunk in that something I dreamed about could be fatal. I've never forgotten that.

I look back at those times when we were acting like fools in our cars and think, okay, that's when the guardian angels were doing a ride-along.

The only tickets I ever got were for things like improper tires and loud exhausts. I put on these big, wide tires on the back that stuck out of the fender wells. The mufflers were bolted onto the header. And when we'd race, I'd just unbolt them and put them in the trunk.

After a race I decided to not put them back on, so my car was roaring when a cop pulled me over. He saw my tires sticking out of the back fender wells and my loud exhaust due to the open headers.

He walked up and said, "Problem with your exhaust, Mr. Evernham?"

Me being the smart-ass I was, I said, "No sir. Mufflers are in the trunk."

Then he slapped me with another ticket. Those kinds of tickets were only fifteen dollars. It wasn't like I was Big John Milner, but I always had a half a dozen of them in the glove compartment. They were usually for the same things: loud exhaust and wide improper tires.

(In the movie, Milner would open his glovebox and say he was filing the ticket under "C. S." for "chicken shit.")

Overall, those were some wild and crazy times. Steve, Frank, and I were just guys who loved cars and didn't have a care in the world.

Growing up in my town was like living in a time capsule. It felt like the early sixties more than the seventies. My friends and I had a few hangouts we frequented, but it all depended on what we wanted to do. If we were just looking for entertainment, we'd go to Leocadia Court Park or the Keansburg Boardwalk. We'd watch a ball game or just walk around and check out girls.

We knew we could almost always find a group of friends at the drive-in restaurants along Route 35. The bowling alley at Airport Plaza was also a popular place to hang out, bowl, and play video games and pinball. Saturday nights in the summer and fall, we'd take my '65 Malibu and cruise the Asbury Park area, home to the premier New Jersey car culture.

Even though my car might have been one of the fastest in Hazlet, it wasn't shit compared to those in Asbury Park. The big guns would come there from all over to show off their amazing hot rods.

There was one guy, Rob Ida, whose father was influential in the Jersey Shore car scene. Rob went on to become one of the best car builders in the country, and he's still hoping to bring back the Asbury Park cruising tradition.

This was street hot rod culture at its finest.

But in addition to parading their cars, they'd street race for money. The rumor was, in addition to racing for cash, those guys also raced for "pinks," meaning title to the loser's car. Amateurs like us never got involved because we'd end up losing money or our car—or both.

———

Going to Friday night football games and dances wasn't my thing. But I'd consider going if I had a girlfriend to hang with. Not surprisingly, there were a couple times I got into some fistfights at dances, and that's when I'd think, "What am I doing here?"

The dances aside, I've always loved music. In my high school days, you'd hear Springsteen, Meatloaf, Deep Purple, or Led Zeppelin blaring from my car. I was always a big oldies fan, too. Even though it was the seventies, I loved Frankie Valli and the Four Seasons, and early fifties doo-wop music. All of it coming out of my eight-track tape player.

Of course, fellow Jersey boy Bruce Springsteen was always part of my music rotation. I've seen Springsteen live several times. I even met him at a concert in Charlotte. It was just him and me for about five minutes, and he gave me his full attention. It was a great experience. What was awesome was when he told me he watched me race at Wall Stadium.

I'd always been curious about the lyrics to a song he wrote when he was going through his divorce, and it was really cool to hear his perspective. The song is "Brilliant Disguise." He'd married actress Julianne Phillips. But it wasn't long until he realized the "Hollywood lifestyle" wasn't for him.

I really relate to all the New Jersey–inspired songs he's written.

———

While I didn't consider myself a lady's man in high school, I did have a girlfriend for a while. She was a cute little Italian girl. She stood about five feet, three inches, with long, jet-black hair and a classic Italian nose. She came from a very Italian family. I'm pretty sure her folks weren't thrilled when this six-foot-two Irishman showed up at their door. Her mom, the stern family matriarch, left me with no doubt how she felt when warning me about getting her daughter home on time. I can still hear her, in her demanding Italian dialect, "You get my daughter home on time, or I'll cut your palle off." Just like that.

Although we had a good run, once I graduated she broke my heart, dumping me for one of the cool kids. It just wasn't meant to be.

Fast forward to when I started working with Jeff, I came back to New Jersey for an appearance. We had just started to hit the big time.

I happened to run into some of her friends during my visit. They said, "We told her she should have stuck with you!" We had a good laugh about it.

Some of my favorite memories of high school were the years I spent with Steve, Frank, and my '65 Chevy Malibu.

———

At seventeen, my focus was working at the gas station and trying to build my race car. I wasn't going to many parties or dances. I was getting ready to race.

I didn't know how I would get into racing, but I knew I was going to do it. I never doubted I would make it. I never doubted I was going to Indy.

I never allowed myself to think, "Oh geez, I'm going to have to get a job. I'm going to have to do something else."

I never wondered what I would be doing for the rest of my life. I already knew that. I just had to figure out how to do it.

And I was in a hurry, too. I had no time for, or interest in, college. I even passed on a chance for a scholarship in art at a local community college. I've always loved to draw. I do a lot of car design work now. So if I'd have gone to college, it would've been to study music and art. As much as I love art and music, my interests in both rank a decidedly distant second to my love for racing.

Beyond art and music, I've always loved movies. Some of my favorite films from my high school years were *Smokey and the Bandit*, *Rocky*, and *American Graffiti*. I actually now own the 1958 Chevrolet Impala driven by graduating senior Steve Bolander, played by Ron Howard, in *American Graffiti*.

There was a drive-in theater a mile and a half or so behind my house. It bordered on a wooded area. Steve, Frank, and I would walk through the woods and sneak in through a hole in the fence. (No idea how it got there . . .)

We did it for years. At one point, we stashed lawn chairs in the woods so we could sit and watch the movie in style. There were speakers close enough to where we sat, allowing us to hear the movie just fine. But, if we were feeling extra bold, we'd just snag a speaker from one of the empty rows of cars, plop it on our chair, and enjoy the show.

It got to the point where too many folks caught wind of our little secret, and the drive-in had to do something about it. But boy, those were the days—sneaking into the drive-in with our lawn chairs, hooking up a speaker, and just enjoying a movie under the stars.

Those were great years spent with great people. It sounds cliché, but Raritan High School was a melting pot of different cultures, which helped prepare me for a life outside of Hazlet. My high school years were full of more "trophies" than scars. In fact, the only real scar was the one on my broken heart.

My first feature win was in June 1976. Eighteen years old and sporting some sideburns. *Ray Evernham Enterprises Archives*

CHAPTER 3

RACING INTO THE BAYSHORE GANG

The Wall Stadium Years

"Let's go racin'!"

As far back as I can recall, I was either racing or thinking about racing: in my imagination, playing with my toy cars, riding my bike, visiting the track with Uncle Nick, or simply tearing up my folk's yard in my go-kart.

In 1975, my birthday couldn't come fast enough. I was as excited for August 26 as Ralphie was for December 25 in *A Christmas Story*. Except, instead of an official Red Ryder, carbine action, 200-shot, range model BB gun, I dreamed of wrapping my hands around the steering wheel of my first race car, finally racing for real.

I was turning eighteen, the legal age to debut at the local Jersey shore short track, Wall Stadium. It sits on fifty-five acres of land off Route 34 in Wall Township, New Jersey. Carved out of an old rock quarry, Wall is a one-third mile oval pathway with thirty-degree banking in the turns—something unheard of when it was first built back in 1950.

I really wanted to run on dirt in a modified, sportsman, or sprint car. Wall was paved, and at that time, ran a six-cylinder racing class called "modern stock" or "hobby stock." I liked it because it was an inexpensive class, really the only class I could afford.

I'd been to Wall Stadium dozens of times. But now, instead of just walking through the pit area and sitting in the grandstand, I would be racing door-to-door against some of the same guys I'd been watching and idolizing for years. Local Jersey dudes like Walter Rogers, Neil Rutt, and Steve Springsteel—they were the kings of that class. If I

31

hadn't watched them compete in person, I'd read about them in the *Asbury Park Press* or the *Area Auto Racing News*. There was no national racing for me. The local guys were the stars on Saturday nights.

I paid a whopping $400 bucks for my first race car: a 1962 Nova. But boy, that baby was hurting when I picked her up. The bottom was rotted out because the last owner had raced on dirt. Still, it had what it needed: A roll cage, a seat, and seat belts. I spent another twenty dollars for a motor I bought from my old pal Tucker Hill and tried to make a pavement racer out of her.

Along with my little brother Willie and my buddies Shay Nappi and Steve Trimarchi, I borrowed Jack Stoddard's wrecker, and we went down to Glassboro, New Jersey, to pick it up. I was so damn excited. Shay, Willie, Steve, and I got the car as ready as we knew how, then used a tow bar to hitch it to the back of Shay's beat-up Chevrolet Impala and headed for the race track.

At Wall Stadium you must be eighteen to race and venture to the pit area. That meant poor Willie had to go sit in the grandstand while the rest of us headed for the pits. (Unlike most tracks, where the pit area is track-adjacent, at Wall, it's positioned up and behind the track, near the exit.)

A track official stopped us to inspect the car just as we were about to drive through the pit entrance. I could tell from the look on his face he knew two things. One, we had no money. And two, we had no clue what we were doing. Pavement cars are low. What caught his attention? Our car sat a foot higher than every other vehicle out there. Also, it sported street tires that had been grooved for the dirt.

I don't know if he felt sorry for us or realized I was just a young wannabe racer. Hell, he knew I wasn't going to beat anybody. I'd be lucky to even qualify.

With a look of concern and a heavy sigh, the official said, "You can run it tonight, but there are some things you're gonna have to do to bring it back again. Okay?"

I noted his list of changes, then he waved us through.

This was one of those moments, like so many throughout my life and career, where I just thought, "I'm going to do this. I'll figure it out once I'm on the track."

As I like to say, sometimes you just have to jump out of the plane and build your parachute on the way down.

As we made our way to our assigned pit space, I soaked in Wall

Stadium's sights, sounds, and smells. Gasoline and burning rubber invaded your nose. Revving motors boomed into your skull due to Wall being a bowl in the ground.

I put on my fire suit, which was really nothing more than a pair of coveralls. It was about as protective as a Halloween costume. But it had my name on it. I had a bandana. I thought I was Mario Andretti.

As I drove down from the pits to the track, I was more excited than scared. While I wasn't frightened, I was so damn nervous rolling out there, my leg shook like crazy as I attempted to push the clutch. Wall may be just a third-of-a-mile Jersey short track, but the first time I drove into one of the thirty-degree banked turns, it felt like I was at Daytona.

"Holy shit," I thought. "This place is steep. This thing's gonna tip me over." I couldn't have been going more than sixty or seventy, but it felt like a million miles an hour.

What added to my nervousness was all the family and friends who showed up to watch me. Every one of them knew I'd been looking forward to this moment my whole life.

Hell, I probably put fifty people in the stands.

When they dropped the green flag for the first qualifying race, I just floored it like I was at Talladega. Then it hit me. I was finally racing. It was incredible.

I had to start in the back, behind a bunch of cars. I remember glancing around, noticing how most were rough-looking. Novas, Mustangs, and '55 Chevys—they were all just warriors, and beat to hell. A lot of the guys would race their car, leave it on the trailer all week, then bring it back, put air in the tires, and get on the track. If their car ever got damaged, they'd take a hammer and beat out the fender.

They'd sometimes decorate them with crazy paint jobs and funky signs. Some would get dolls and position them in their car so the head would stare out the back window at you.

Guys like me that started in the back had no concept of what we were doing. It was almost like a demolition derby. Bangin' bumpers and doors. The racers up front, folks like Walt Rogers, they were more serious.

In my very first race, one of the cars, a giant '55 Chevy, pulled out in front of me. Coming off the corner, he got sideways. The track had wooden fences on the outside. As I whizzed past him, I watched the Chevy climb up the fence, then flip and roll back on the track upside down. I couldn't believe it.

While I had a blast, I didn't qualify for the feature race that first night. Unfazed, my buddies and I kept working on the car, making it lower, trying to make it faster weekend after weekend. I finally won my first qualifying race before the end of that year.

I was proud of myself and my makeshift crew. In the span of just a few weeks, we went from being a bunch of clowns to winning a qualifying race and making it into a main event. That was a big accomplishment.

In my imagination, next stop, Indy!

———

I realized if I was going to be competitive, I needed a faster car. So I sold the '62 Nova and bought the car that won the last race of the year: a 1968 Camaro. It was owned by a really decent guy from Jersey City named Ed Moench. I agreed to pay him $1,000. A real class act, he let me take the car to go racing after I gave him a deposit of $600, promising to pay him a hundred bucks monthly for the next four months.

I wound up winning my first two feature races and winning rookie of the year. But I still had much to learn about setting up cars, tire pressure, and generally how to compete. Even so, that car gave me a better way to race. I was all in.

———

I won my first race on Father's Day weekend, 1976. My crazy buddy, Walt Rogers, had the fastest ride, a Plymouth Valiant. That Valiant was also the loudest vehicle out there. The headers came right out of the fender, and it made the weirdest noises. It didn't sound like any of the other cars. It was more like a megaphone.

Sure enough, I managed to get into the lead where I drove my butt off. Racing in those big old modern stocks was wild. Back then we didn't have good racing seats. They were the same kind you'd find in normal street cars. So with every whip of the wheel, I bounced around and slid all over the freaking place.

I was out front with five laps to go, expecting friggin' Walt Rogers to pass me at any second. In my mind, Walt was the man. There was no way I could stop him.

While I couldn't see him, I could hear him. Then suddenly, I didn't anymore. No more megaphone blast. Driving on the front straightaway something caught my attention. I quickly glanced to the infield and damned if I didn't see Walt's white No. 27 with its hood in the air. Outside his car, Walt's head was buried under the hood trying to discover what happened.

"Holy shit," I thought. "He's in the infield and I'm going to win this race!"

It turned out Walt had some throttle linkage come off. Walt's bad luck was good for me. Sailing beneath the checkered flag, I grabbed my first race victory.

Man, that felt good.

For some unexplainable reason, Father's Day weekend continued to be lucky for me throughout my career. I won many races that weekend, especially during my Cup career.

Then the guys and I took on the New Egypt Speedway. It was a flat, paved, quarter-mile, NASCAR-sanctioned track thirty miles from Hazlet. My first race there turned into a rematch with Walt and, somehow, I'd gotten in the lead again. We raced ten hard laps together, and again I beat him across the finish line. This victory tasted even sweeter than the last because this time his car didn't break down. I'd just driven the wheels off mine and won fair and square.

I had just beaten my "Earnhardt." Right then and there, my confidence shot through the roof. People started taking notice of this new kid from the Bayshore.

By and large, racers like Walt and the rest were blue-collar Jersey Shore guys. Walt was a roofer by trade. Others were fishermen and construction workers. Racing was for those of us who weren't great baseball players, footballers, or white-collar businessmen. Generally, they were all good people, and those were great times. Saturday night at Wall Stadium and the neighboring tracks was our chance to perform in front of a crowd of 3,500 to 4,000 and maybe get our name and picture in the local paper.

We all raced for the love it. The Jersey Shore racing culture was our whole world.

In the 1977 season, I racked up eleven wins. But I had built a car that pretty much killed the modern stock class, unfortunately. There weren't a lot of rules in that designation; the ones they did have, we found a way around them. Or at least most of them.

First off, there was no weight or height rule. For added strength you could add stock frame rails. Some racers used Camaros or Novas that were only half-frame cars or sub-frame. (You were permitted to connect frames from another car.)

My buddy Charlie Koijza helped me a lot in this department. A great welder and body man, he said, "Ray, I know this guy that's got a car he started, but he's not gonna finish it."

It was a Camaro with a sub-frame. Charlie took the sub-frame and welded 1955 Chevy frame rails on the back of it. It was feet lower than everybody else's. The roof was only forty-two inches from the ground, and it weighed just 2,200 pounds. Most other cars were a foot or two higher and weighed 3,000 pounds.

We were excited to race it. But the first time out I couldn't get it to handle correctly. It was terrible. I couldn't drive it.

We made all the adjustments we could think of and took it back to the track the next week. Then it was too loose. Instead of turning, it would spin out. I was so frustrated. We had custom built a race motor. I'd even spent $120 bucks for what was advertised as a "secret" six-cylinder cam from Clifford Research. It was supposed to give the car a real boost of power. They probably just boxed up some standard six-cylinder shit and claimed it was something special. That's why I thought I should have been flying.

Finally, we took the car over to Walt and asked if he could help us figure it out. Looking it over, he said, "This car's so light, it's too stiff."

The spring rate was too stiff relative to the weight of the car. The springs in our suspension were meant for heavier cars. So Charlie and I took the car to his garage and changed to softer springs.

Honestly, we really didn't know what the hell we were doing. But the races had started at Wall Stadium, and we needed to get there fast. Loading the car on the trailer, we drove a gazillion miles an hour to get there.

We got there just in time for my heat race. Charlie and I quickly unloaded the car. I got on the track—and won. "Whoa, this isn't the same car!" I thought.

That night I also clinched the main event. Thereafter, we just kept on winning.

We even won three races in one night.

That's when everybody realized they'd have to trade in their "cheap cars" and start custom building if they wanted to stay competitive. That's what I meant when I said earlier about Charlie and me killing the six-cylinder modern stock class.

———

I capped off the 1977 season at Wall Stadium by capturing the six-cylinder modern stock class championship. Not only did we win it, but we set the record for number of wins. Not bad for only my second year of full-time racing.

As a result, I was becoming a local celebrity. My name was always in the *Asbury Park Press*. But it was also in the *Area Auto Racing News* and that was big time to me. That meant people throughout the Tri-State area could be reading about me. I sported a mound of long blonde hair and always wore my sunglasses. I looked fairly stylish— by Jersey standards.

Track announcer Charlie Roberts took notice and dubbed me "Hollywood Ray." People who have seen pictures of me from back then actually mistook me for NASCAR legend Tim Richmond. That's about the best compliment I've ever gotten.

I was convinced that at any minute I'd pick up the phone and some giant owner like Roger Penske would be on the line: "Hey, aren't you the kid that won those ten races at Wall Stadium last year?"

One of the great things about being champion was becoming a full-fledged member of the Bayshore gang. A colorful bunch of Wall Stadium racing diehards, they were all from the same five-square-mile seaside fishing community. On average, they were a decade older. Walt, who was considered the leader, brought me in.

Most of us were related in some way. We were all first, second, or third cousins. While I never formally traced it, I suppose I was related to some of them.

The three main members were the Rogers brothers. Walt was the youngest, but he was the biggest, standing at an intimidating six feet, two inches tall, with 200-plus pounds of solid muscle. A roofer by trade, he was capable of flinging bundles of shingles over his shoulders while climbing a ladder or carrying multiple heavy, steaming buckets of hot tar.

As I said, he was the Earnhardt of our Bayshore gang, sporting the mustache, attitude, the whole deal. He was a crazy bastard. And I mean that in a respectful, endearing way. Walt was always ready to fight it out, on and off the track. And if I was ever in a tight situation and needed backup, I always knew I could count on Walt.

The two other Rogers brothers were small. I mean feet shorter than Walt. The oldest was Charlie. He owned a little general store and was more the "social" racer. He raced a Dodge Dart slant-six, and it never had a mark on it.

The middle brother, Gary, was a roofer with Walt. He raced a six-cylinder Chevy Nova and took his racing a bit more seriously than Charlie. Years later, his son, Gary Jr., worked for me at IROC and went on to enjoy a great career as a car builder.

Then there were Walt's cousins Neil, Warren, and Roger Rutt—the Rutt brothers. They were big guys, on the heavy side. They kind of reminded me of the actor Terry Thomas. They wore mustaches and had a gap between their front teeth. Good people.

Then there was Richie Baradino, a champion before Walt. He was the first of the Bayshore gang to win the modern stock championship at Wall Stadium. That little Port Monmouth group owned the modern stock series. We thought we were the shit.

As colorful and crazy as these men appeared on the outside, they were smart and methodical about their race car mechanics, and I soaked it all in, giving me a foundation for my own mechanical prowess. Such know-how aside, I also learned early on that survival meant holding my own around these older racers.

One time, when I was still new to the Bayshore gang, I bumped Neil Rutt in a race because he was running slower and he tried to block me from passing. Pissed, he came charging over to me afterward. I doubt he'd have taken a swing at me, but I wasn't sure in the moment.

I knew I had to hold my ground. "Look, Neil, you were in the way. You knew I was there, and my car was faster. You've gotta gimme a lane: the outside or the inside, but don't block me."

And just like that, Neil calmed down. If I'd have said, "Oh geez, Neil, I'm sorry. It was an accident," he'd have marked me as a wimp, and I would've never been able to race with Neil again, or any of the gang for that matter.

That was a code of conduct in the gang, you had to be willing to stand up for yourself and for each other. If you were out with those guys and one of them got into trouble, they needed to know you were there to back them up. I always felt I could count on them, and I hope they knew they could count on me.

There were some tough guys in that group, and it'd be nothing for Walt Rogers to take on two or three guys at once. One night, we were in this bar and there were a bunch of rowdy, drunken softball players. One was a team of cops, the other firemen. They got to drinking and trash-talking. The next thing you know, the insults became fists and it erupted into a brawl. It was old-school, the type Walt loved. He was the kind of guy who'd say to the other side, "Let's make it a fair fight. Why don't two or three of you jump in here with me right now?"

In August 1977, I was walking through the grandstand at Wall Stadium, collecting donations in my helmet for an injured racer, when I noticed this beautiful tall brunette out of the corner of my eye. I turned to her, and she just looked at me and laughed. I thought, "Well, she's not too impressed with me." (Later, she said, I looked scared. That's why she laughed.)

After my race that evening, I was in the pit, and here she came walking up with Gary Rogers. Turns out, she was friends with most everybody in the Bayshore gang.

Gary Rogers said, "Hey, I want you to meet Mary Dowens."

I thought to myself, "I already did meet her, and she wasn't all that impressed."

This time she flashed a smile without a laugh. The group was headed back to my house for my twentieth birthday party. They invited Mary along because they knew she was interested in me. She and I got a chance to talk, and the next thing I knew, we were dating.

———

Even though I was known to have a cocky streak, I like to think I wasn't delusional. While I was proud of the championship, I knew it was only for six-cylinder modern stock. I had to get to the next level. I eventually needed to get to the modifieds.

That's when I decided to move up a class and build a faster, more expensive sportsman car. But as usual, I had no money. I wasn't going to let that stop me.

I was a big fan of Charlie Jarzombek, who built these cool Chevy Vega modified cars. Charlie Koijza and I decided to model our sportsman car after his modified. One day at the track, Charlie and I took pictures of Jarzombek's car. From these, Charlie drew the schematic of a sportsman on the cinder block wall of his garage with chalk. Then we built our car based off those drawings.

The two things you can't skimp on at that class level and above are motors and tires. So I did everything I could to get more money. The motor cost around $2,500. Thank God I was working at the railroad where I made decent money.

I took what I made from selling my modern stock, combined with the money I'd saved from my day job and my winnings, and put it all into building the new car. It still wasn't enough. God bless Charlie. He'd buy parts so he could keep building and I'd pay him twenty-five dollars a week or whatever I could until I paid him back.

By the time we finished, we'd built a car ahead of its time. Even so, I realize now we didn't have enough experience or money to finish it properly. We didn't get the front-end geometry right, and I couldn't afford the good shock absorbers and springs. If we'd have known a little bit more about suspension and geometry, and if I had a little more money, that car would have been as good as any modified back then.

Opening night at Wall Stadium came fast. We rushed to get the car as ready as we could. In hindsight, there were two more things I wished we'd have put on the car before racing: nerf bars and window netting. Nerf bars attach to the rear frame extending from the rear bumper. They keep the tires from becoming entangled with other cars. The netting keeps your arm and upper body from being tossed out the driver's side window should you wreck. Neither were mandatory in those days.

We would've put them on eventually, but we had to get the car to the track, and we had run out of time.

————

Starting positions in both the qualifying race and main event were points-based. Being new to the sportsman class, I had to start from the back. That car was so good I had no problem qualifying. In the main event I was cutting through the field like a hot knife through butter: flying, passing people on the outside, then dropping back down on the inside and swinging back out again.

Then I made a dumb move. Going down the front straightaway, I passed a guy on the outside, then dropped down to pass another on the inside. As I tried to get back up to the outside, I hooked my back bumper right around his left-front wheel—having the nerf bar would have prevented that—and my car yanked at about a forty-five-degree angle, sending it straight up into the wooden fence. The fence grabbed the car's front end, tossing it into the air. It came down hard on the rear bumper and cartwheeled. The hit's force jarred me out of my seat, and without window netting, my head, left arm, and shoulder dangled outside the car.

Fortunately, the car landed flat on its wheels and spun a few times before stopping. In that moment, I realized how different modern stock was from sportsman. I used to race at 60 or 70 miles an hour in the modern stock. I was flying at over a hundred in this thing.

It was a big wreck. I sat there stunned and dazed. It occurred to me, just like motors and tires, you can't skimp on safety, either. I was lucky. But it was another one of those nights where if I was gonna be dumb, I had to be tough.

We missed the next few weeks to repair the car. But Charlie got it fixed.

The next couple of times out, we had overheating problems and finally the motor blew. I thought, "I'm done." I went from being a champion, winning weekly, to a guy that can't even race. Plus, I'd blown ten times more money on this car than I'd spent on my modern stock. I had spent more money in the first two weeks on tires alone for the sportsman than I paid in a year with the modern stock.

I was in a hell of a spot. I had no motor and no money. It was a hard lesson. For the first time it started to sink in that, "Shit, maybe I ain't goin' to Indy."

It was the first time something happened that I didn't think I could do anything about. The motor was pricey. We weren't talking about hundreds of dollars, more like thousands of dollars. I couldn't get a motor from the junkyard and be competitive like when I raced modern stock.

Yet, through the generosity of some good people in the racing community, I managed to rally and give it another shot. An engine guy named Ron Buck worked on my motor, allowing me to pay him over time.

I still owed him about $300 or $400 bucks when I happened to be walking through the pits one night at Wall Stadium and ran into Bill Wishnick. Bill was CEO of Kendall Motor Oil. We used to call him Bearcat Bill. He ran modern stocks, and he was a fun guy.

Bill said, "Hey, how come you're not racing?"

I told him my motor blew up and I didn't have enough money to get it fixed.

"I always liked to see you race," he said. "You're fun to watch." Then he asked, "How much do you need?"

"About $400."

Bill reached into his pocket, peeled off four $100 bills, and handed them to me. "Come race next week!"

So I paid off Ron Buck and we got the car ready.

―――――――

I always promised myself I'd be driving modifieds by the time I was twenty-one. I'd been talking to Jim and John Bauma, trying to coax them into letting me drive their modified. The Bauma brothers were farmers who sponsored a modified car. Well-known and well-liked in the racing community. As much as I wanted to drive for them, they didn't seem too interested in putting me in their car, especially John.

John was tougher than Jim. He'd always say, "Maybe you can drive this modified someday. But you gotta get more experience."

On my twenty-first birthday we were at Wall Stadium getting ready to race my sportsman with the newly rebuilt engine. Mary and my mom and dad surprised me with a brand-new set of tires as a birthday present, and I went out and won the feature race that night.

The next day my phone rang.

It was John Bauma. "Saw you won last night. Would you like to try the modified?"

I couldn't believe it. The next week—I drove the modified for the Bauma brothers. While I'd kept my promise to myself, it turned into a classic case of be careful what you wish for.

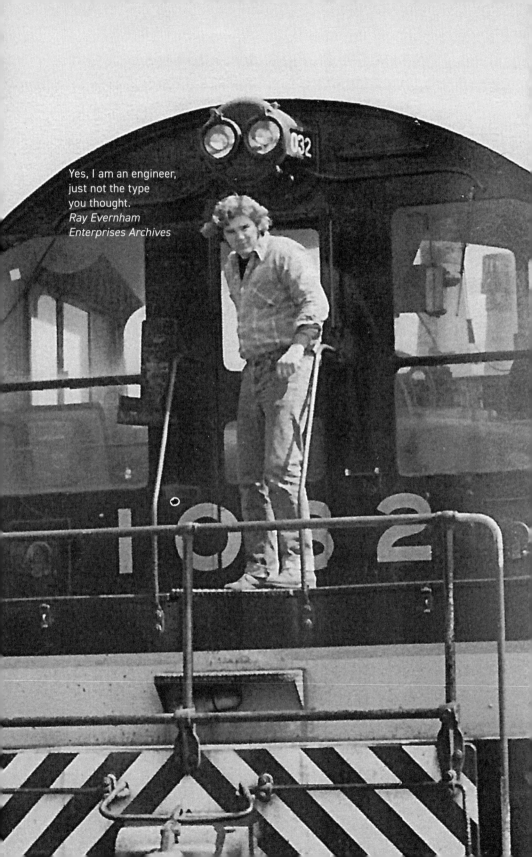

Yes, I am an engineer,
just not the type
you thought.
Ray Evernham
Enterprises Archives

CHAPTER 4

A NEW KIND OF TRACK

The Railroad Years

"Yeah, I can drive that."

My mom's brother, Bob Bailey, worked for a short-track railroad in Bayonne. The short track was used for transporting goods back and forth between the docks and Conrail's main rail line.

He knew I was a big healthy boy and mechanically inclined, and he also knew I needed money for racing. When the railroad needed a new switchman, Uncle Bobby came through with a job for me.

As a switchman, I hung onto the side of the train and hopped off when it slowed down to manually throw the switch so the train could go where it needed to for loading, unloading, or changing direction. I also had the task of connecting and disconnecting the boxcars. It was hard work, even harder in scorching heat or during a blizzard.

Working around trains can be a lot riskier than people think because they're surprisingly quiet. They move silently, which leads to a lot of accidents. Workers not paying attention often end up getting run over or crushed between boxcars. Thankfully, we were fortunate enough not to witness such incidents in our yard, but I've personally been hit by a train before and knocked off my feet because I couldn't hear it approaching. If you're lucky, you might catch the faint sound of a squeaky track, but railroad workers always have to stay alert. Some people think railyard trains aren't dangerous because they don't speed down the tracks, but plenty of people learned the hard way just what a train can do to the human body.

Another thing you had to watch out for was going around bends. When trains make turns, the boxcars come closer together. If you're hanging on the side and not paying attention, you can slip in between them and get crushed. I had a couple of close calls myself.

To learn the ins and outs of the job, they paired me up with a couple of railroad lifers named Jim Clancy and Frank Kalanack. They knew all the tricks of the trade, how to save time, and how to stay alive. When a man has spent a career working on trains and has all his fingers and toes, you pay attention to him. These guys were my mentors.

Frank Kalanack was a lifelong bachelor. He was in his fifties at that time. He lived in the Jersey City area and took care of his mom.

Jim Clancy was a lively guy who would get really animated when explaining something, and he had a great sense of humor. But he wasn't exactly the most politically correct person. He might have a hard time fitting in today.

Jim's looks, mannerisms, and personality reminded me of James Caan and his character of Sonny Corleone from *The Godfather*. It was a persona that worked to his advantage around the docks. In those days, between the unions and organized crime, the docks operated under a code. If you went above and beyond or did someone a favor, you could expect a little something extra in return. It was just the way things worked on the dock.

Jim eventually moved on to a different, bigger railroad, which was something he had always wanted to do.

When I first started the job, we used a trackmobile to pull the box-cars. It was the coolest damn thing to drive. A trackmobile looks like a great big bulldozer without the blade on the front. It has retractable steel wheels and rubber tractor tires enabling it to travel on rail tracks or on roads.

I would drive it on the road at about 20 miles per hour and line it up on the rails. Once I was on the track, I'd hit the switch and drop it down on the steel wheels and jam it into gear, shooting sparks off the rails. It looked like a drag car going down the track. Whenever Jimmy or Frank didn't want to go get a boxcar, I'd jump in before they could reconsider. It was so damn fun to drive, and I drove the piss out of it. It was my race car on the rails, even if the speed didn't live up to the name.

I started on the second shift, 3:00 p.m. to 11:00 p.m., which wasn't the best shift to be on when it came to working on my race car. My guys were volunteers, so they could only work on the car at night after they got off work. I'd work on it during the day and leave notes on what I needed done that night.

The cool thing about the night shift was, once the boxcars had been delivered or emptied, there was nothing to do. I could leave. So, there were a lot of nights I was out of there at seven or eight o'clock. Then sometimes it might be 10:00, 10:30 p.m. It was a tradeoff. Regardless of when I could leave the train, my mind was usually on my race car around the time I knew my guys were going to show up.

––––––––

Business with the railroad started to pick up. We were moving so many boxcars, they decided to upgrade from the trackmobile to a locomotive. They bought a used 1,000-horsepower diesel electric locomotive from Southern Railway. Manufactured by General Motors, the giant diesel engine would power the electric traction motors on the wheels in place of the old-fashioned coal boilers.

It took a couple of months for our locomotive to get delivered, but they sent all the operating manuals ahead of time. I read through every one of them. I even talked to the salesman and the technician who delivered it. I wanted to learn everything I could on how to drive it.

Since Frank was already our engineer, he assumed he'd continue in the locomotive. Jimmy thought he'd get the shot at moving up to engineer on the second shift.

Once the locomotive was delivered, I said to Uncle Bobby, "I've studied the operator's manual and know how to run it." So, I jumped into the engineer's cab and fired it up. Uncle Bobby asked if I'd teach Jimmy and Frank. I said, "I will, if you name me the engineer on the second shift." So, he did. I don't think Jimmy was happy about it. In hindsight, he probably should have had a shot at it based on seniority.

Driving the locomotive was so cool. In the 1970s, locomotives were not computer controlled like they are now. Even though I'd studied the manuals, Uncle Bobby asked, "Do you really think you can drive that?"

"Oh yeah, I can drive that," was my immediate answer, not really knowing if I could or not.

I learned really quick that the most important control in the engineer's cab was what they called the "dead man's pedal." The engineer had to keep their foot on the pedal because if they somehow became incapacitated, simply lifting their foot off the pedal would shut off the engine, causing the train to slowly come to a stop. Back then, that's how they prevented runaway trains.

I should have been fired a couple different times. Once I was going a little faster than I should have been as I approached a bend. When you're going around a corner, the switches would position the tracks to direct the train to turn in one direction or another. But if you were going too fast, the front wheels on the locomotive would "pick the switch," which meant the locomotive would open the switch on its own. In that case, the locomotive doesn't go either way. It goes straight. Well, that day, the train picked the switch because of my speed and the next thing I knew, the locomotive jumped the tracks and drove out into the middle of the street.

I was like, *holy shit*. I had knocked a train off the tracks more than once, but that day I had driven it completely off. The train was blocking the road. People were honking their car horns at me. I was thinking, "What the hell do you want me to do? It's a freakin' train!"

I had to call for help. So, I left the train in the middle of the intersection and walked about a mile down the road to get to a phone to call my uncle. That was not a fun call to make.

"Hey, Uncle Bobby, we're derailed."

He said, "Where is it?"

"Ah, in the middle of Port Jersey Boulevard," I replied.

I learned that day trains are not race cars.

————

One of the other things I really appreciated about that job was the life lessons I received about a lot of things. I came from a small Bayshore town in New Jersey, and the docks were up in the Jersey City area, not far from New York. Even though it was only forty miles by car, culturally they were worlds apart.

The docks were mostly under the control of the unions. I say "mostly" because the unions had to share some of that control with the mob.

Navigating in and around some of the wise guys showed me how things worked under the surface. As I said, there was a code, and as long as you followed the code, you'd be fine. I'm not suggesting they were the Sopranos. But you quickly learned, do what you're told and you're rewarded for it. If you run your mouth and do things that you're not supposed to do, you pay a price for it.

I was never involved with organized crime. Far from it. But as I learned more about the docks, I learned a lot of the operation may have been controlled by people connected to organized crime.

I quickly learned to keep my eyes and ears open. There were a couple of guys there that looked out for me. They'd say, "Hey, if somebody asks you a question about this. You say that . . ." If I did as I was told, all of a sudden a new set of tires for my race car would appear.

There was this small coffee shop close to the docks run by two guys. We used to go there for breakfast before starting work. One day, I noticed that one of the guys had a black eye and bruises on his face. Uncle Bobby whispered to me that those guys were involved in some illegal gambling and were accused of "skimming," which means they were stealing money from the boss. They messed with the wrong people, and the beating was a warning.

About a year later, we arrived at the coffee shop around six in the morning, and we saw fire trucks and police cars all over the street. Our favorite breakfast place had been burned to the ground. They had bit the hand that fed them one too many times.

That was the world I was in at the time. As harsh as it was, it wasn't a terrible experience. It taught me a lot about how some parts of the economy operate.

One of the more powerful guys at the dock was a man I'll refer to as Mr. Z. Mr. Z was one of the people in charge of the distribution there at the dock and he liked me. One day, Uncle Bobby said, "Hey, come with me. Mr. Z wants us to come to his office."

Mr. Z was seated behind his desk when he waved us in. He looked like he meant business. Another guy was seated in a chair facing him. When Uncle Bobby and I walked in, the man turned to look, and his face visibly changed. He suddenly looked uncomfortable. I'm thinking, "What am I doing here? Mr. Z and the guy are in suits. I'm in my jeans and boots." I looked every bit like a railroad guy. Without getting into specifics, Mr. Z just unloaded on the guy. And now I'm concerned. My thoughts became more urgent. *"Why the hell am I here?"*

Mr. Z ended his tirade by saying in his thick accent, "Don't let what happened to him happen to you. Okay. Because what happened to him was not very good. Understand?" I started wondering, "Who was 'him,' and what the hell happened?"

As we walked away from Mr. Z's office, I said, "Bobby, that wasn't a friggin' warehouse safety meeting. What was that all about?" He just looked at me and grinned. Then it dawned on me. I stood at six feet, two inches, 225 pounds. I was "muscle" for Mr. Z and didn't even know it.

I had developed a reputation for being willing to drive anything. One time, the docks were buried under three feet of snow. So Uncle Bobby and Mr. Z asked, "Hey Ray, we gotta move this snow. We're gonna rent a loader. Can you drive it?"

"Yeah, I can drive that!" (I had no freaking clue how to drive it.) But I climbed in it, fired it up, and quickly scanned the controls. I pulled a couple of the levers to see what they'd do. Soon enough I felt like I had a handle on it.

I was scooping up snow when suddenly the rear wheels were in the air. Sure enough, I forgot the loader pivots in the middle. The bucket swung around and knocked a hole in one of the warehouse buildings. Mr. Z was not happy with me that day.

———

Every once in a while, I'd see boxer Chuck Wepner in and around downtown Bayonne. He was famous for his 1975 championship fight against world heavyweight champ Muhammad Ali. Chuck fell just nineteen seconds short of a full fifteen rounds. He was also the inspiration for Sylvester Stallone's *Rocky*. Chuck's a great big guy. He was huge, standing three inches taller than me, and everybody loved him.

The train tracks cut right across Port Jersey Boulevard, one of Bayonne's busiest streets. I don't know if you've ever been caught in traffic as a train is dropping cars, but you can be stuck there for twenty or thirty minutes if you aren't lucky. I hated to do it because it pissed people off. But at some point, you have to get your work done.

If Chuck Wepner got caught behind the train, he'd get out of his car, walk up, slap a five dollar bill on the cab window, and shout, "Hey kid, do me a favor and break the train?"

The champ was such a good guy, I'd unhook the boxcars from the engine and pull forward out of the way. I broke the train for very few people. Mr. Z and Chuck were at the top of my list.

Another character I got to be friends with was a guy we nicknamed "Billy, the Conrail kid." He did the same job I did, except for Conrail railroad company. Billy was my age and just as crazy.

If we'd go for drinks after work, it was usually to one of the bars in Bayonne. But one time we decided to run into New York City and wandered into a place we shouldn't have.

We stumbled into this dive bar, and Billy started buying champagne and drinks for the girls. When the bill came, it was hundreds of dollars. Neither of us could afford to pay it. Billy decided, "Screw this, let's get the hell outta here." As we skulked toward the door, the bouncer came toward us. Billy just spun the guy around, threw him up against the bar, and we ran out the door. That's when I heard gunshots.

Now, I have no idea whether he was shooting at us, into the air, or if he was shooting blanks. I didn't care. I promise you I have never run so fast in my life, and I'm the slowest guy on the planet. Carl Lewis would've been proud of me that day. We ran until I was about to puke. And you know what? Billy was laughing the whole time.

———

I worked at the railroad for three-and-a-half years. When Dad needed a job, Uncle Bobby hired him. I suggested that I go back to working on the ground so Dad could have the job running the engine. We made it work for a while, but eventually, the railroad business started slowing down again.

Around 1982, they had to let someone go, I had more seniority than my dad, and they were considering laying him off. But I had lost interest in the job. Racing was my true passion. I told them to keep my dad on and lay me off instead, so I could fully pursue my racing career. And that's exactly what happened. I left the job in '81 to prepare for the 1982 racing season.

During that time, I didn't really have a steady job. Dad continued working at the railroad until it eventually slowed down to the point where they closed it down for good.

Looking back, the experience of working with my uncle on the train and being around the docks shaped my personality and taught me the importance of respect. Respect for people from different worlds, and respect for machines that will kill you just as easily as they will carry goods across the country.

There's a final lesson I learned on the docks that I didn't grasp for many years. No matter how far you go in life, you carry a part of every place you've been with you. I realized this many years later as I was prepping the No. 24 car for the race season ahead in the mid-to-late nineties.

My phone rang, and I picked it up. Expecting the call to be from a crew member or my wife, I answered with a simple "Yeah?"

A gravelly voice that sounded older than I remembered but was still unmistakable came down the line. "Hey, big shot, I need some passes for the Daytona 500."

It brought me right back to the docks. I didn't have to think about my answer. "No problem, Mr. Z. How many tickets do you need, and where do I send them?"

No matter whether he did or didn't have an affiliation with organized crime, Mr. Z was always nice to me in my youth, and I trusted him completely during my time at the railroad. That experience taught me the importance of loyalty and respect. I thought Mr. Z was a great guy no matter what the government may have thought of him. I know that if I needed him today, all I'd have to do is call him. So, if he wanted tickets to the "Great American Race," he was gonna have them.

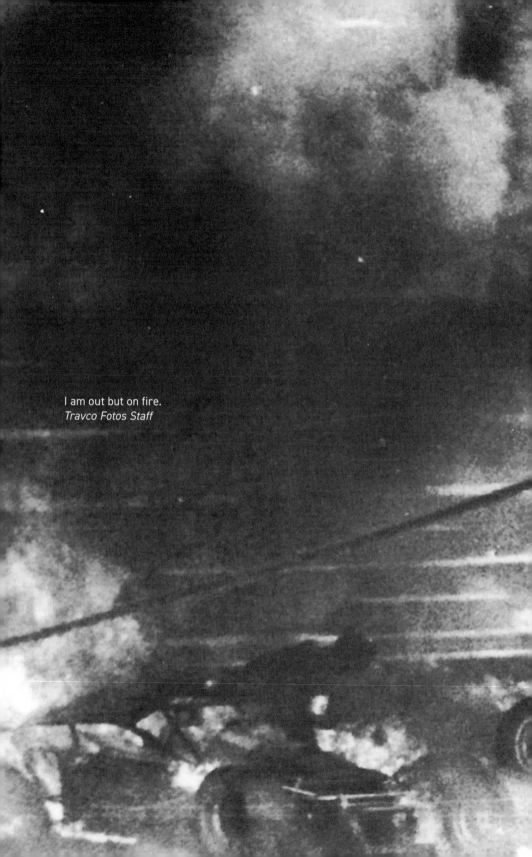

I am out but on fire.
Travco Fotos Staff

CHAPTER 5

INTO THE FIRE

The Modified Years

"I'm not supposed to die like this."

That sportsman feature victory must've been more impressive than I thought. Now heading into the 1979 season, John Bauma figured I had just enough experience to make him comfortable with me behind the wheel, and he offered me the full-time ride in the No. 61 modified.

I was going to step up, to show 'em what I've got.

The No. 61 was a big ole car—bigger than the other cars, and heavy. The first night out, I did pretty well. Finishing sixth. Well enough for the Baumas to keep me in the car.

I drove the No. 61 for about a year. Then the Baumas bought an even better car. Again, I was doing okay, but I still hadn't won.

But it looked like my luck was about to change.

I was leading with one lap to go to clinch my first win in a modified main event. Wall Stadium offered a bonus to the driver who could pass the leader on that last lap. So, as you can guess, all the other drivers near the front were gunning for me.

The crowd was going wild. In the final lap, I was barreling for the start-finish line when Tony Siscone comes up and spins me to take the checkered flag. I was so pissed!

But the loss stung a little less when the officials realized what had happened. They penalized Tony by taking away the win and the bonus. His selfishly aggressive driving that night may have actually helped my popularity and hurt his. He later told me he didn't mean to spin me, which I knew was bullshit. When you hit somebody in the corner, odds are you're going to spin them out

Our relationship wasn't the greatest. Costing me my first modified win didn't help. It was the damnedest thing, it didn't seem to matter where we were racing, somehow we always ended up side by side or bumper to bumper.

———

The truth is, I wasn't running as well as I'd hoped. John Bauma was right. I lacked experience and needed guidance.

Great people surrounded me when I was driving in the modern stock and sportsman classes. But the leap to modified took a different level of commitment and knowledge. Getting behind the wheel of the modified was a much steeper learning curve.

I needed an ex–modified racer or crew chief to do for me what the Bayshore gang did when I started running modern stock.

I discovered modifieds require more maintenance, a more detailed setup, and a real understanding of how to keep the motor tuned properly.

Then there was the huge step up in competition level.

It wasn't like I was racing the Bayshore gang. I was going up against modified legends like Jim Hoffman, Charlie Kremer, Don Stives, and the winningest driver at Wall Stadium, Gil Hearne. I even raced against Cup-level drivers like Geoff Bodine and Ron Bouchard. Real pros.

I didn't want to admit I was out of my league.

I kept thinking, "I just have to drive better." Then I'd drive the piss out of the car. I had a bad habit of keeping it sideways, which would burn the rear tires off, and I'd ultimately wreck the damn thing. I just didn't have the know-how to get the most out of it.

Truth be told, I wasn't mature enough in my life outside of racing, either. I was eating a lot and probably drinking too much beer. It wasn't like I was a drunk, but I certainly wasn't thinking about switching to water or hitting the gym anytime soon.

My mentality was, I'm going to drink with my friends during the week, work on the car when I feel like it, and go to the racetrack and drive the hell out of it.

If I truly wanted to level up as a driver, that was the wrong approach. My focus should've been on improving myself as well as the car.

The Baumas were the nicest guys; they should have fired me a dozen times. I didn't know how to set the car up properly, and I really didn't know how to race it.

When you're used to winning a lot, and suddenly you're not, it weighs on you. But if it wasn't for them taking the chance on me, I may not be the person I am today.

———

By 1982, it was just Jim Bauma and me. He got a new car, switching from the Number 61 to the Number 19. We were competitive, but I crashed a lot.

Regardless, Jim was there for me.

He just loved racing, and I don't think he was as "accomplishment oriented" as much as he just liked me and my family. He liked owning a car and going to the racetrack. He wasn't a wealthy man. So, I felt I had to find ways to keep our partnership up without asking him for money all the time.

I was glad I ended up winning several races for Jim during the time we were together. Jim believed in me, and that gave me the confidence to start winning again.

That's happened to me several times in my life.

For example, the night of my first modified win. I was sitting on the nerf bar of my car and Jamie Tomaino's dad, Speedy, who I loved, a really cool guy—with a good nickname—sat down beside me. (Coincidentally, he had an Italian accent, too.)

"Tonight is your night," he said. "Understand me? You can beat these guys. You're gonna win this thing."

His voice and words—"Tonight is your night"—echoed in my mind lap after lap. And damned if I didn't win—even beating his son Jamie, who took second.

After that, I gained confidence and ran pretty good. Then we got to Martinsville, Virginia, for the annual Cardinal 500 NASCAR Winston Racing Series Budweiser Modified event. It was October 31, 1982.

Our car was fast, but we had tire trouble. The tire manufacturer I'd used throughout my career didn't have the kind of tire I needed for that race, and the kind we chose to use kept blistering and blowing out. We were running well, but the tires weren't holding up, putting us behind.

With eighty-four laps to go, I pitted once again to replace another blown tire. This time I also fueled up.

No sooner was I back on the track than a right-rear tire failure sent me careening into the wall. It knocked the car sideways, and the rear scraped along the concrete.

The car finally came to a standstill.

I was pissed!

I sat there thinking, "I'm done. Screw this." Then, as I watched cars whizzing past, it dawned on me they hadn't thrown the caution flag.

The officials obviously didn't see I was stalled. I was a sitting duck.

Just then, Tony Siscone was barreling down the straightaway, nose to tail behind another car. (Front ends of modifieds sit so low and the tails ride so high, there was no way Tony could've seen what was just ahead of the car he was chasing.)

The car in front of Tony whipped to the side to avoid me. With no time to react, Tony crashed into me at a hundred-plus miles per hour.

I'd never felt that kind of an impact in my life. My whole body took the shock. He hit me with tremendous g-force, knocking the wind out of me. Which, as it turns out, probably saved my life. More on this later.

My car started spinning.

I wasn't unconscious, but I wasn't totally coherent. Everything stopped for a second.

My full fuel cell was ripped open by the impact, dousing mine and Tony's car with fuel. A second later it ignited, shooting flames forty to fifty feet in the air, consuming both cars in a huge fireball.

I found myself in an inferno. Fire everywhere. Even creeping under my helmet. I knew I had to unbuckle my belts, but I couldn't see my hands through the flames.

I started feeling burning pain from the heat. I couldn't breathe and I started panicking. As I fumbled to get my belts undone, I realized my shoulder harness was literally melting. The heat was so intense.

I kept thinking, "I'm not supposed to die like this. Not now, not this way."

I don't know how, but I finally undid my lap belt. Reaching for the roll bar, I fought to pull myself through part of the roof that had been torn off in the crash.

I knew I'd finally gotten out of the car, but I still couldn't see, and my back and shoulders were on fire. I didn't know which way to go so I just blindly ran.

A car owner named Jim Soucy flew over the pit wall, soaking me with his fire extinguisher.

Meanwhile, fellow driver Jerry "Magee" Miller, who'd pulled up alongside the wreck, helped Tony out of his car.

They put me in an ambulance and rushed me to the hospital. My lips hurt. So did my eyes and my neck. My hair had been burned to the helmet line. My beard was completely charred. I was in shock.

Paramedics applied ice to my face and gave me something for my eyes. They put a damp cotton cloth in my hand and told me to keep wiping them as my eyelashes had singed together. That's why I couldn't see.

When I could finally pry one eye slightly open, I noticed the damp cloth was actually a Kotex tampon. It's odd. After everything I had just been though, damn near dying in the crash, one of the lingering memories is seeing that Kotex in my hand.

They were treating me for second-degree burns, but they wouldn't give me a mirror, which scared me. I thought, hell my face must have burned off.

By then, Mary and my mom had arrived.

They assured me I still had my same old face. I realized Tony Siscone had been brought to the same place when I heard his voice in the ER.

Tony had it worse than me. Both of his hands were burned horribly, third degree. Apparently, just before the accident, his hands were sweaty, so he took off his driving gloves. He endured months of skin grafts and rehab. He had no use of his hands during much of that time. His wife, Margie, was his rock, she did everything for him. It really changed the way I thought about Tony and Margie.

I'd always been somewhat envious of Tony. Not only was he driving the best car on the track, he was also getting paid to drive it. He was beating me regularly. He seemed to have all the luck. He was no longer the lucky one. Now he and Margie were two young people facing a serious, life-changing incident.

I remember going to visit him after he was transferred to a burn center in Philadelphia. I was still hurt, with open burns myself, but I needed to see him for some reason.

Between seeing his burns and the scent of burnt flesh in his hospital room, I started to feel sick and almost passed out. The nurse came in, pissed off that I was in a sterile area with the open burns around my neck. So she kicked me out. I'll never forget that day.

Tony's successful comeback to racing has always inspired me. One night after the feature race (I don't think either of us won) I watched as Margie carefully unbuckled his helmet. Then Tony took off the driving gloves he wore over the compression gloves that covered his bandages and burns. I could see his hands were bleeding through the bandages.

I understood right then why Tony was the champion and I wasn't.

I made a decision, no more whining or excuses. My racing rival had just overcome something that would have ended most people's driving careers. I needed to toughen up. (By the way, a year later, Tony went back to Martinsville, the track that almost killed us, and won. I went back too, but in typical Ray style I was fast but couldn't close the deal.)

———

The fire's intensity, and all the time I spent in it, should have burned me much worse. But I was always good about wearing my safety equipment. I had quality stuff on that day, thank God, because I was in that inferno for quite a while.

Before, when I said getting the wind knocked out of me may have saved my life, that's because it stopped me from breathing in fire when I was panicking.

The car was all but destroyed.

Part of the rear suspension came right through and over my left leg, pinning me in. Had it gone two or three inches more toward the car's center, it would have pierced right through my back.

My helmet took a beating, too. The face shield melted, and the interior burned as flames climbed up the insides. The paint on the outside bubbled. I sent it back to the manufacturer Simpson so they could see how it held up.

That horrific accident happened in 1982, but I can still feel and see it in my imagination, as if it happened only yesterday.

———

The Martinsville wreck set me way back. I had nothing. No job. No race car, and I was hurt again. But I didn't quit. I had every reason in the world to do so, but I didn't.

I just knew I needed to find a way to get some money in the door.

I started flipping through "help wanted" ads in the paper.

A local car dealer, Straub Lincoln Mercury, needed a salesman. I applied and got the job, and I worked there from November until the following April. Turned out I was a pretty good car salesman. So good, in fact, when I told the owner Charlie Straub I was leaving to go back to racing, he did everything he could to convince me to stay.

"Ray, look, you need to stay here," he said. "You can make a lot of money. You're a good guy. People like you." Then he added, "You're never gonna be able to make a living in racing."

I said, "Charlie, I gotta go. I want to go race."

He shrugged his shoulders, shook my hand, and told me I'd always have a job there.

Fast forward. Over the years Charlie expanded his dealership group with other manufacturers, including Dodge. Bringing this relationship full circle, when I started Evernham Motorsports with Dodge, one of our sponsors was the Dodge Dealers Association, and Charlie was among them.

Once when I was home for a visit, I decided to stop by and see Charlie. He came out to greet me and asked how I was doing.

"Charlie, not only have I made a damn good living in racing, but you're also sponsoring me!"

We both had a big laugh over that. I'll always be grateful to Charlie for giving me a job when I needed it.

Meantime, I kept my expenses as low as I could. I had a truck payment and some nominal living costs. Other than that, every dollar I made or saved went 100 percent into building another race car. Hell, I even lived with my folks. I did whatever I could to make or save money.

Jim Bauma and I salvaged what parts we could of our wrecked ride. He and I decided we'd split expenses fifty-fifty for our new car, a brand-new chassis from Troyer Engineering. We got a lot of help from various people to build that car. Ralph Critelli, who owned a body shop, even painted our car for free. In exchange, we let them slap his name on it like a sponsor.

Bottom line: We begged, borrowed, and traded to get this car on track.

———

Here we'd just built a new car for the 1983 season, but for the first two or three weeks I ran like crap. There were some who suspected the Martinsville wreck shook my confidence.

Detractors would say, "Hey, he's had a tough time. Maybe he's scared." My dad even said, "You know, you don't have to do this. If the memory of the wreck is stopping you from going fast, it's okay."

I'm thinking, "Bullshit, it's not me. This thing drives like shit."

So we worked on it and worked on it. And I was driving the hell out of it trying to prove to everyone I could still do this. But, back then, I still didn't know that much about race cars. I'd just put them together based on what people told me to do, not because I necessarily knew what I was doing.

Sure enough, we raced the car at Wall Stadium, and damned if I didn't wreck it again. So here I am, I've got no money. I've wrecked this brand-new car. People are thinking I can't race anymore.

Still, I knew in my heart I could do this.

By now, there were many more naysayers than supporters in my corner. Even so, I was determined to fix the car. I wasn't quitting. I didn't care if people thought I sucked.

That's when I borrowed $2,500, which was a lot for me. Some came from a personal bank loan that my folks cosigned for and some from friends and family. Then I got to work putting the car back together.

The first thing to do was fix the bent chassis. Luckily, my friend Jamie Tomaino owned a car frame machine and jig system. The jig holds the chassis, keeping it square and positioned while you work on it.

Once we put the chassis in the jig, Jamie noticed it did not fit properly. Turns out, the chassis was a half inch shorter on the right side.

That's why the car drove like crap. It wasn't straight, so the wheels weren't pointing in the right direction.

We added a piece to the right side, put the car back together, went to the racetrack, and won the race. Boom! I was back in business.

But I was still far behind in points, so I had some catching up to do.

We won a total of three times that year. Believe it or not, the last night of the season, the battle for the points championship was between me and Tony Siscone.

While we raced each other hard and clean that night, I couldn't make up the points. Tony beat me to clinch the championship.

Still, taking second in points had people looking at me in a different light. The haters who thought I couldn't drive out of sight on a dark night, now were thinking I could be a true challenger for next year's championship. This was all thanks in no small part to Jamie, who by the way, went on to a great career in modifieds, becoming a NASCAR modified champion himself.

I was starting to realize I needed more knowledge when it came to the car, and I needed to be more committed to success.

I needed better cars, and I figured my lifestyle had to change, too. Besides losing the championship to Tony, I learned a painful lesson during the 1983 Garden State Classic at Wall Stadium.

The first Garden State Classic was in 1957. It began as a three-hundred-lap race, but in the early 1980s it dropped to two hundred laps. Regardless, it was a hell of an endurance contest on the one-third-mile track.

My car was wicked fast, and I won the pole. I had the equipment to win the race, and it would've been my biggest triumph at Wall Stadium. Instead, I was so out of shape, I literally had to take one hand off the wheel just to hold my head up. I was flat-out exhausted by the end.

This was a major wake-up call. I had never been as mad at myself as I was after that race. It wasn't the car's fault. *I* lost that race. It was me not being physically prepared.

Humiliated, right then and there, I thought, "Okay, if you wanna do this, you gotta get your shit together."

That's one race that still haunts me.

I've racked up about thirty-five victories in my driving career. While I can't tell you when or where all of them happened, I can describe in detail just about every race I lost.

Those hurt. You just never let them go. The thought that I could've won the biggest race on New Jersey pavement at that time, had I been in better physical condition, pisses me off—even now.

Until this point, I was sure I'd be discovered by some big owner or team. The combination of the Martinsville fire in '82, the crash in '83, and losing the Garden State Classic, which I believe cost me the championship, made me ready for a change.

Although I had guys offering me rides, telling me I stood a great chance of winning the championship the next season, I realized any big opportunity wasn't going to come to me at Wall Stadium. I had to get going. If I stayed, I'd end up just like some of my heroes. I would be a star at Wall Stadium, but all the real opportunities would be gone.

Right around that time, I'd heard the International Race of Champions (IROC) was setting up shop in New Jersey. IROC was the brainchild of former race car driver and business genius Roger Penske, TV marketing wiz Mike Phelps, and former LA Rams linebacker (and later Riverside International Raceway track president) Les Richter.

The idea was an auto-racing competition, featuring identically prepared stock cars set up by a single team of mechanics, to make the race purely a test of driver ability.

It was obvious—if I was ever going to make it to the Indy level, I'd have to stop racing at Wall Stadium and get a job with IROC. If I could figure out a way to get to test drive those cars, I could showcase my ability.

Fine then.

It was time to put the burgers and beer down and get a haircut.

IROC cars at Daytona. *Ray Evernham Enterprises Archives*

CHAPTER 6

ACADEMY OF SPEED

The IROC Years

"Professor Penske and the school of IROC."

The rumors turned out to be true; IROC opened its shop in Tinton Falls, New Jersey. Résumé in hand, I showed up and was hired on the spot by Barbara Signore. Barbara was the wife of Jay Signore, who was president and part owner of IROC and responsible for much of its operations. Barbara thought I was what they needed to get started in New Jersey. I dove right into setting up the shop with her and Jay.

The first few months involved transforming an empty building into a racing shop. One bitterly cold morning I faced a hell of a problem. A delivery truck was frozen to the loading dock after snow melted and refroze overnight. I needed that truck free because more deliveries were coming in.

I was banging away at the ice with a hammer when a beautiful, slant-nosed Porsche pulled into the lot and Roger Penske stepped out. I must have been an odd sight to the racing legend. I was twenty-five years old with long hair, a bushy beard, and wearing a flannel jacket. Certainly not the uniform of a Penske team member.

His greeting was straightforward: "Hi. Roger Penske. Who are you? What are you doing?"

After introducing myself, I said, "We gotta get this tractor trailer out of here, so I'm busting this ice."

He nodded. "Is Jay Signore inside?"

Mustering as much politeness as the bitter cold allowed, I replied, "Yes sir. He is."

He walked inside as I continued with my job. I didn't know the memorable part of meeting Roger was still to come. Twenty minutes later, he came back out.

"Hey, got any spare change?"

I didn't know what he meant. "What kind of change?"

He gestured to the tollway. There was a toll booth right by the new IROC facility. "That thing only takes change, and all I have are twenties."

I happened to have a quarter, so I proudly handed it over.

When I went inside, Barbara said, "Mr. Penske really likes you, but you should get a haircut and shave off the beard."

I took that advice to heart, cutting my hair short and losing my big beard. I lost thirty pounds for good measure, which I've kept off my whole life.

I've had a relationship with Roger ever since I worked for him at IROC. When his team wins, I often text, "Hey sir, great job," and he always texts me back because he's that much of a class guy. Many years later I got to tell the tale about paying Roger's toll at an event honoring him in Amelia Island, Florida.

I stood at the podium and said, "In 1983, I loaned Roger a quarter to get on the Garden State Parkway, and he never paid me back."

The crowd chuckled but Roger just looked at me like, "What the heck?" Apparently, he didn't remember the incident.

I continued, "Even with interest right now, that'd probably be about five bucks. Still, it's the best investment I ever made."

Why was it the best investment of my life if my dreams of driving an Indy car for Team Penske didn't work out? IROC taught me discipline and gave me the skills to run a winning team. It also exposed me to a network of racing legends, friends, and mentors who've lasted to this day, starting with the great Jay Signore.

———

I had little awareness of professional racing at the time, which is why I didn't know much about Jay when I started working for him. Early on, I learned he was close friends with legendary racer Mark Donahue. I was left thinking "Oh my god, this guy's a star."

Looking back, my career closely paralleled Jay's. Through our work together, I discovered he was a former race driver and skilled mechanic working on Mark's cars. For a while he was away from the sport working as a schoolteacher. That is, until he got a call from the Penske organization.

When Penske hired Mark to drive for him, he said, "Hey look, Jay is my mechanic, you should bring him in because we can win together."

This is not far off from what happened when Hendrick Motorsports hired Jeff Gordon to drive for them.

Working for the professional organization Jay put together was a brand-new concept for me. I was used to being on my own, running my own life. Now I was traveling as part of a professional outfit, getting meal money and other allowances, and working damn hard to make IROC a success.

We used to joke when we came to work in January that the job hours were "8:00 a.m. till August" because we'd typically put in sixteen-hour days, seven days a week until our season ended. At times I was unhappy with the hours and conditions, but looking back, all I can think about is how much Jay taught me about racing, business, and building for success.

The hard work and attention to detail that was characteristic of how Jay ran IROC became the blueprint for my career. The experience taught me not to fear big projects. I've been asked a million times in interviews how I assembled the Dodge deal or worked out the SRX deal. The truth is, I used the same process Jay taught me. I've even found a way to remind myself and my team of Jay's approach to work by buying up old IROC cars.

The incredibly detailed paperwork that comes with IROC cars is a direct reflection of Jay's unique organizational skills.

He was always buttoned up and efficient. I'm sometimes embarrassed to compare one of my record books to the one that comes with an IROC car. I can only think, "Damn, I'm such a slacker. I better fix this before Jay sees it."

Jay's IROC also had a certain culture it shared with Penske. It was a bit like the military. You had to fit in, or you wouldn't make it. At IROC, that meant there were certain things we did right—no matter how long they took. You could then look at that completed task with satisfaction even if you were tired as shit and needed a shower and a bed, never mind dinner.

The funny part is I don't think Jay was consciously setting out to teach us these lessons. It was Jay's personality and the way he did things that inspired us to want to do things the right way. I can't say I was always happy or that I always agreed with him, but looking back at my time at IROC, it was the most valuable education I could have hoped for.

People in the racing world know Jay Signore has a big fingerprint. During my time at IROC, guys would move on to Team Penske, NASCAR, and other highly regarded organizations, taking the Jay Signore way of doing things with them. Half of the No. 24 team was made up of guys I brought over from IROC, including Michael Landis. Seven-time NASCAR Cup champion, Chad Knaus, learned Jay's systems from working with me and being one of the original members of the No. 24 team. I believe that's what helped him become an exceptional crew chief.

It reminds me of the "Six Degrees of Kevin Bacon" game people play, connecting actors via various productions back to Kevin.

You can play "Six Degrees of Jay Signore" just as easily. Good guys educated by Jay started to spread far and wide to NASCAR, IndyCar, IMSA, and other organizations. Teams began to steal crew from IROC once they realized how well we were all trained, and that they'd gain access to Jay's techniques, like the impeccable check sheets everyone who worked for him learned to use.

He set a higher standard for crews, influencing the sport in other ways, too. If you've ever seen the gray interior found in practically every NASCAR Cup car, you're seeing an idea of Jay's in practice. In the early days, most of the stock car interiors were painted black. Jay and Roger felt the neutral gray color gave the car a much cleaner appearance and made it easier to maintain.

When I began working for Jay and Barb, I wanted to improve at every aspect of racing. It was immediately obvious that there would be more opportunities in motorsports for someone like Jay than someone like the twenty-five-year-old version of me. I wanted to get better organized and better at racing, and Jay was how I'd learn to make it happen. All I really needed? To be around a different group of people who were on the success trajectory I wanted to join.

That's what happened at IROC.

I was suddenly beside Jay, Roger, and world-class drivers. It dawned on me: these guys are champions and I'm not, and it's not just because I haven't had my shot yet.

I realized I wasn't working hard enough.

I wasn't putting in the effort the way champions did. I wasn't thinking about the right things, either. I realized it wasn't just going to come to me, I had to go get it. I wasn't going to magically take a tenth-place car and win with it. I'd keep crashing it weekly, looking like an idiot. I had to learn how to build a first-place car, race it differently, and, most of all, manage my life differently.

That's why I immediately took Barb's advice about a shave and a haircut.

————

Up to the time I joined IROC, I was building race cars for myself. When I'd weld the seat belt mounts and roll bars, I was thinking of my own safety. Suddenly, I was welding safety equipment in cars that would be driven by others. That didn't really register until the first big IROC crash I saw, when Neil Bonnett took a violent ride through the air at Talladega in 1984.

In the split second it took him to go airborne, it hit me. Oh my God, I welded his seat brackets and seat belt mounts in the car. His life depends on my welding job.

Neil came out of the crash okay, but I was forever changed.

I never forgot what I learned that day. I am personally responsible for the lives of the men and women who drive what I build. I preach that to all my crew members to this day. Watching that car take off like a rocket changed my perspective on the level of detail that was needed to prepare a car to race at high speeds.

My new attitude, focus, and hard work paid off.

In short order I became team manager instead of just chief mechanic. I was the guy everyone reported to for work, and I was responsible for accomplishing everything Jay wanted done, including car setups and other normal tasks.

When Jay allowed me to take the team and cars out to racetracks without him, it showed me he trusted me completely. This legendary guy having confidence in me meant a lot at the time—and to this day. I never made him regret that confidence, although there was one embarrassing incident that occurred on the way to Watkins Glen International in New York.

From the Glen I made a phone call I'd have paid anything not to make. It was about the new vans Chevrolet had provided us.

I called Jay, blurting out, "The cars are all fine, but we wrecked a van."

Jay sounded pissed off. "Who'd you hit?"

"Well . . . we hit the other van."

Jay was so shocked and angry he couldn't even form a sentence.

I quickly explained how one of our guys panicked when he came to a traffic circle and jammed on the brakes, causing our second driver to smash into the back of him. As a team, it wasn't our brightest moment, but it could have been worse—all the race cars were fine, and the trip continued.

Despite his no-nonsense approach in the garage and in business, Jay was funny. Normally, he didn't get angry at all the stupid pranks the IROC boys pulled, like moving all the hotel vending machines into my room one time in Ohio.

But he was madder than hell when cops showed up at his hotel room in Talladega, Alabama, after a couple of our guys wound up in the Talladega jail. Still, he loved jokes and had an easy laugh.

Another time at the Glen, Al Unser Jr. was going to race, and his uncle Bobby Unser was going to call it for TV. We had a special two-seater IROC car, and the TV crew wanted to tape Al driving Bobby around the course for a promo.

This gave me a devious idea to screw with the plans. I shared it with Al, who loved it, and I immediately got to work.

The IROC cars had a water braking system. A little hose would shoot water onto the brake rotor to keep it cool. So I rigged one of the water hoses to point directly at where Bobby Unser would be sitting in the car. Every time Al would hit the brakes, Bobby would get shot right in the face by the water braking system.

The plan worked beautifully.

As soon as they hit the course, Al was pumping those brakes as much as possible, leaving Bobby Unser soaked. When they came back in, they were both laughing hysterically. The TV people were pissed because they had to do a reshoot. But Jay was laughing his ass off, too. He knew it was a good way for us to blow off steam, so he couldn't be hard on us for pranks like that.

By April 1987, Mary and I had been dating nine years, engaged for five. It seemed as good a time as any for us to get married. It's what you did.

The ceremony was held in a small Catholic church in Port Monmouth, New Jersey. Mary had grown up going to that church, and the priest who wed us was the same who had baptized Mary as an infant. A typical small-town wedding, the usual family fun and drama ensued: The drunk uncle. The out-of-control dancing cousin. And the friend hitting on anything in a skirt.

Because it was early in the IROC season, I had to be right back at work by 8:00 a.m. Monday morning. The honeymoon would have to wait.

———

Certainly, one of the coolest things about working for IROC was that I was suddenly getting to know the absolute best racers in the entire world. I got to be friends with A. J. Foyt. We later did business together. I built several motors for his race team. At some of the IROC races, he would hold court with all these other amazing drivers, swapping stories.

I recall a rainout at Cleveland Burke Lakefront Airport where he was telling stories with Cale Yarborough. I was standing there, mesmerized, and I couldn't believe I was listening as these legends traded tales about being in plane crashes, being bitten by rattlesnakes in Texas, and even getting struck by lightning.

There is nothing like that feeling. Holy shit, I'm sitting among royalty.

Included among the royalty was Dale Earnhardt, whom I got to know well through IROC. He was an incredible competitor. But as much as I loved him, it would really get under my skin when he'd mark off the height of each car's spoiler on his suit to ensure he had the same setup as everyone else. It was so annoying when he complained his spoiler was a sixteenth of an inch lower than somebody else's.

I also formed a relationship with Mario Andretti, a classy gentleman, and the very definition of racing royalty. Thirty minutes with Mario can change your life, and I'm privileged to say I spent far more time with him than that.

Mario was respectful to me when I was an IROC mechanic, and that hasn't changed over the arc of my career. My favorite story about him came years after IROC. He gave me a tour of his home during a television show we did together, and he took me into his trophy room.

Along with gleaming trophies from the Indy 500, Daytona 500, and Formula 1, there was a rusty little one I recognized from Pinebrook, a midget track back in New Jersey. I asked him about racing in my home state.

Mario said, "Yeah. Early in my career I won a midget race there."

"Wow!"

"You know why that trophy is there next to world championships and the Indy 500 trophy?"

"I don't know, Mario."

"It's there because it's just as important as the rest."

Like I said, thirty minutes with Mario can shift your perspective.

Darrell Waltrip was another great driver, strategist, and clever dude. He was a great manipulator, forever trying to swing things in his favor. Picky about cars, he'd get upset if his race car wasn't just right.

One time he grabbed me by the shirt and shook me, yelling at me about his car being junk.

Later, Darrell and I joked about it. I said, "Hell, I thought you were gonna beat me up at Michigan!"

"I wasn't gonna beat you up. But that car was junk!"

I could mention a whole list of other drivers. Each was amazing in their own way, but to keep this chapter a readable length I'll finish by mentioning Hurley Haywood, whom I consider one of America's greatest road racers.

Hurley is a special driver and remains a friend. His enviable record includes five overall victories at Daytona's Rolex 24, three at the 24 Hours of Le Mans, and two at the 12 Hours of Sebring.

He suffered a terrible injury in a crash years before I met him at IROC. He felt pain during every lap, but he kept racing with incredible spirit.

Despite a variety of challenges, such as facing persecution for being gay in a time when the sport was less accepting, Hurley never allowed them to hinder his track performance. I hold Hurley in the same high regard as the other greats I've mentioned, mostly due to his exceptional driving skills, but also because of the genuinely admirable individual he is and for the class and dignity he consistently exhibits. Hurley was a racer's racer, and I enjoy every chance to be in his company today.

———

I never got a shot to race for Penske. Years later, Jay Signore let me know that it wasn't for a lack of talent, as much as it was poor timing. That answered a question that had haunted me for years. Even though I didn't get the ride, IROC was an incredible experience. It taught me lessons that would make me a future success.

Plus, I did get to test the IROC cars. Once, I even passed Rick Mears and Al Unser Jr. during a practice session at Michigan. I'll never forget when Al walked up to me on pit road and said in an incredulous tone, "What the hell? I thought you were a mechanic."

I think Jay was grooming me to take a senior position at Penske, but I wasn't ready to leave my racing dreams behind. The IROC brass made some minor moves to help me pick up rides at various racing levels, but nothing big materialized.

Still, my dream was driving race cars. That's why I ultimately left IROC.

I wanted to find a job that would let me build cars while having the chance to race them myself. Although I didn't race a ton after IROC, I was able to put all the lessons I'd learned into action. My winning percentage went up dramatically after my education with Jay and working around those racing legends.

I immediately went to work for Australian racer Dick Johnson in his NASCAR operation. It was a smaller outfit and I was handling everything. It was fantastic for me because I learned about NASCAR, the business side of racing and sponsorships, and about TV. I was doing everything from paying rent on the shop and ordering parts to hiring mechanics.

I was making good money and getting the chance to race on the side, but what I was really doing—without knowing it—was preparing myself for a jump to the NASCAR big leagues a few short years later.

Somebody said something funny on the radio in Daytona 1989.
Ray Evernham Enterprises Archives

CHAPTER 7

PUSHING A NEW PARTNERSHIP

Busch Grand Nationals: 1990

"Ray, I'm Jeff Gordon."

I got a call from my friend Andy Petree in September 1990—a time when I was still focused on my race driving career. Andy was the crew chief for the No. 33 Winston Cup car driven by Harry Gant and owned by Leo Jackson. He explained that Jackson's son-in-law, Hugh Connerty, had just hired a kid to drive for him in the last few races of the NASCAR Busch Grand National season and wondered if I'd consider becoming the crew chief for the team.

"Who's the kid?" I asked.

"His name's Jeff Gordon," Andy replied, "heard of him?"

Hell yes, I'd heard of him. The first time I heard Jeff's name was when I learned he drove in sprint car races at just thirteen years old. And of course, I'd watched him compete in the races on ESPN's *Thursday Night Thunder*. He was fast as hell, and he was beating the veterans. It didn't matter what he was driving. He jumped in several different cars and was fast in all of them. He was seventeen or eighteen by that time, but he looked twelve.

At that time USAC was made up of these midget and sprint car guys whose history could be traced back to the old days in Indy. And here comes Jeff, just some kid with long hair, whacking these guys week after week on national television.

I told Andy I'd take the job, and I headed for Charlotte, North Carolina.

I arranged to meet Jeff at a local hotel. He and his mother, Carol, had just arrived from their home in Pittsboro, Indiana. Carol had to accompany Jeff because he was too young to rent a car.

That was always a memorable aspect of our first meeting. I'd come from working with seasoned drivers like Andretti, Foyt, and Unser at IROC, and now I was about to go to work for this kid who's not old enough to get to the meeting by himself because he can't rent a car.

When I watched them walk into the lobby, I was instantly struck by how small Jeff was. Despite his size, he seemed poised and confident.

He introduced himself with a firm handshake, "Ray, I'm Jeff Gordon. This is my mom, Carol."

I used to carry a carbon fiber briefcase, because everyone seemed to have one in those days. I noticed Jeff had one, too. As we sat for our meeting, we both opened our briefcases to get a pad and paper. My briefcase had my notepads and books and my notes for Charlotte Motor Speedway, things like that. In Jeff's briefcase? He had a Nintendo Game Boy, some gum, a stock car magazine, and peanuts. It was kind of funny.

We hit it off immediately. We talked about open-wheel racing and drivers we were fans of. I learned we both shared a love of Indy car racing. You want to work with people who are really excited to do things, and Jeff was.

The next day, we rolled Hugh Connerty's No. 67 Outback Steakhouse Pontiac onto the speedway at Charlotte. There were several other Busch Grand National competitors running the track, including Davey Allison and Chuck Bown, who claimed the series championship that year. Because Jeff was inexperienced, untested, and potentially risky, it took some maneuvering to secure him a practice spot. This would be his first time driving a stock car since attending Buck Baker's driving school.

He was doing pretty well but needed some advice on negotiating Turn Three. So, I went over to Chuck Bown and said, "Jeff's having some issues in Turn Three. Can you help him out and get in the car and make some laps?" Chuck agreed to lend a hand. He took the car out and drove three- or four-tenths of a second faster than Jeff. It was an eye-opener for Jeff. He didn't know the car was capable of going that fast.

Chuck pulled into the pit and said, "Nope, y'all, the car's really good." In true Gordon fashion, Jeff got in and drove it three- or four-tenths of a second faster than Chuck did. As soon as he knew the car could go that fast and he could push it that hard, Jeff unleashed it.

Throughout the day, he kept getting faster, and by the end of practice, he was second only to Davey Allison in lap times. Not only was his speed impressive, but Jeff's ability to analyze and explain what was happening with the car and the track struck me. He conveyed the situation to me with such clarity and precision that it became easy to understand what adjustments were needed.

The last time I experienced that kind of driver-mechanic dynamic was at IROC. There's something special those guys have when it comes to communicating with you. It's like a sixth sense. And that first day I worked with Jeff, I realized he could communicate at that level. When somebody is that young, it's not based on experience. It's just natural ability and instinct. I knew he was a special kid right then—he was living up to his reputation.

I could tell that Jeff valued my feedback just as much as I valued his. Even though he didn't have any real knowledge about driving stock cars, I was able to understand and interpret what he was trying to tell me. Later on, I discovered that our dynamic was similar to how Jeff collaborated with his stepdad, John Bickford. It turns out, John and I are similar in many ways.

John wasn't there for our meeting—he'd stayed behind in Indiana to work on Jeff's sprint car for an upcoming race. John later told me Jeff called him that night after the practice and said, "You're not going to believe this guy. He never stops working on the car, ever." He told John how organized he thought I was, and that I wrote everything down. "He's just like you!"

John jokingly replied, "Well, I'm sorry to hear that." We've laughed about that ever since.

Jeff's initial Busch race at Charlotte didn't go well. Rain ruined individual qualifying, so the starting positions were determined by drivers' point standings. Jeff had zero points, which meant he had to participate in a short race alongside other drivers at the bottom of the standings, called a "hooligan race," where only the top finishers could qualify for the main event. Despite running decently for a few laps, he ended up colliding with Randy Baker, ironically his former instructor at the Buck Baker driving school. Just like that, our day was over.

Instead of heading back to New Jersey between races, I went straight to Arden, North Carolina, where the car was kept. It was the only car we had so we had to get it back together before the next week. I worked three days and three nights with the crew, straight through, rebuilding it. We had to put a rear frame section on it and redo the body and a bunch of other mechanical stuff.

Despite the disappointment from the previous race, we stayed positive and hoped for the best at Rockingham. Qualifying went better than we anticipated. Jeff went out there and recorded the second-fastest time, surpassing thirty-eight other racers, including major Winston Cup stars like Darrell Waltrip, Dale Earnhardt, Dale Jarrett, and Davey Allison. In his very first NASCAR race, he would be starting on the outside of the front row.

Suddenly, fans who'd never heard of Jeff Gordon were now asking, "Who's that kid? Where'd he come from?" His mom, Carol, wasn't nearly as excited. She was afraid for his safety and preferred he'd have started in the back. I could tell it was nerve-racking for her.

During the final practice, we were trying to figure out the proper car setup for the race. Although he knew the Pontiac needed to be tighter during the race, he wanted it to be loose initially to make turning easier.

We talked to Harry Gant's car owner, Leo Jackson, before the start of the race. Leo was a tall, thin, bearded mountain man, and quite a character. He was also a mechanical genius. We told Leo we felt the car was pushing too much in practice and Jeff wanted it to turn easier for the race.

Leo said, "Are you sure? Because I think you need to be pushing at the start of the race or you're gonna get too loose."

I said, "No, Leo, we feel like we're pushing too much. We're gonna adjust the car to make it turn easier for Jeff."

Leo replied, "Well, if that's what you wanna do."

Unfortunately, things didn't work out as planned. Jeff became too loose and ended up sliding into the outside wall on the thirty-third lap, placing us in thirty-ninth at the finish.

After the race, Jeff and I were sitting on the back of the hauler looking at our crashed car, all torn up for the second time in two weeks. Leo walked up to us, looked at both of us and then at the car and said, "Well, the next time you two boys come here, you won't worry about if you're pushing, you'll worry about if you're pushing enough." Then he spit a big wad of tobacco on the ground and walked away.

Later, all through our Cup career, every time Jeff and I raced at Rockingham, where we won four times, we'd always jokingly ask each other, "Are we pushing enough?"

The team only earned a meager $400 for the race, but we all considered it a minor victory. We demonstrated that we could set up a car that could compete with the best, and Jeff showed that he had tremendous potential.

The last race at Martinsville wrapped up the season similarly to how it began. Qualifying got canceled because of rain, leading to another "hooligan race" that concluded with a broken crankshaft. Any expectations of Hugh Connerty continuing the program into the 1991 season vanished due to the Iraq War. With an uncertain economic future, no sponsor was willing to invest. The members of the Outback Steakhouse team headed home.

Jeff made the trip back to Indiana to finish out the last few events of his midget and sprint car seasons. I returned to Jersey and my modified racing.

If I ever needed proof of the axiom, "Things happen for a reason," that short Busch Grand National season was it.

The final argument between Alan
Kulwicki and I at Daytona in 1992.
George Tiedmann / GTimages

CHAPTER 8

ONE LAST RIDE

The Alan Kulwicki Year

"Boys, I've had enough."

B y 1991, after all the valuable lessons I'd learned at IROC, along with a renewed perspective and being in the best physical shape I'd been in for a long time, I was genuinely excited to dive back into racing on a full-time basis for the first time in seven years.

I was going to drive two new modifieds: the No. 2, owned by Tom Park Autobody and the Bauma Farms No. 19. Two very different rides.

I raced the No. 2 car at Flemington Speedway in the new "dirt/asphalt" series. These cars were basically designed for dirt, but the series would run on pavement. The seat was in the center and the motor sat so far back it was practically in my lap. The body was a big square box with huge wings on the inside. It was incredibly fast.

The Bauma Farms No. 19 was my Wall Stadium car. It was a low-slung, left-seated, NASCAR-style pavement modified with a 1991 Ford Probe production body. Like most Northeastern modifieds, we only used half of the body, leaving the front wheels exposed.

I also had a TQ midget and one of the Redkote cars I'd acquired from Dick Johnson's racing team, which I planned to drive in the Automobile Racing Club of America (ARCA).

I kicked off my return to racing by setting a track record and scoring the checkered flag opening night at Wall Stadium in the No. 19. Then I took second behind Doug Hoffman in my first race at Flemington the next week in the No. 2.

Those tracks couldn't be more different. I averaged 92 miles per hour at Wall Stadium, which was a one-third-mile paved oval with high banked corners.

There wasn't another track in America like Flemington. Flat, square, five-eighths of a mile; you could drive it like a circle. It had guardrails inside and out and was wicked fast. I averaged about 130 mph there.

The year 1991 started off well. With my win at Wall Stadium and second at Flemington, I was feeling pretty confident.

I raced regularly at Flemington on Saturday nights. On Saturday, May 18, instead of one main event race, they ran triple twenties. I hated that kind of racing. It just meant running twenty laps with the hammer down, causing us all to drive more aggressively than usual.

In the first twenty-lap race, points and money earned determined the lineup. The fastest cars were relegated to the rear.

The field managed only one lap before we were all bunched up, banging bumpers. I got a little bit sideways. Quickly, I jerked the wheel right to save my car. In that instant, somebody hit the left side of my rear bumper, turning me. I shot straight across the racetrack at a hundred-plus miles an hour and slammed into the ambulance gate at Turn Four. The impact was so severe it picked the car up, flinging it out into the middle of the speedway.

Mary, who was seven months pregnant, was sitting in the grand-stand and saw the whole thing.

She watched the track crew rush to my aid. As they waved for the ambulance, officials escorted Mary from the stands, and we took off for nearby Hunterdon Medical Center.

I was in and out of consciousness for about a day. At one point, I woke up and saw my brother Willie and my car's owner sleeping in chairs in my room. I was confused about my whereabouts and asked, "What are you guys doing here? What's going on?"

Willie, relieved to see me awake, said, "Well, Ray, you had an accident. You're in the hospital."

"What? On the way home?" I assumed I had wrecked the hauler driving back from Flemington. The concussion had knocked any memory of the crash out of my mind.

Willie said, "No. You wrecked the number two."

"How bad is the car?" I asked. He just rolled his eyes. So, I said, "Well, call Bauma and tell him I'm going to be late for New Egypt." I was supposed to drive Jim Bauma's No. 19 car in a race on Sunday.

Willie looked at me and said, "Oh, you're going to be late all right. Ray, that race was yesterday. Today's Monday." I was stunned.

My brain continued to swell, causing me to be belligerent at times. At one point I refused to use the bedpan. I insisted on getting out of bed to go to the bathroom. As soon as I stood up, my blood pressure dropped, I passed out, and crumpled to the floor. I'd "coded."

When I woke up, I was in a different hospital. Due to the severity of my concussion, I was moved to a hospital in Red Bank, New Jersey. I was still in and out. I was awake but unaware. At one point, I called a couple of guys who worked at my race shop and told them I was being held against my will. I asked them to come pick me up and get the car ready as we were racing in Flemington on Saturday.

To my disappointment—but thankfully—nobody came to get me. I ended up spending almost a whole week in the hospital.

After I got out, the impact of my injuries didn't lessen. I experienced bouts of dizziness that kept me from racing for weeks. I wasn't allowed to race until my doctor said it was okay.

Knowing what we know today about head injuries, I shouldn't have been allowed back behind the wheel for the rest of the season.

But I did everything I could think of to speed up my recovery. I worked out at a gym daily to get back in shape physically. I sought recommendations from doctors on steps to rehabilitate and retrain my brain. I was constantly reading, did exercises to improve my depth perception, and played video games to regain my agility and mental focus.

During my recovery, Jeff Gordon was among the many friends and associates who called to check up on me.

I'd also received a call from Alan Kulwicki. Alan was trying to convince me to come work for him in North Carolina. While flattering, the idea of joining an owner/driver NASCAR Winston Cup team with limited funding wasn't something I was interested in. I already experienced that with Dick Johnson. I was focused on my comeback, putting all my efforts into rehabilitation so I could get back behind the wheel as soon as possible.

During my recovery, I also had to rebuild the car. But to this day, I don't recall who helped me, or how we did it. I just know five weeks after the accident, I was back at Flemington hoping to convince track officials I was in good enough shape to race.

But it wasn't just the track officials that watched me that day. Ken Schrader was there testing his Busch Grand National car, along with some other modified drivers.

Ken was completing laps in the twenty-two-second range on the five-eighth-mile track. When he took a break, it was finally my turn.

Emotionally, it felt great getting back behind the wheel. Physically? I was still sore. My rib cage and hip bone still hurt. And I worried about my depth perception. The high-speed turns at Flemington created a tremendous amount of g-force. You could easily run 130 mph—on an oval! I also thought, "Man, what if the car doesn't handle well? Everybody's gonna think I'm not ready to come back."

I rolled out onto the racetrack, scrubbed my tires, and did a couple of caution laps.

I got up to half speed. Then I began to gradually increase my speed. I checked all my gauges and floored it.

My track record was a 16.0, but I achieved that time at night.

I believed I had to run strong to please the officials. I felt pretty good. Coming out of Turn Four, my car stepped out a bit. I caught it. But then the son of a gun whipped around, which those cars were prone to doing. Then it whipped around the other way, spinning twice on the front straightaway.

"Don't hit anything," I thought. "Just fire it up and keep going."

Despite my concerns, and the unexpected spin, I started clicking off one quick lap after another. At one point, I clocked a 16.5-second lap.

When I pulled into the pit with a smile on my face, Schrader walked over and asked, "Isn't that the car you just got hurt real bad in?"

"Yeah."

"How fast were you going?"

"I think I ran a sixteen point five."

"Well, why don't you just take a gun and shoot yourself? It'll be quicker." Schrader said, as only Schrader could.

Despite the spin, I was given the green light to resume racing.

The comeback race I had planned for the following Saturday at Flemington was canceled due to rain. Restless and eager to race, I couldn't sit still.

I called Jim Bauma to ask if I could race his old No. 19 car that night at Wall.

"Yeah, I ain't doing anything with it. Let's go race it!" he said. It was sitting in my shop but hadn't been used in months. It was under a layer of dust, and the tires were totally flat. Didn't bother me. I wiped it off and filled the tires. Then Jim, Willie, my crew, and I quickly loaded it onto the trailer and hurried off to Wall Stadium, arriving just in time for the heat races.

The lineup for the main race showed me starting toward the back of the field, but I managed to finish fourth.

The following week, I was back at Flemington. Despite it being wicked hot that night, the fans made me feel great. Whether they love or hate you, when you come back from an injury, they give you the warmest welcome.

That night I competed against one of my favorite racers, Jimmy Horton. Jimmy's among the greatest in the sport and a fantastic guy. I hadn't had the chance to race Jimmy often, but that night we put on a hell of a show.

We were side by side for a lot of the race. At one point he passed me. No sooner had he gotten ahead of me than the caution came out, which meant we reverted to the positions in the previous lap. So, I was back in the lead. He stayed on my rear bumper for the rest of the race. I barely breathed until I drove first under the checkered flag.

I had beat him, but it wasn't easy by any stretch. Later, the promoter told me how exciting the race was. He described it as electric. The fans were on their feet because it was so close.

I was worn out. It was so damn hot. My fire suit was soaked with sweat, and it felt like it weighed a ton. I was dehydrated and woozy, barely able to get out of the car.

Still, I fulfilled a dream that night.

As a kid I'd tell my Uncle Nick, "I'm gonna win a race at Flemington someday." Now I had.

Everyone came over to congratulate me. While fans seemed genuinely thrilled about my comeback, deep down, I felt something wasn't right. I didn't feel like the same driver I used to be, but I was too damn stubborn to admit it.

Unfortunately, the next week at Flemington, I got into another serious accident. I was racing wheel to wheel with Kevin Collins, both of us fighting for a top-five position. As we entered Turn Three, a lap car spun out right ahead of us, blocking Kevin's lane. The driver panicked, rolling his car right into my path. I crashed into that lap car at 120 mph.

I slammed into it with such force my car reared up on its front tires, almost flipping over. We hit so hard, I thought I killed him. My car came crashing down and barreled straight into a fence.

The other driver was okay; the front of my car was totally destroyed. I was banged up again.

My ankles got bashed up badly when the drive shaft whipped around wildly. The impact was so intense a knuckle in my hand was dislocated (still is today) and it felt like all the air got punched out of my lungs.

Here I was with another wrecked race car and every bone in my body hurting.

The crash also flared up an injury I'd suffered back in '82. I had shattered my kneecap and sternum driving the midget, and my sternum had never quite mended right.

The wreck that night at Flemington knocked me off my feet for another month. Back then, I just accepted injuries as the price you paid for being a race car driver. But I also started to question everything I was doing. Was I not feeling like myself because I was hurt or was I just not good enough?

I missed a few weeks fixing the car and recovering from my injuries. The next race I was able to compete in was at Thompson, Connecticut. I always loved Thompson; I felt good and my car ran well. We finished fifth.

Then we shot up to Toronto Motorsports Park in Cayuga, Canada, where we logged another top-five finish.

Then we raced at Nazareth, Pennsylvania. Roger Penske was there so I made sure I was on my A-game. Doug Hoffman, Mike Stefanik (a fellow NASCAR Hall of Famer), and I were battling it out.

We finished first, second, and third. Hoffman won, I took second, and Stefanik was third. It was one of the greatest modified races I ever competed in. We were on a one-mile track, in front of the Indy car crowd, and we put on an unforgettable show.

Immediately after the finish, my crew and I hightailed it to Flemington, where I got another second-place finish. My next big race was the Flemington 200, where I had a guaranteed starting position because of my earlier win at Flemington.

But just before that race, I got a call from an owner wanting me to drive a car I'd driven years earlier in a modified race. I took the car out for practice before making a final decision. It felt pretty good in warm-ups, but on the first lap of the heat, I banged wheels with Ken Woolley and broke a tie-rod.

The crew repaired the car. I entered the consolation event and earned a starting position for the feature race. I was competing against some of the best pavement modified racers, including Reggie Ruggiero, George Kent, and Jamie Tomaino.

I drove my car from the back, on the outside, and passed the entire field to take the lead. But my vision started to blur, and my depth perception was failing me. That's when I bumped into the rear of a lap car and spun out.

I just couldn't judge distances the way I had before my head injury. It was really frustrating because there was no logical pattern or explanation for when it would occur and when it wouldn't. Here I had deftly driven through the field of cars, inches apart, only to then misjudge the distance between me and a lap car.

Finally, the moment arrived for the Flemington 200. Just before it started, I headed out on the track to scuff my tires. I was about to discover why running a dirt car on pavement wasn't such a great idea.

I was ripping down the front stretch at a blistering 140, 145 mph. As I started to turn into the corner, the force broke the car's aluminum spindle. The right-front wheel, the hub, the brake rotor, the brake caliper, everything just ripped away from the car. I felt the car drop and I watched as the wheel flew over my head. To this day, I can still hear the scraping sound the chassis made as it was dragging on the racetrack.

I had no brakes and no steering. I thought, "Damn! I'm heading right for the wall."

I held on for dear life as the car just plowed into the foam barrier. I hit the blocks with such force the car got wedged in with the back tires hanging off the ground.

Again, I had the breath bashed out of me and I sliced open my chin, making me think I must have hit the windshield. Turns out, my head was thrown forward so fast and hard, I cut my chin on the chest buckle of my shoulder harness. There but for the good Lord, I could have easily wound up like drivers Corky Cookman, Richie Evans, and Charlie Jarzombek, who all died from basilar skull fractures caused by similar circumstances.

They needed a forklift to tow the car back to the pits. There I was, back in the pit after another clash with the wall during a prerace practice run.

Since I had a qualified spot for the 200, my guys went into action. They cut the damaged front snout off the car, straightened it out, and welded it back together.

I started dead last. As I was coming through the field, actually making good progress, two cars spun out and crashed in front of me. I hit the brakes and slid right into them at about 25 mph. It just bent my front axle.

I got out of the car and walked back to the pit area, leaving my car with the other two crashed cars. My crew came to me and said, "Don't worry, man. It's not that bad, we can fix it."

I just looked at them and said, "Well, I don't know who you're gonna get to drive it."

"Boys, I've had enough." I turned the lights off on my driving career right then and there.

There were moments in my life when I believed I had what it took to pursue a racing career. I had instances where I proved, both to myself and others, that I was at least as good, if not better, than the guys I competed against. However, there were also times when I questioned my abilities.

The inconsistency was irritating, to say the least. I had the ability, but I couldn't showcase it consistently. Ultimately, I believed it boiled down to a lack of sufficient experience and the absence of proper coaching and mentorship behind the wheel. I was incredibly tough on myself, and this self-criticism only led to misery.

Moreover, the injuries I sustained added more fuel to my frustration. It would be a long time before I truly felt good again, both physically and mentally.

So, I decided I'd pack my bags, take Mike Joy's advice, and head for North Carolina to take the job with Alan Kulwicki.

While I was disappointed and hurt to be giving up on my driving career, Mary was relieved. She knew it was one of the hardest decisions of my life, but she was also grateful I'd made the choice to get out of the car. Our son, Ray J., was born July 18, 1991. We were a family now and financially we were in trouble. I needed to rise to the occasion. That's why I thought taking the job with Alan Kulwicki was the right thing to do.

Being a professional race car driver was the only dream I ever had. Now I literally had no idea what was going to happen with the rest of my life. Needless to say, it was a very confused and scared thirty-four-year-old who packed up his belongings, kissed his wife and child good-bye, and headed to North Carolina.

I arrived in January 1992. Alan's shop was located behind Charlotte Motor Speedway. The only apartment I could afford was in Concord, about fifteen minutes northeast of the speedway. It was a one-room apartment so tiny I had to sleep on a pull-down Murphy bed. But with

Mary and Ray J. still living in New Jersey, it suited me just fine. Besides, the rent was only $350 a month.

Alan and I had had lots of productive and friendly telephone conversations throughout the previous year. But once we got into the same room, we were like oil and water.

While I did know a great deal about race cars, at that point I didn't know a whole lot about Cup racing. Consequently, I felt like Alan didn't respect anything I had to say.

Alan and I were arguing constantly. The insults flying back and forth between us were soon replaced by small tools being thrown across the shop.

The problem was simple: in many ways, we were too much alike.

After five weeks, I'd had enough. I couldn't take one more day of his belittling me or his constant condescending attitude. During the Friday practice before the 1992 Daytona 500, things came to a head. Alan and I got into a minor physical altercation outside of the garage area. While we were shoving and screaming and yelling obscenities, A. J. Foyt was perched above us on his hauler enjoying the whole thing. He still kids me about it today.

So, after I quit/got fired, I headed to the parking lot, feeling like I was at the lowest point in my life. I ran into Lee Morse and Preston Miller from Ford Motor Company.

They asked me how I was doing, and I told them the whole story. They then asked me to walk with them to see Bill Davis. They knew Bill's driver, Jeff Gordon, was struggling and Bill needed a chassis specialist. They were also aware of the good relationship between Jeff and me.

As I was following Preston and Lee to see Bill Davis, I wasn't sure what their plan was.

We met him at his race car hauler. After some discussion, it was decided I would go to work for Bill as his chassis specialist and Ford would pay the bill.

Jeff and I clicked immediately, winning poles and races. Davis planned for Jeff to race one more year in the Busch Grand National series and then move up to the Cup circuit. But our quick success drew the attention of other car owners.

PART II

BUILDING A CHAMPION

1992–1999

The original DuPont crew in 1992. *Ray Evernham Enterprises Archives*

CHAPTER 9

HALLOWED GROUND

First Days with Hendrick Motorsports

"If we can't win there, we can't win anywhere."

In May 1992, I got a call from Jeff Gordon's stepfather, John Bickford. John managed Jeff at the time. He told me Rick Hendrick had reached out. Apparently, Rick saw Jeff's victory in the Atlanta race and was so impressed he wanted to build a third Hendrick race team around him.

Although well respected, Hendrick Motorsports current performance was in question. It was known for spending a lot of money but had yet to win a championship.

John and Jeff asked me to go on a reconnaissance mission to Hendrick, meet with their rep, tour the facilities, and report back my findings.

This was a huge deal.

For me personally, to prepare for the Hendrick meeting, I had to stop my damn head from spinning. You must remember how fast things had happened for me. I got hurt in May 1991 and quit driving altogether in November. I relocated to North Carolina in January of 1992. I moved into a one-room apartment and started work as a crew member for Alan Kulwicki.

My life was changing faster than one of our Daytona cars.

Suddenly, here I am interviewing and analyzing one of the biggest teams, if not the biggest, in motorsports. Hell, they'd just done the Tom Cruise movie *Days of Thunder* based on Hendrick.

So even though it intimidated the shit out of me, I had to somehow stay focused and objective. I also had to look past all the money and Hollywood stuff and ensure there was real substance at Hendrick.

––––––

The Hendrick Motorsports complex was impressive. Some of it was built on Harry Hyde's property. Harry was a top Cup series crew chief from the 1960s through the 1980s, winning fifty-six races and eighty-eight pole positions. He was also the inspiration for the Harry Hogge character played by Robert Duvall in *Days of Thunder.*

Half of the property was the venerable Hendrick Motorsports, home to some of NASCAR's biggest stars like Tim Richmond, Geoff Bodine, and Ken Schrader. On the other half sat Harry's shop where the storied K & K Dodges were built and maintained.

So here I am, this Jersey short-track racer, rolling up to hallowed NASCAR ground. Hendrick HQ was in this beautiful building. The first thing I spotted walking in was a black-and-silver Corvette GTP parked right in the damn lobby.

The receptionist, a kind lady, sat behind this big round counter. I told her I was there to see Jimmy Johnson. (To clarify, the Jimmy Johnson I was coming to meet was Rick's general manager, not the seven-time Cup champion.)

Jimmy was a straight-up guy. But I think he was a bit insulted, maybe even a little pissed off, because I was there to judge them and not the other way around. (Believe me, if I'd have been there for myself, I'd have begged them for a job!) But I came for John and Jeff.

Jimmy gave me the full tour. I looked at the shops, their resources, the equipment, and tools. I met with other crew chiefs, and they described their systems, how they built their engines, and the way they produced their vehicles.

Their engine shop was impressive. They had some of the best guys in the business and everything was brand new. Some of the top fabricators worked there, too. Jimmy even laid out their sponsorship process. Clearly, Hendrick had great people, great resources, and great equipment.

Okay. So if their issue wasn't resources, I thought it must be how they were using them.

I can't say that Jimmy and I ever had a solid relationship. I never saw him as a race car guy; he was more of a dealership guy. There was no cohesion among the drivers and crews. They were locked into some old school ways, and it showed in how they built their cars.

Crews and drivers also didn't share information among the teams. Teams actually lied to one another. They also weren't very open-minded about some of the new things I'd learned at IROC.

Nevertheless, Rick had the foundation for the juggernaut organization he has created today. He also had good people who had accomplished much in the past. But I wasn't yet convinced they had a clear vision for the future. I didn't hear they had any sort of a master plan.

And I believed I could help fix that.

After spending the day with Jimmy Johnson, gathering all the intel I could, I returned to Jeff and John to tell them what I thought.

"Rick gives his people everything they could want," I explained. "They just aren't doing a great job at using what he's giving them. It's got nothing to do with Rick Hendrick."

Now, knowing what a great driver Jeff was—combined with Hendrick's resources—I said this next, "If we can't go there and win, we can't win anywhere."

Jeff and John both smiled before the latter delivered his verdict. "Okay, now we want you to go back and meet with Mr. Hendrick, 'cause you're coming with us."

"Wait, what? You've already decided?"

Oh, man. I didn't think I was ready to make that jump. Plus, as much as I wanted to go with Jeff, I felt a little guilty because Bill Davis and the Ford people had been so good to me.

Still, I knew with Jeff leaving, they didn't really have a place for me. It was suggested I might consider going down to Bud Moore's team, but I didn't want to go to Spartanburg. Frankly, I wanted to stay with Jeff.

For those reasons, I did want to follow Jeff to Hendrick, especially due to everything I saw there. But I was afraid I wasn't good enough.

Even so, I went back to talk with Mr. Hendrick. The meeting included Rick himself, Jimmy Johnson, and chief engine builder Randy Dorton. They took me down to this warehouse filled with *Days of Thunder* memorabilia.

It was really cool. Once again, this drove home just how big Hendrick Motorsports was in the NASCAR Cup world. Intimidating, to say the least.

Rick Hendrick and Jimmy got right to the point in our meeting.

"You're hired."

While I don't recall my exact phrasing, my response was something like, "Okay, let's see if we can get Andy Petree to come and crew chief and I'll be the chassis guy and mechanic."

Their faces went blank at that.

Rick said, "Uh, no. We don't need Andy to be the crew chief. You're gonna be the crew chief."

"But I don't have any experience being a Cup team crew chief. This is Winston Cup, Mr. Hendrick. I'm a good car builder, worker guy, you know. I'm a second or third in command."

In his characteristically calm, reassuring, and certain tone, Rick said, "No, you're the crew chief. Jeff wants it."

Still feeling overwhelmed and underqualified, I shot back, "But I don't wanna be the crew chief."

"Well, that's the only job I've got for you." With a smile, he added, "Take it or leave it." Then he said, "Look, Ray, you'll be all right. The chassis shop will build your cars for you. You just tell them what you want. Plus, Randy Dorton will craft your motors. And Jimmy Johnson will make sure you have what you need. You'll have a ton of support. The other crew chiefs and the people that work here, they'll all help you."

Like a scene out of one of my all-time favorite films, *The Godfather*, Rick just made me an offer I couldn't refuse.

Then we all talked about how talented Jeff was and how they wanted to establish a competitive race team. Rick Hendrick was all about winning, but he didn't put pressure on you. He was incredibly supportive.

I would later see how Rick would split his time on each pit box throughout race day. Whoever was leading or furthest up toward the front at the end of the race, he would go there for the finish.

But the first car he would go to after the race would be the car who finished furthest back. Sometimes he'd be late for Victory Lane because he would go see the other drivers before joining in the celebration.

Working with Rick made you put more pressure on yourself if you're not winning. There was never a doubt he was the man in charge. And yet his leadership style was quiet. Determined. You always knew where you stood.

His message was undeniably clear: he wanted to be victorious.

In all the years I was there, I don't ever recall him saying, "Damn it. You guys better get out there and win or else!"

Instead, he'd say, "You know, the Charlotte race is pretty important. It's our hometown race."

Or he'd just let you know, "This race matters to me . . ." for whatever reason.

After a while you understood which races were critical. It was always good to win those for him. If we weren't winning, he'd say, "Okay, what's going on? How come we're not winning? What do you need? What can I do?"

That's leadership.

After the meeting, I jumped back in my little piddly ass Nissan pickup truck and headed home. My mind was moving so fast. I kept thinking, "Holy shit! Did that just happen?"

It was such a rush.

Hell, only six months earlier I was lying on my back in Flemington, New Jersey, putting quick change gears in a damn modified. Now I was working for Rick Hendrick as the crew chief for a new Cup team.

How does this happen?

It's like being a walk-on for some third-level college football team, then six months later you're playing the Super Bowl.

After composing myself, I called John and Jeff, telling them my big news . . . which they most likely already knew.

Then it hit me. Now I have to tell Bill Davis. We've still got races to do. I had to get the Baby Ruth car ready for the Memorial Day weekend race at Charlotte.

———

I can't remember my exact words. But I do remember Bill wasn't at all happy. I don't blame him. He was dealt a one-two punch. First, he lost his star driver. Then he learned I was taking off, too.

Bill wanted me to stay.

He had Bobby Labonte coming onboard and was convinced he was about to get a sponsor. He said, "I want you to be the crew chief here."

But again, it wasn't about the job. At that point, it wasn't even really about the money. I wanted to be with Jeff.

Still, I did feel a sense of loyalty. And the fact is, I loved Bill. We had a great time working together, and I still think highly of him.

To his credit, Bill saw there was no changing my mind. Instead, he asked me to stay on just to get Jeff through the Charlotte race. I assured him I would. Then I'd start with Hendrick the day after.

Naturally, the whole time I was prepping the Baby Ruth car I was also talking with Jimmy Johnson about all the things and people we needed to get our team started at Hendrick.

It's amazing how lives and careers unfold.

You think you're headed in one direction then wind up in another.

I can look back now, especially since working on this book, and realize just how the dots connect. From starting my own race teams, to managing IROC for the best drivers in the world, to running the Cup team for Dick Johnson or being at Daytona helping Phil Barkdoll. Even my time with Alan Kulwicki and Bill Davis. All of it prepared me for what I was about to take on with Hendrick.

––––––––

I had so much fun working with Bill Davis partly because I got along well with his crew. I especially connected with his engine builder Keith Simmons. Keith was a bit of a nutball back then, but so was I.

Remember the "tomahawk chop" gesture you'd see the Rainbow Warriors make when Jeff would do something cool on the track? That started with Keith. He's an Atlanta Braves fan, and when we raced the Baby Ruth car in Atlanta Keith would swing his forearm up and down like a tomahawk every time Jeff would pass a car.

After winning the pole at Charlotte on Friday, then backing it up with a win on Saturday, Keith decided we should go out and celebrate. I reluctantly agreed, knowing I had to be in the Hendrick suite the next morning for the formal announcement of our new team and to meet with sponsors and other Hendrick folks before the race.

Keith and I sauntered into this local bar that night, Coyote Joe's. Approaching the bartender he said, "Give me twenty-five VO whisky and waters." Then he looked over at me and said, "Evernham's a pussy. He'll only drink twelve. I'll drink the other thirteen."

I'm not a big whisky drinker., but I managed to slam all twelve. And man, we got hammered. Bad.

Sure enough, the next day I woke up late. Luckily, my apartment wasn't too far from Charlotte Motor Speedway. But by the time I headed out the door, the traffic was just jammed, practically at a standstill.

My head was pounding.

I felt like I'd gotten no sleep, and I could throw up at any minute. I was in bad shape, thinking, "Oh God, what are these people gonna think of me?" I prayed I didn't still have whisky on my breath.

Given the snarled traffic, my only choice was to hoof it the mile and a half to the Speedway.

I was not doing well by the time I got there.

Sweating, I felt nauseous. But I put on my best game face, smiled, and shook every hand in sight.

As soon as I could, I got back to my apartment and went back to sleep.

———

I guess I didn't embarrass myself too much at the Hendrick suite because I started full-time the next day. Priority one? Putting my team together. Fortunately, I already knew some guys who would be perfect for the team's key positions.

Ed Guzzo worked with me on my race cars in New Jersey before he became a mechanic at a Ford dealership. He had also gone to Kulwicki's with me. Ed always got the job done; I knew I needed him in the No. 24 shop.

Michael Landis was another strong mechanic I'd worked with in the parts department at IROC. A sharp guy, he was living in New York at the time, and I knew he'd be excellent at handling purchasing and procurement. I'm so glad I convinced him to come down and join the team.

I also wanted an engineer to build our systems. Brian Whitesell, yet another super good guy I met at Kulwicki's, came to mind. I brought Brian in from the Freightliner Truck dealership he worked at in Charlotte.

Lastly, I'd met a former Stanford University football player during my time with Alan: Andy Papathanassiou. (Don't even try pronouncing Andy's last name. We shortened it.) Andy "Papa" was a volunteer on the Kulwicki crew. He had great team-building ideas. So I brought Andy on to run the recruiting and conditioning of our pit crew.

(Side note: Back then, it was unheard of to have a dedicated over-the-wall unit, separate from the guys that worked in the shop five days a week. But Andy and I were convinced a well-conditioned, highly trained, and choreographed pit team could bring efficiencies to a sport where hundredths of a second can mean the difference between winning and losing.)

The only problem?

Jimmy gave me a specific headcount and budget. But we didn't let that stop us; we knew building the right team was critical. Those first early Rainbow Warriors got paid very little money, if anything at all, to pit the car. They were basically volunteers out for some experience.

Still, Andy and I knew if we proved our theory, the money would come.

———

I will never forget the first day Mr. Hendrick visited the shop.

I said, "Hey guys! Come meet the boss."

The four of them—Guzzo, Whitesell, Landis, and Papa—dropped what they were doing and came over.

I introduced Ed first. "Mr. Hendrick, this is Ed Guzzo. He's going to be our chief mechanic."

"Wow, Ed, that's great," said Rick. "So, what's your background? Your experience?"

Ed told him he was a Ford mechanic.

Impressed, Rick then asked, "Oh, with Jack Roush? The Wood Brothers?"

"No, Mr. Hendrick. I was a mechanic for Tom's Ford, a dealership in Keyport, New Jersey."

I could see Rick was like, "What?"

But I kept going. "And this is Michael Landis. Mike's gonna be in charge of our procurements and parts. He knows a lot about that business."

"Okay, so what's your expertise?" Rick asked.

"Plumbing," said Michael.

"Oh, so you know oil tanks, radiators, fittings, stuff like that?"

"No. Toilets, sinks . . ."

By now Rick's face has assumed an unmistakable look. If it could be put in words, it might be something like: "Are these guys messing with me? Is this a prank?"

But I was on to the next introduction. "Brian's the engineer that's going to help with our systems. But he's gonna pull double duty by driving our hauler to and from the races."

Visibly girding himself for the response, Mr. Hendrick then asked, "Okay, did you come from Penske and IROC?"

Brian swallowed hard before saying "No. I was working at the Freightliner dealership down the street."

By now Rick's thinking, "Okay. Great, I've hired this young new hotshot and he's brought in guys with zero Cup experience between them."

He wasn't far off. While a few of us had done work for Kulwicki, and I was crew chief briefly for Dick Johnson, we were pretty much at square one.

When at last I introduced Andy Papa and explained our theory about having a separate dedicated pit team, Rick saw the potential right away.

I explained how a car going 200 mph equals 300 feet per second. "We spend all this money trying to perfect cars. But if we can beat other teams on pit road and get out ahead of them, it's easier than passing them on the racetrack. Under green flag, we're gonna make big gains."

Further defending the idea of a dedicated pit team, I said, "I don't know how I can work these guys fourteen, sixteen hours a day building race cars, getting them ready for the weekend, then expect them to be good on pit road. We're gonna lose on pit stops if we do that. The pit crew doesn't need to be experts on the car. They only have to know what happens over the wall. If we have damage, we'll bring the pit guys back and put our mechanic over the wall."

(By the way, you can't do that nowadays. The rules were different back then. Though you were allowed only seven men over the wall, it didn't have to be the same seven guys. You could keep changing guys back and forth. Teams can't do that now.)

Rick knew we were onto something. "I understand Jimmy's got his budgets, but we'll figure it out." The man always found a way to feed us extra dough when he could see even the potential for a good ROI.

When I accepted the job as crew chief, I thought that meant all the responsibility and accountability for winning fell on me. It wasn't just about car and driver. It was car, driver, and pit stop strategy.

We won a lot of races with a fast car. But we also won a good percentage by simply being smarter on pit road. Not making mistakes. There were plenty of days we took the trophy away from those with faster cars.

But like I used to tell the guys all the time, "Look, we don't have the fastest car today. But at some point in the race, the team with the quickest car is gonna fumble. They're gonna screw up, and we're gonna take advantage of it."

And we did.

———

In those first few weeks and months, I was just buried.

Building our team, building the shop, building our cars, and building my confidence, just hoping I could rise to the job. My goal? Get to the same level as the other two Hendrick teams.

I didn't want us to look like the new guys on the block. Even though that's exactly what we were.

So I put in the hours. A lot of hours.

With Ray J. and Mary still in New Jersey, this schedule, though serious, worked in my favor. I'd open the shop at seven in the morning. And while I can't say I did the Joe Gibbs thing of sleeping in my office, I bunked there more than once.

Working that hard in the early days never bothered me. Frankly, it doesn't bother me today. But in the immortal words of Captain Tom "Stinger" Jordan from *Top Gun*, the difference between then and now is today my mind writes checks my body can't cash.

Back then it was all so interesting. So new. So exciting. I could have worked twenty hours a day. I knew it was the chance of a lifetime.

Even though the goal was to be ready for the 1993 season, the more I considered it, the more I didn't want our first Cup race to be the Daytona 500.

I went to Rick and Jimmy to ask what they thought about us entering the final race of the 1992 season in Atlanta. My rationale was that Jeff and I had just won there in the Baby Ruth car. "Plus, it'd be cool to have Jeff make his Cup debut in Richard Petty's farewell race," I put in.

We could make some noise with that. Sort of the passing of the torch. At the time, I had no concept how prophetic that idea would turn out to be.

Racing in Atlanta also gave us the chance to work out the inevitable kinks in our systems, to ensure we had all the right equipment. That we weren't just a bunch of guys who started up a new team. We were a new unit inside of the Hendrick organization.

Yes, we had a lot of support, but we also had a lot to prove.

Rick and Jim agreed that racing at Atlanta would be a good move, but we'd have to really hustle. On top of that, Jeff was still under contract with Bill Davis through the rest of the season. Rick would have to get him to agree to let Jeff race.

As Rick's luck would have it, Jeff hadn't won a single race since I left to work full-time at Hendrick. With the October race at Charlotte coming up, Rick used me as a bargaining chip. He had a hunch Bill would want my help getting the Baby Ruth car ready and that he would want to use me as Jeff's crew chief for the big race. To Bill's credit, he was smart enough to know if he got me back to work with Jeff for that race, we could win it.

Rick's hunch proved true. The thing was, our shop wasn't even close to being fully operational. My hands were full. There was no way I could split my time between running our shop and going to Thomasville to work on the Baby Ruth car. So guess what? When Bill agreed to the deal, he had the Baby Ruth car delivered to Hendrick.

We started building the two DuPont Chevy Luminas for Atlanta in one corner while the Baby Ruth car was being prepped for Charlotte in another, all while constructing a spray booth and storage decks.

Mike was ordering parts and more chassis. I hired more mechanics and fabricators. Besides the two cars bound for Atlanta, we wanted eight or nine cars done by the time we headed to Daytona.

Meanwhile, Andy onboarded our over-the-wall pit crew, adapting every conditioning trick he learned from his playing days at Stanford. He kept me posted on what guys he had coming in. He was begging, borrowing, and stealing all the conditioning equipment he needed. Jeff even donated some.

I'll never forget, and neither will Mr. Hendrick (he talks about it to this day), the time he thought the military was training in the large vacant field outside his office. He just stood there watching these guys running, carrying each other on their backs, flipping these giant tires and doing calisthenics.

Rick was like, "What the hell? Do we have the army here today?"

Then he realized it was just the guys preparing for the No. 24 pit crew.

————

At times, I felt like I was drinking from a fire hose, given everything I needed to learn and do. I knew if I wanted the team and Jeff to be all they could be, I had to learn more about Cup race cars. I had to learn more about NASCAR. I had to learn more about how to lead.

Thankfully, I realized there's a world of free knowledge out there in leadership books. Honestly, I was a lazy student back in high school, not known for picking up a whole lot of books. If you were seeking me out, the library would have been about the last place you'd check back then.

But racing gave me a reason to want to learn. And having a team at this level motivated me to become a better leader.

Still, there's a difference between leadership and authority.

Just because you have the authority to manage a team, doesn't mean you're leading. I've seen so many people who are supposed to be leaders but they're unclear about where they're going.

People need to believe the leader knows where they're going. The leader must explain why they're going there, and as a team, they will figure out how to get there.

I needed to figure out where we were going as a team, so I spent a lot of time sizing up our competition. I looked at the teams who were winning races and clinching championships. I studied their strengths and their weaknesses.

I decided we'd focus on Richard Childress Racing and the black No. 3 driven by the man, Dale Earnhardt. That's the only car I thought about. I didn't give a shit about the rest. The way to a championship was through No. 3. Period.

I preached this to my guys all the time, "If we can beat that black number three, then we can beat everybody else."

I believed it was possible. I had a young team with major potential, an incredible driver about to hit his stride, and Rick Hendrick standing behind us.

Our first cup race was at Atlanta in 1992. The rainbow would stay but the mustache would go. *Nigel Kinrade*

CHAPTER 10

A ROUGH START

Battling with the Big Boys: 1992

"If this doesn't work, it's your ass."

When Jeff and I learned Rick had given the green light for the Atlanta race, we were stoked. We had just kicked ass, winning at Atlanta in the March Busch Grand National race.

We felt good about the track and about our team. Moreover, we couldn't wait to go up against those Cup guys in our brand-new race car.

We thought, "Yeah, we're moving up to Cup, but we'll be racing on the same track, with the same driver, same crew chief. How different could it be?"

We blindly stood at the dangerous intersection of cocky and ignorant.

We didn't know how much we didn't know.

The difference between Busch Grand National and Cup goes way beyond car and equipment. You go from racing maybe five Cup guys in the field of a Busch race, to competing against forty Cup-level pros. Weekly.

We were in for a big lesson.

Our schooling began in October, when Charlotte Motor Speedway hosted open test days. Teams were invited to test their cars, and media was invited to watch. We thought it was the perfect chance to assess our cars for the November race in Atlanta.

To make it even more fun, the track's general manager, Humpy Wheeler, offered $1,500 in cash to the driver who set the fastest lap for the day.

Beyond us, Darrell Waltrip and a bunch of other Cup guys showed up. I said, "Rick, we can get that $1,500."

He looked at me. "You think you can beat Darrell?"

"Yep!"

I'd watched Darrell's team put a big bag of ice on the manifold to cool the engine down, giving the car more power. Since there was no inspection, nothing was deemed illegal. I knew exactly what to do.

We took all the weight out of Jeff's car and put on four left-side tires. (Left-side tires have a softer compound that gave us more grip.) It wouldn't work in a race, but for that one lap, it was the perfect trick. Jeff went out and blew that lap away.

We made the Charlotte paper, with good press for Rick, Jeff, and DuPont (now known as Axalta). Plus, Rick was $1,500 richer . . . which is probably the same amount we dropped on those four left-side tires.

Our second track test came when Chevrolet invited us to Atlanta. They rented the track for a whole week. We went down there and ran around for four days until we just didn't have any more to do.

We felt like we were in good shape and ready for the No. 24's Cup debut.

Boy, were we wrong.

———

On October 11, 1992, Jeff and I were back at Charlotte Motor Speedway for the Busch Grand National race we'd promised Bill Davis in exchange for allowing Jeff to test and race in Atlanta. Having been so focused on building the No. 24 team, I'd almost forgotten how much fun Jeff and I had running in those Busch races.

We especially enjoyed the chance to race Cup guys like Mark Martin, Harry Gant, Rusty Wallace, and Dale Earnhardt. They were among the best Cup drivers at the time. Earnhardt used to rip us pretty hard with his trash talk. He'd always say something like, "Hey, I'm gonna kick your ass out there." Stuff like that. It was cool. Cup drivers aside, there weren't many slouches in the Busch Grand National field back then, either.

Just like in May, we won the pole and the race. I was so glad we could do that for Bill.

The least fun part? The head-splitting hangover that came with Bill Davis's engine builder Keith Simmons and his crazy celebrations.

———

Building the team and trying to introduce some new systems caused conflict between myself and some of the long-term Hendrick team members.

I know I was ready to go toe-to-toe on more than a few occasions.

If the conflict was between one of the higher-level Hendrick folks, whether it was me and another crew chief or an engine guy, you got called to Mr. Hendrick's office for a "help me understand" meeting.

I was brought in there more than once.

Mr. Hendrick would always start off with, "So, help me understand . . ." and you knew before that meeting was over you were going to get your ass chewed and it was you who would understand.

Meanwhile, Jimmy Johnson and I fought. A lot.

Jimmy had his job to do, and it wasn't being crew chief. We got into some pretty heated arguments about how I wanted my cars built, and he'd push back on critical things I needed to make our cars better.

Here's an example. I wanted to change the front-end geometry on our Hendrick cars to the one designed by another car builder, Ronnie Hopkins. His cars were winning a lot of races.

One day when quarreling with Jimmy over doing something different with the geometry on the No. 24 car, Jimmy just glared at me and said, "Okay, you got what you wanted. But if this doesn't work, it's your ass."

Look. I knew how to build a car. And although Hendrick cars exhibited beautiful engineering and craftsmanship, they were just too heavy and didn't work well. We had to change them.

So, one day when Mr. Hendrick dropped by the shop to ask if we needed anything, I seized the moment.

"Mr. Hendrick, your cars are really good. They're beautifully fabricated. But . . . they're heavy and they're not consistent. No two cars are the same."

Rick is a good listener, and as I've said, he loves to win. I could see that what I said registered. Next thing I knew, he brought in some top-notch race car engineers and builders.

He hired Rex Stump, a brilliant engineer, along with Eddie Dickerson, one of the best in the business, to run the fabrication shop. Then he brought on an extraordinary car builder from up north named Steve Leavitt.

Those guys took our ideas and turned them into reality. I could ask for something I'd only imagined might work, and they'd figure out how to get it done. When Rick decided to bring them on, it was a real game-changer.

Though Jimmy said he would've fired me, I'd like to think Rick wouldn't have let him.

Despite our differences, I believe Jimmy had the best interest of the team at heart. Even so, he wasn't a racing guy, which I felt thwarted progress. So sometimes I had to go around him to Rick directly.

That didn't help my relationship with Jimmy.

Rick knew Jimmy and I didn't see eye to eye on everything. Still, he had enough confidence in me to know it really wasn't about me trying to get Jimmy's job. I just wanted to make the team better, make the cars faster, and sometimes that required Rick's intervention.

––––––––

The Hooters 500 in Atlanta on November 15, 1992, was going to be a special race for several reasons. It was where Jeff would be making his Cup debut. It was also seven-time Cup champion Richard "The King" Petty's final race of his thirty-five-year career—an event with a bigger place in NASCAR history than any of us realized at the time.

The race was also the battle for the series points championship, with six drivers mathematically eligible to win. Finally, it marked Hendrick Motorsports's return as a three-car team.

If we hadn't felt like the new kids on the block before Atlanta, we sure as hell did once we arrived. We didn't know a lot of people at the Cup level back then. And nobody gave a shit that we were there except for maybe our friend Andy Petree, who had the Skoal Bandit car. A great dude, he stopped by to wish us luck.

Honestly, when we rolled into the garage at Atlanta, no one cared. It wasn't like Dale Earnhardt walked over to say, "How y'all doing? Kill it today." You know what I mean? It'd been more like, "Hey, you! Get that piece of shit outta my way."

People knew who we were. But guys like Dale, Rusty Wallace, Mark Martin, Davey Allison, and Bill Elliott—they couldn't have cared less. They were focused on themselves.

Well, the first blow to our collective ego came in qualifying.

We qualified like shit. We just couldn't figure it out. We were the blind leading the blind. Jeff didn't know if or when he was over driving. I tried to adjust the car but only made it worse.

Somehow, we got through practice and thought we were ready to race.

I have always been a fan at heart. So on race day when we got to the drivers' meeting, I was excited to see who would be there. I looked around and wow, there's Leonard Wood, Bill Elliott, Tim Brewer, Andy and Harry Gant, Jimmy Fennig and Mark Martin, Buddy Parrott, and Rusty Wallace.

Burt Reynolds, who was there as part of a *Smokey and the Bandit* promotion, got up and spoke. The King Richard Petty was celebrated. He handed out special money clips to all the drivers, commemorating his final career race. That drivers' meeting was another one of my career Forrest Gump moments. I thought, "Holy shit, how the hell did I get here?"

Yet as cool as it was being in that session with so many of my heroes, I had a job to do. It was time to focus on the race.

Afterward, I scheduled a team huddle in the hauler. Gathering everyone, we went over all the things we should be ready for. We discussed fuel and tire strategy. I told them to be on their toes. It's a big day for us.

Then I reminded them, "We got here because we earned it. But it's our first Cup race and we're gonna make mistakes. If we have a problem, let's handle it professionally. Keep good notes, this is our test for Daytona. Let's make it count." (I was always big on tracking things we did wrong and things we did right.)

Then Jeff and I went over the notes we took from our test days at Atlanta. We felt like we really knew what we were doing.

When it was time for him to get in the car, I let him go by himself. Jeff and I came from open-wheel racing. We were used to losing a lot of drivers in fatal crashes, so I never put Jeff in the car. I know most crew chiefs walked their drivers to their vehicle, made sure they were buckled in, shook their hand, or patted them on the back, before fastening up the window netting. I never did.

It may sound crazy or overly superstitious, but I always felt if I didn't say goodbye to him at the car, then I'd always see him again. I don't think Jeff ever knew. He probably thought, "Shit, Ray's never around when I get ready to go."

———

Our race day ended miserably, finishing in thirty-first place after Jeff crashed on lap 164. We didn't take into account how much of an effect the increased weight and horsepower would have on our race setup.

To reiterate, we totally missed the race setup. It wasn't a V6. It was a V8, and it was a Hendrick V8, which meant plenty of power. And the car was 200 or 300 pounds heavier than our Busch Grand National car.

I know what you're thinking, what were you doing during those four test days in Atlanta?

First, we were by ourselves. There weren't thirty-nine other Cup cars to chase around the track.

Now we were dealing with rubber on the track. There were other competitors going faster in practice than we had at the test. Not only were they faster in practice, but they somehow picked up a bunch more speed for qualifying.

On top of that, they were adjusting their cars throughout the weekend in ways I wasn't familiar with.

What an embarrassment.

We thought we were such hot shit. But that day we got a big lesson in how much we didn't know. Again, I was so thankful we ran at Atlanta first. We didn't fully realize how crucial that experience would be until we did it.

If we would have begun at Daytona, it could have been an even bigger disaster. As much as we prepared and practiced, it wasn't the same as racing. Everything changes in a race.

I was pretty hard on myself. I felt like I should have known better instead of thinking, "Hey, Jeff's the best. We got this. I got good guys working for me. We have the best equipment."

That was my fault. And even though it probably wore through my stomach lining, it made me a better crew chief because I took responsibility.

A leader has to be accountable.

Later, Jeff and I talked back in the garage. We agreed. Nothing worked the way we thought it would. We realized testing and racing are two different worlds. The Busch car and Cup car are not the same animal. And racing with thirty-nine Cup guys versus five or six is way different.

That day it hit us: We've got a lot of work to do. We weren't in Kansas anymore, Toto.

To Rick Hendrick's credit, you could have your worst day, totally screw up, and if he knew you put in the work—you did everything you could to win—he'd come over and say something like, "Look, we'll get it next time."

I also believe this to be true: Rick saw something in me and Jeff that we didn't even see in ourselves. And what he saw, he enjoyed. It gave him confidence.

Rick was patient when it came to cultivating talent. There aren't many owners that would've been tolerant enough to let Jeff and me get through our first two seasons together.

But Rick could sense the chemistry. He saw our ability. He recognized the unique way Jeff and I communicated.

Rick knew even before we did, we were going to get it done.

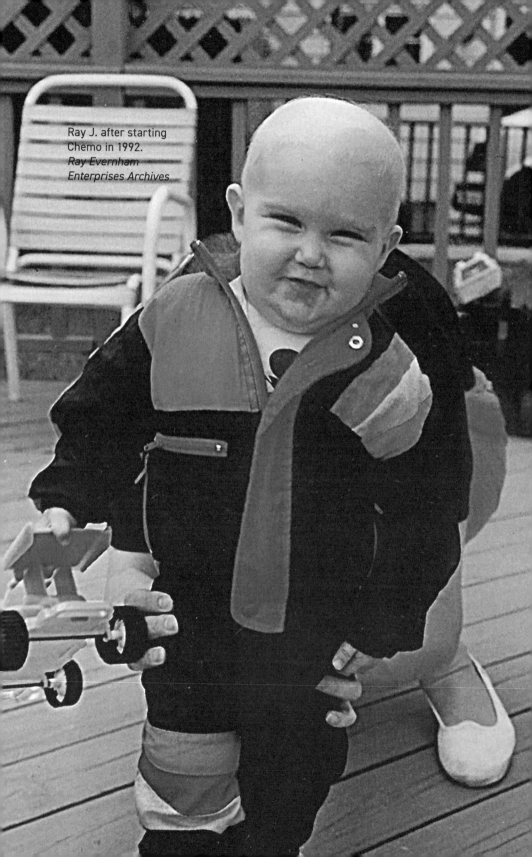

Ray J. after starting
Chemo in 1992.
*Ray Evernham
Enterprises Archives*

CHAPTER 11

I CAN'T FIX THIS

Hard Times at Home: 1992

"Ray, I need you to come home."

I'd been at Hendrick less than six weeks, working nonstop between building the No. 24 shop and getting cars ready for Atlanta.

We hadn't yet had time to move Mary and Ray J. to Charlotte. I would sometimes fly back to New Jersey on Friday or Saturday, be home Sunday, then fly back for work Sunday night.

One week, Mary and Ray J. came down to Charlotte for a visit. I could tell Ray J. wasn't well. He just didn't look like himself. Then again, I thought kids just got sick and bounced right back.

This time, he wasn't bouncing back.

In fact, he'd developed a limp in his walk and was fighting a temperature. Fortunately, my mom was a trained nurse and lived next door to Mary and Ray J. Between these two women, I felt he was in good hands.

But then I went home for Ray J.'s first birthday on July 18.

Everybody was there for his party. Here he was supposed to be having fun, and instead, the poor little guy just wasn't feeling well. Mary said she'd made a doctor's appointment for the next day.

Still believing it was nothing to worry about, I returned to Charlotte.

I went to work that Monday as usual. The next day, my phone rang. It was Mary. All she said was, "Ray, I need you to come home."

I knew it was about Ray J., but I had more than a plateful of responsibilities in front of me. I calmly asked, "Well, how sick is he?"

"I just need you to come home."

"Well, does he have the flu?"

I now know she was panicking inside. Still, she wouldn't tell me any more than that. In hindsight I feel guilty for challenging her judgment.

But I never, ever dreamt this was life-threatening.

I wasn't going to continue arguing with her. I could tell she was upset. "All right," I said. "Let me call you back."

I rang my father because I knew he'd shoot straight with me. I told him about the conversation I just had with Mary.

"Dad, tell me what's going on. I need to know what's happening before I jump on a plane."

"You need to come home, Ray," he said in a concerned voice. "The doctor thinks Ray J. has leukemia."

Silence.

Time stopped. Growing up, if I heard somebody had leukemia, it was a death sentence. It was over. I'm standing there on the phone thinking the worst possible thing a parent could imagine.

I was going to lose my child.

Everything became a blur, though I do recall going back into the shop to tell the guys. After that I said, "I gotta go," because I knew I'd start crying.

Then I went to see Wayne Stemler; he was the controller at Hendrick. "Wayne, I got to go home."

Those are the only words I could muster before I started crying.

"Whoa, what's the matter?" Wayne asked.

I told him. Next thing I knew, Hendrick had made all the arrangements to get me back home. They got me out on the next commercial flight.

Dad's friend Jack Stoddard picked me up at the airport and drove me the hour and fifteen minutes to the Monmouth Medical hospital. I was grateful he came to get me, but I couldn't speak a word the whole trip.

When I entered the hospital room, Ray J. was sitting on Mary's lap. He looked terribly sick.

The doctor came in right after and began explaining his thoughts. To this day, I can't tell you what that guy said. I just wanted to see Mary and Ray J.

All I could think while listening to the doctor explain Ray J.'s condition was, "You're ripping my heart out of my chest."

That's when my mom came over to me and offered the best advice: "Look, we need to put Ray J. in an ambulance and get him to Memorial Sloan Kettering Cancer Center in New York as soon as possible."

116

Having been a nurse, my mom noticed petechiae, tiny bleeding spots in the mucous membranes of the eyelids. Not a good sign.

She reiterated, "Get Ray J. to New York immediately."

After staying awake all night from worry and fear, the next morning, Mary and I did as she said. We put our little boy in an ambulance bound for Memorial Sloan Kettering in New York City.

Once admitted, he was seen by Dr. Peter Steinherz, an amazing specialist in Pediatric Hematology-Oncology with a focus on leukemia.

Thank God for Dr. Steinherz.

He looked like a scientist from a movie. A shorter man, his wrinkled lab coat was way too long for his height. His beard was disheveled, and although nearly bald, the few remaining hairs surrounding his head stuck out in all directions.

Like I said, he looked like a man who spent most of his time in a lab, hunched over a microscope, hoping to discover one more puzzle piece that might bring humanity closer to ending childhood cancers.

In fact, it was Dr. Steinherz who wrote the protocol to battle acute lymphoblastic leukemia, ALL, which was the type that Ray J. had. The most common childhood cancer, it's also one of the most treatable.

It's also one of the most aggressive.

Now retired, it's hard to say just how many kids Dr. Steinherz saved. The number would have to be well into the hundreds, if not thousands. Mary and I desperately hoped Ray J. would be one more.

In a kindly voice, affected with a thick German accent, Dr. Steinherz asked us his age.

"One year and one week," Mary responded.

Then leaning down, focused on Ray J. seated on Mary's lap, he asked, "And how are you today, Ray J.? How are you feeling?"

You could tell by his tone and demeanor this was an all too familiar experience for Dr. Steinherz. The way he looked at Ray J., I just knew 100 percent of his focus and brain power was on my child.

As I listened to him speak, I began to realize there was actually a chance Ray J. could beat this.

It would be a tough fight, but I cautiously allowed myself a little hope.

And in an effort to reinforce this dream, I went to the hospital chapel. I get emotional just thinking about it now.

Entering, I noticed rows of empty chairs and a stained glass window at the far end. I had the place to myself. Just me and God.

As I sat down and stared at the scene before me, the dam burst. All that physical and emotional pain I'd kept at bay caught up to me.

I took a deep breath but couldn't hold back. I started to cry.

Wiping away my tears, I folded my hands, fingers intertwined, praying harder than I ever remembered praying in all my life. "God, you know, if you can save him . . . if I can keep him . . . I'll never ask for another thing."

I sat for a moment, calmed myself, and hoped God took me at my word.

———

I got back to the room.

Mary, Ray J., and I were relaxing as best we could, when we heard someone tapping on the door frame. It was Rick Hendrick at the door.

Again, I get emotional recalling and writing about that moment even now.

I'd been working for him only four or five weeks and yet here was the man himself coming to check on me and my family.

He stood there in his suit, characteristic friendly grin on his face, with this big basket full of food and snacks. As we talked and I told him what we faced, in a reassuring tone he said, "Look, we're going to get through this. We've got people that can take care of whatever needs to get done while you're here. And when you're able, I'll fly you back and forth if you need to."

That's just what he did.

And the fact that he said, "We're going to get through this," speaks to the kind of man he is and the family-like culture that he's built at Hendrick Motorsports.

It's why I love the guy to this day.

———

I won't kid you. Those early days at Sloane Kettering were some of the worst—if not the worst—experiences of my life. I'm a fixer and there was nothing I could do to correct any of this. Mary or I would just hold our sick one-year-old son while the doctors and nurses stuck him with needles while performing spinal taps.

Awful doesn't start to describe it.

One night I spoke with a Vietnam veteran whose grandchild was there. I remember him saying this was the worst thing he'd ever experienced. Now, here's a guy that had gone through the shit of that war and yet he said there was nothing more horrible than seeing his grandchild go through such suffering.

Once Ray J. stabilized enough, I'd leave for a few days, work Monday through Thursday from 7:00 a.m. until midnight or one or two o'clock in the morning. I'd put in half a day Friday, then fly to New York or New Jersey, spend Saturday and Sunday there, then fly back to Charlotte Sunday night.

As rough as this got at times, Ray J. was at least responding well to the treatments. He was improving. Our fingers stayed crossed as we hoped for some kind of remission.

That didn't mean he'd be cured. He'd still be on a protocol.

Fortunately, Ray J. did go into remission within a couple of months. He had some flare-ups, but the medical team got it under control. Then he had to stay on his chemotherapy for another twenty-two months.

I was in Dover at a race when Mary called with the news we'd long been hoping for. "Dr. Steinherz said Ray J. is in full remission. We're done with chemo! He's going to have to take some pills here and there, but otherwise we're done."

Holy shit, we were both so relieved.

We went on to win the race that day, making me the happiest I'd been in a long time. When I got home, we celebrated with a "flush party."

Anyone who's battled cancer knows what kind of a celebration that is. It's when you flush all the unused chemo pills down the toilet . . . along with all those worries and fears you've been carrying during the cancer fight.

Still, we weren't a hundred percent out of the woods. We had to take our son to New York at least once a month. Eventually, though, it became an annual checkup.

He fought infections and other related illnesses until he got into kindergarten, then first grade. But he lived and has happily grown into manhood.

God did answer my prayers.

———

At the start of the ordeal, I realized how fortunate I was to have had my captains, Ed Guzzo and Michael Landis, manning the ship at the No. 24 shop. Of course, Jimmy Johnson was making sure all the financial stuff got handled.

I was flying back and forth from Charlotte to New York or New Jersey. But once we started racing, sometimes I had to go months without seeing Mary and Ray J. That's one of the reasons I give her so much credit for Ray J.'s recovery.

She was a rock.

I also have to say how incredibly supportive Jeff and John Bickford were. John is the kind of man you can lean on in times like that. He would check on the guys at the shop for me and got to be good friends with Mike, Ed, and Brian.

Everybody respected John. He's always been a sounding board for me.

If Jeff ever worried about whether my absence would affect our performance, he never mentioned it. Ray J. was a baby when Mary first brought him to visit me at the track. I've got pictures of Jeff holding him when he was just six months old. I think Ray J.'s struggle with leukemia was emotionally tough for Jeff. Still, neither he nor Rick ever put their worries about the No. 24 team's projects ahead of my issue with Ray J. And the measure of my gratitude for them and everyone else at Hendrick Motorsports during that time is impossible to put into words.

I told God in the chapel that first night, if he spared Ray J.'s life, I would never ask for another thing. And I never have.

Christmas 1992. Ray J. was sick, and I got to spend some time in New Jersey with him. *Ray Evernham Enterprises Archives*

CHAPTER 12

DIALING IN

The 1993 Season

"Our rookie year . . . here we go."

Our performance in Atlanta was a jarring wake-up call. After that, I got right back to work with my tail squarely between my legs to prepare for the 1993 NASCAR season.

People mistakenly think NASCAR has an offseason. Some in NASCAR might, but we sure didn't. During that so called offseason, we were building speedway cars for Daytona. And I had the least amount of experience with speedway cars.

I had no idea how incredibly important aerodynamics were. Most of my life had been spent on cars that didn't even have fenders. Now my world was filled with fenders, grills, spoilers, things like that. We were spending a lot of time either at the wind tunnel or in the body shop while trying to get things prepped for a full 1993 season.

When we weren't building, we were testing.

There were no testing restrictions in those days. We tested at Daytona a couple of times for three or four days. We also tested at Talladega.

Plus, we were still building our team.

As embarrassing as it was, thank God we ran that Atlanta race. If for no other reason than to learn just how much we had left to learn.

While there was plenty to do with the team, I did fly home for Christmas. But given Ray J.'s uncertain future, it wasn't the greatest.

Still, people in town were so kind. Something about the combination of a sick child and the spirit of Christmas brought out the best in people. They rallied around us. That's what small-town folks do. My uncle was with the fire department, so he brought over one of their trucks for Ray J. to see.

Mary and I were incredibly grateful. It's heartwarming as a parent knowing people are going out of their way because of your ill child.

When it came to Ray J.'s illness, I let Mary handle it. Honestly, I just couldn't deal. I shielded myself from the pain by not thinking about it.

Consequently, I spent a lot of time being angry.

Everyone tells you, when dealing with cancer, you must keep a positive attitude. You've got to think the best. Easier said than done when the one who's sick is your only child. Plus, every kid I had ever heard about with leukemia, which might have been one or two, had died.

I blocked my emotions. Became numb. Compartmentalized.

It's how I dealt with things that were out of my control or too emotionally draining. I put all my focus on my work. Still today, people who know me well will say, "If you want something done—if you need your car fixed—just piss Ray off. He goes to work when he gets mad."

I tried my best not to let my emotions spill over into the No. 24 shop, but they did. Back then, I knew how to build cars, not relationships. The way I saw it, if you didn't dedicate 100 percent of your life to getting our cars to go faster, I didn't have much time for you. And I know my temperament was on a hair trigger. I just didn't want to be around people who wanted to talk about my problem, no matter how well intentioned.

The fact is, everybody's always battling something. Everybody's got their scars. That's why I'm careful what I say to those who are going through things. You really don't understand what they're dealing with unless you've been through it yourself. When you do come out the other side of whatever challenged you, you just pray you're somehow better because of it.

I had a select few I confided in. As team leader I never wanted to show any weakness. I didn't want to offer even the slightest hint I might be thinking about anything besides Daytona and the season.

It was a lonely time.

I moved from my tiny apartment to a slightly bigger place when Mary and Ray J. were supposed to come down. Even then, the décor consisted simply of a blowup air mattress and outdoor lawn furniture.

Ray J. wound up having another setback with his leukemia, so he and Mary couldn't come down for another six months.

So Andy Papa, our pit crew coach, lived with me for a while. That didn't go well. Don't get me wrong, Andy's an awesome guy. But being

Greek, he used to fry up all kinds of peppers and smelly food that stunk up the whole house.

The long separation from Mary added to our disconnect.

As selfish as it sounds, I was scared of getting closer to this child I thought I would lose. I was not the person I wanted to be, and I was doing things I really regret doing. In my head, I could fully justify my actions. But then came the inevitable day I realized there was no justification for what I was doing.

Thereafter, I doubled down on my work.

I was the first one at the shop in the morning and the last to leave at night. I started at 6:30 a.m., and the rest of the guys would arrive around 7:30 a.m. We'd have a meeting first thing to plan out the day's "must do's."

I would also attend Hendrick meetings with all of Rick's other managers. Then I had a weekly meeting with the motor shop.

Back then, the teams were small, we wore several hats. I built the shocks, set up the cars, and even worked with Michael Landis on ordering parts and equipment. In those early years, I tried to put my hands on every single car that came out of the shop.

There were weeks we'd need to go to Detroit to spend two or three shifts in the wind tunnel. Getting ready for Daytona, it meant those trips were in the winter and we would freeze our asses off loading and unloading cars from the truck. It could get brutally cold.

Most times, wind tunnel testing would start at three or four o'clock in the afternoon and go to six or seven o'clock the next morning. The race teams worked the graveyard shifts because the manufacturers would get the day shifts.

The main focus? Preparing for the Daytona 500. It's the biggest race.

You work like crazy, but then guess what? The checkered flag drops, and you have just four days to get to Rockingham, then four days after that to get to Richmond, and four days after that is the next race on the schedule.

As we prepared for Daytona, we also had to make sure the cars for the other tracks were ready. We always had the schedule posted right up on the parts department wall of the No. 24 shop, showing us which cars we were planning on running for the next four or five weeks.

Back then, you could build custom cars per racetrack if you wanted.

And we did that. At any one time, we'd have fourteen or fifteen cars in our rotation.

We had two speedway cars and three or four cars for midsize tracks. Then we had two or three short-track cars. And then a couple of road-course cars. But we also had cars built as hybrids, something in between that could run several tracks.

Beyond getting cars ready, the team was still coming together. I was hiring and firing people right up until the day we left for Daytona.

We had a pretty good rotation of folks, a solid core group. But we kept adding to it. It really was a work in progress.

Along with all the building and testing, Andy Papa and I were fine-tuning our dedicated pit crew team. People thought having a team solely focused on pit stops was revolutionary. But what we were doing was really more or less evolutionary.

The guys who deserved credit for innovating pit stops were the Wood Brothers. Richard Petty and the Wood Brothers would not be the first- and second-winningest motorsports teams in history if they hadn't had smart, coordinated pit personnel and protocols.

We just took their strategies and choreography to the next level by having a separate team that only worked pit stops. That was the game changer. It didn't make sense having a guy work sixteen hours a day on the race car, then expect him to have enough time and focus to go through intense pit practice.

Andy came up with a well-synchronized choreography. It differed from most other teams. While NASCAR only allowed seven men over the wall, it didn't have to be the same seven.

Depending on what I'd call for, Andy had the appropriate crew members jumping back and forth. The left tire guy would hop over the wall. While he's in the air, the guy that would make the wedge changes is in the air, too. When the gas man finished fueling the car, he'd throw the empty dump can back over the wall for someone to catch. So technically, we never had more than seven men over the wall at any one time.

Truly, our pit stops were a show unto themselves. It was wild as hell.

The secret? Choreography and pushing the limits on rules. Again, drawing from his days as a Stanford football player, Andy worked with the team on specific drills as well as strength training and conditioning.

We'd even film the pit stops so later Andy and the team could evaluate their performance. He would work on the small details to speed things up; even the number of steps the jackman takes mattered.

By shaving tenths of seconds here and there, our pit stops were consistently getting faster. We had our routine down, and it took a while for other teams to catch on. It was fun.

Having a smart, efficient, well-choreographed, and dedicated pit crew was low-hanging fruit for gaining positions during the race. For us, at that time, it was a hell of a lot easier to beat them on Pit Road than on the racetrack.

————

As the season drew closer, I developed a "take no prisoners" attitude and a strong sense of duty to the team. There were days I was not a nice guy.

Looking back, I regret being so stern and showing so little empathy. But my job was to win races. I felt a responsibility to Rick Hendrick, Jeff Gordon, and all of those who were working sixteen-hour days.

Bottom line, winning was the goal.

I didn't think it mattered if I hurt somebody's feelings or if I was being too tough on a guy. I wasn't a politician. I believed you either wanted to win or you didn't. Because of my attitude, I knew I wasn't going to make many friends.

Still, there was one guy I regretted pissing off: Rick Hendrick. He got me riled up about something that I can't even remember.

But I shot back at him with, "Look, you wanna win races or you just wanna talk about winning races?" That was a big mistake!

It was one of those moments when you wish you could just grab words out of the air and stuff them right back where they came from.

Oh, shit. He was so pissed off at me.

He should have fired me on the spot, and probably more than once.

Thankfully, Mr. Hendrick chalked my remark off to the pressure I was putting on myself.

I'd been to Daytona International Speedway several times. As someone who's loved racing his whole life, it never got old rolling through the tunnel in Turn Four. The track is intimidating *because* it's Daytona. Since it opened in 1959, it's been the home of the Daytona 500, our sport's equivalent of the Super Bowl. It's a track with character. History.

It became one of my favorite places. Although you'll occasionally hear drivers talk about running it wide open, Daytona's still very much a handling track. You have to make sure your car handles in different lanes.

The track gets hot, and it gets slick. At the start of a run, drivers can be wide open on the banking, but as soon as the tires start to wear and the fuel burns off, they must start lifting off the gas.

It's not like going to Talladega where you're flat on the floor all day long. Daytona changes a lot more with the weather than Talladega, and it has a bumpier surface. There's also more opportunity for collaboration between driver, crew chief, and pit crew at Daytona. On the other hand, at Talladega, you need three things: a fast car, a driver who's skilled at drafting, and no mistakes.

Though I had some knowledge and experience, I knew there was much about running speedway restrictor plate racing I didn't know. Fortunately, I could lean on good friends like Dave Marcis, who I knew from my IROC days. Andy Petree and Tony Glover also helped me a ton.

Tony's won the 500 three times as a crew chief. He answered every question I had about the car, the proper setup, and about the racetrack. He advised me on what four springs to run. We put those springs in, and I never changed them the whole time we were there.

I trusted Tony. I still do.

Honestly, it took us a while to learn speedway racing. Even though we were good at Daytona, we crashed every time we raced at Talladega. We never ran good there. It was 1995 before we won our first restrictor plate race. Even though we'd finished in the top five a couple times, we didn't crack the code until '95.

To be sure, I've always enjoyed racing at Daytona. To me it's a lot like Indy. Legends have raced there. You can almost feel the eyes of history's greatest drivers and mechanics staring down at you to see if you're really worth a damn. I know it sounds weird. But when you walk through the gates at Indy or Daytona, you can almost feel those ghosts.

I actually did have one of those greats literally staring at me in the flesh at times. Legendary crew chief and engineer, Smokey Yunick, used to stand in the garage peering right over my shoulder as I worked on the car.

He intimidated the hell out of me.

Years later at a sponsor dinner meeting, I asked Smokey why he watched me but rarely talked to me. He said, "Well, I wanted to see if you really knew what you were doing, and I heard you were a smart ass." So I asked, "What do you think?" He replied, "You do know what you're doing . . . and you are a smart ass." Smokey and I became friends, and he visited me regularly until he passed.

The first competition of our rookie season was the Gatorade 125. While we qualified well, we did qualify with our race setup, which meant our car was actually better than people thought. Normally, your race setup is more conservative than your qualifying setup because in qualifying the driver only has to hang on for one or two laps. During the race there could be up to one hundred miles between pit stops, so the race setup is typically slower.

During practice, I played with the tire camber settings and a little bit with the shocks, mostly minor stuff. Jeff was comfortable. He liked the way the car drove, and he drove it like a frigging veteran. I've always said that Hendrick's engine builders, led by Randy Dorton at that time, made great drivers and crew chiefs out of a lot of plain folks.

Jeff did do an amazing job running that race.

He looked like he'd been racing with those guys for a gazillion years. He used his mirror. He drafted. Never panicked. Made no mistakes. He had confidence and the ability to control his emotions.

To be twenty years old, in his first NASCAR competition at Daytona on national television, with all those pros breathing down his neck, was amazing to watch. Again, demonstrating his extraordinary talent, he held them off and, in winning that race, stunned the motorsports world.

After we won, you'd have thought the whole team would have been high-fiving and celebrating. Here I am, the rookie crew chief. The team and I built this car, and Jeff won the 125. But instead, we just acknowledged everyone did a great job—then got to work figuring out how to win Sunday's race.

We didn't get caught up in our own success. We honestly never did.

I was still working on my communication with Jeff and the team during a race. For some reason, early in my career, I wasn't comfortable talking on the radio. I'd become nervous. My finger shook every time I went to push the radio button. I just wasn't comfortable talking to everybody as the director, the crew chief.

Funny thing was, I did have confidence in the car we'd built. I was confident in Jeff. I was not confident I'd say the right things on the radio. And to be a great crew chief back then, you had to be almost a play-by-play announcer as you made decisions and instructed your crew and driver.

It sure took me a while to get comfortable doing that.

So here's what I did in the meantime.

I picked three or four crew chiefs I admired and eavesdropped on their conversations with their drivers. Then I decided to record my radio calls and listen to them all week long.

Then we started recording the conversations of other crew chiefs and drivers. Eventually, we got printed transcripts made of the other team's conversations. It gave us great intel.

It's a common practice today. But it started with the No. 24 shop back in the early nineties.

———

The night before the 500, I had an early dinner in my room and went over all the notes from the week. I reviewed the shock data. Jeff's comments. All the changes we made were based on time of day and weather.

From that, I came up with a plan for how we would set the car up in the morning. (It used to be you could wait until Sunday morning to do your setup. You could even change shocks, springs, and the front end right up until prerace inspection. You can't do that now.)

Then I started to look at the fuel mileage and determine my fuel strategy.

Next thing I knew, I woke up lying on the bed, still in my clothes, halfway through the night. The shock and race sheets and notes were all over the place.

At that time, the gate at the track used to open at six in the morning.

Aware that close to 200,000 people would soon be heading to the track, I made sure we got there extra early. It was a chilly Florida morning, so the crew and I just waited in our cars for about an hour until the gate opened. The pit crew could come a little later.

The first thing I did was give the crew a schedule of what I wanted done and by when. I let everyone know what time I expected to be rolling through inspection and when the car had to be positioned on Pit Road.

Then we uncovered the car and got it prepared.

My guys were focused, they weren't social butterflies in the garage. They knew we were there to race.

I told them if those others aren't paying attention to their race car, they're giving us a chance to improve and beat them. My guys were really good about being focused, staying close. I'd always say, if you've got time to be over talking to somebody about some bullshit, then you've got time to do something to help make the car better and prepare to race.

When the pit crew arrived, the pit captain Andy Papa coordinated with me on the setup of our pit area. We decided on how many sets of tires and dump cans of fuel we'd bring and what equipment was needed on Pit Road.

I wasn't concerned about the inspection.

Shit, by race day, we'd been there for a week. We'd been constantly grinding Bondo, jacking it up and down, and checking our templates.

We were always concerned about our heights and our templates, but we'd been through inspection enough by then that I really didn't have much to worry about.

The NASCAR inspectors did a safety check of the seat, the belts, the fire extinguisher—all driver-related safety stuff. Then an inspector got underneath the car to make sure there was nothing illegal.

Afterward, we rolled over to the inspection line where they checked the height, weight, and templates. From there, we were off to Pit Road.

I didn't see Jeff much that morning. I think that's when it hit me. It was going to be a little different for us. This was the big time. Jeff was a rising star.

He was getting pulled to hospitality meet and greets for our sponsor DuPont, for Hendrick, and for NASCAR. I'm sure his stepfather John prepared him. But now his schedule was filling up with "have to do's" and not "wanna do's."

Still, that's how the money gets made. Therefore, I needed to make the most of the time I did have with him.

He and I attended the drivers' meeting together. Since we ran in the Atlanta race the previous season, we were somewhat established. Plus, we were part of the Hendrick team.

Still, I got the feeling those veteran drivers and crew chiefs took one look at us and thought, "Who the hell are these guys? One from New Jersey, the other from California, and they show up with a rainbow-colored car? What the hell's NASCAR come to?"

But there was no question in anyone's mind we'd be gunning for Rookie of the Year.

In the early nineties, drivers' meetings were not held in the big media centers like they have today. We sat on folding chairs in the garage area. David Hoots, NASCAR race director, along with NASCAR president Bill France Jr., and Bill's number-two guy, Mike Helton, stood at the microphone, giving us prerace instructions about things like how and at what speed to exit Pit Road.

David was the lead official. His word was law.

Since we'd won the 125, I had no doubt the other drivers knew we had a pretty fast car, and they might want to think about following the kid with the rookie stripe if they wanted to get to the front.

The Rainbow Warriors getting it done on Pit Road. *Nigel Kinrade*

CHAPTER 13

BUCKLING DOWN

Rookie of the Year

"Fun's over, time to go to work."

I had to work like hell to suppress my inner racing fan in the early days. I was in awe of most of the guys sitting around me in that Daytona 500 drivers' meeting. But then I had to remind myself, "Ray, your job today is to figure out how to beat them."

Still, every once in a while, that little Jersey race fan would jump up and go, "Holy shit! Dale Earnhardt just patted you on the back. Bobby Allison just said, 'Good job.'"

After inspection and the drivers' meeting, I held a prerace team meeting in the hauler.

"Look, this is our first Daytona 500," I began. "Somebody's going to win this race today so that might as well be us."

I'd caution them next about making mistakes. Then I'd lay out the tires and fuel strategy. I'd tell them to be ready for any damage. Again, we had to stay in the mix because at some point, the fastest car would give us the chance to capitalize on their mistake and we must be ready.

We had a pretty basic formula: common sense. The old Vince Lombardi strategy of blocking and tackling. We couldn't afford to get penalties. We also had to stay sharp because all day long, people were bound to make mistakes, to give their lead away—and when they did we'd have to be ready to take it from them.

Standing on pit road with my nerves fired up, hearing the national anthem always centered me. Looking around, seeing all the fans and the flags, takes your breath away. I did that more than two hundred times with Jeff, and it never got old. It always felt the same way. Honestly, sometimes it'd bring a lump to my throat.

I don't know if NASCAR would admit this or not, but the Rainbow Warriors were the first crew to deliberately line up on Pit Road for the playing of the national anthem.

If you look at the North Wilkesboro race in 1993, the only crew lined up at attention on Pit Road was the Rainbow Warriors. That was my doing. To develop my leadership and team-building skills, I used to read a lot of books about great football and basketball coaches. I read about one particular coach who said what separated his team from others, what created unity, was having his players line up at attention during the anthem.

Not only was it a show of respect, but the coach also believed in some ways the uniformity of it intimidated the other teams.

When our first Daytona 500 was over, we had survived a wreck-strewn afternoon. Jeff had jockeyed into second place behind Dale Earnhardt with twenty laps to go. He went under the white flag in second or third, before Dale Jarrett overtook him and Earnhardt.

Earnhardt got blocked, and he and Jeff lost momentum. Dale Jarrett was there to take advantage with a great finish.

I always preached, the fastest way to the front is to follow Earnhardt's black No. 3 car. That's exactly what Jeff did that day. Most of the time, you wouldn't end up any worse than second place following Earnhardt.

It was Dale Jarrett's first-ever Daytona 500. For us, placing fifth was an impressive showing.

I look back on it now and I'm almost glad we didn't win that race. We weren't ready.

Now, if we had won that race it would've been great for NASCAR history—and it would've been an achievement for us—however, we may not have become the same team had we clinched the Daytona 500 right out of the gate.

I learned a lot from that race.

I discovered my guys were really good. There's a lot more to winning races than just having a fast car. If we were going to secure that big prize, the Daytona 500, we had more dues to pay.

We didn't deserve to win it that day. It sounds corny, but had we won the Daytona 500 that day, we would've assumed we were great already.

We weren't. Yes, we were destined for greatness; however, had we won, it would've stopped us from ever becoming an excellent team.

Mom trying to get me to smile. *Ray Evernham Enterprises Archives*

Me and Cousin Danny at seven years old. He was more like a brother than a cousin. *Ray Evernham Enterprises Archives*

Captain Baldy, my barrel racing horse, in 1972. *Ray Evernham Enterprises Archives*

The Bob Weiss No. 201 was the first modified I ever worked on and the first dirt car I ever raced. *Ray Evernham Enterprises Archives*

My boss, Bob Bailey, and me working on the railroad in the late 1970s.
Ray Evernham Enterprises Archives

Modern Stock Champ. *Ray Evernham Enterprises Archives*

Left to right: Me, Gil Hearne, and Chip Graves with our championship jackets.
Ray Evernham Enterprises Archives

Working on my homebuilt No. 19 in 1978. *Ray Evernham Enterprises Archives*

I never liked that nickname. *Ray Evernham Enterprises Archives*

My first checkered flag in John Bauma's No. 61 was in 1979. *Ray Evernham Enterprises Archives*

The crew at my garage in 1979. Left to right: Charlie K., Bobby Thomas "Bulkhead," Scotty "The Hammer," and me. Shay Nappi is under the car. *Ray Evernham Enterprises Archives*

Driving Ted Siez's ATQMA Midget at Pinebrook, New Jersey, in 1982. I broke my knee and my sternum later that year in that car. *Ray Evernham Enterprises Archives*

Me and Tony Siscone side by side at Wall Stadium in 1983. *Ray Evernham Enterprises Archives*

About to finish the body molds on the IROC prototype at Diversified Fiberglass in 1983. *Ray Evernham Enterprises Archives*

A big win at the Bud Crown Classic held at Wall Stadium in 1983. *Ray Evernham Enterprises Archives*

Being introduced at Pocono Speedway Race of Champions. *Ray Evernham Enterprises Archives*

Making some last-minute seat adjustment for Dale Earnhardt in 1984. Left to right: Me, Rick Frank, Jay Signore, George Follmer. *Ray Evernham Enterprises Archives*

Working on Dave Marcis's car at Bristol in 1984. *Ray Evernham Enterprises Archives*

Darrell Waltrip and
me talking shop.
*Ray Evernham
Enterprises Archives*

Me, Dave Marcis, and Jay Signore working on the IROC prototype in 1984 at
Daytona. *Ray Evernham Enterprises Archives*

Me and Dale Earnhardt at North Wilkesboro in 1988. I'm wearing his fire suit. *Ray Evernham Enterprises Archives*

Earnhardt bustin' my chops for wrecking my modified while qualifying at North Wilkesboro Speedway in 1988. Jim Bauma is on the left and my brother Willie is looking on. *Ray Evernham Enterprises Archives*

My first shop was in Manasquan, New Jersey. I was building cars for Australian Dick Johnson. *Ray Evernham Enterprises Archives*

Nazareth, Pennsylvania, 1991. Finished second to Doug Hoffman in a one hundred miler. *Ray Evernham Enterprises Archives*

Flemington win, June 1991. It was my first race back after my head injury. I am as proud of that as anything I have ever done in racing. *Ray Evernham Enterprises Archives*

One of my favorite photos. Winner's Classic with some dirt racing legends on a one-mile dirt track in Syracuse, New York. *Ray Evernham Enterprises Archives*

The foam blocks saved my life. My right-front tire is headed for the stands. Thank God, it didn't get there. Flemington Speedway, 1991. *Ray Evernham Enterprises Archives*

What was left of the No. 2P after hitting the lap car at Flemington, 1991. *David Pratt Photo*

Building the DuPont No. 24 shop in 1992. *Ray Evernham Enterprises Archives*

The first No. 24 car done at the Hendrick shop in 1992. *Ray Evernham Enterprises Archives*

Jeff, Mr. H, and me at the Charlotte test in 1992, the day we took $1,500 from D. W. with four left-side tires. *Ray Evernham Enterprises Archives*

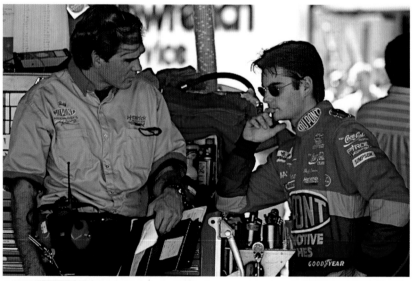

Jeff's thought process when describing the car was a level above most drivers. *Nigel Kinrade*

On the other hand, Rick was thrilled as hell with our top-five finish. Rick loved to race, and he loved to do well. Plus, now he realized he'd found a driver, a crew chief, and a team that could take him where he wanted to go.

The Hendrick team had performed well with Geoff Bodine. Rick had an incredible relationship with probably one of the most exciting drivers in NASCAR history, Tim Richmond, whose career ended too early. Rick had been instrumental in *Days of Thunder*, and I think down inside, he felt, "Holy shit, I have the real Cole Trickle right here in Jeff Gordon."

———

Next was Rockingham.

Here we had just come from running in the top five in the Daytona 500, and Jeff spins out leaving Pit Road during qualifying. The crowd went wild. He tore the front air dam off the car. Needless to say, we qualified horribly, and we finished thirty-fourth.

Rockingham brought us right back down to Earth.

That was an eye opener. So now everybody was thinking, "He may have been Cole Trickle last week, but he's coal in your stocking this week."

In Richmond, we placed sixth. We had a good run, and people were like, "Hey, these guys are legit."

After that we went to Atlanta in March and got caught in a damn blizzard. In Atlanta! Our van slid around on the highway. Cars were all over the road.

I was thinking, "Shit, we gotta get to the track."

So, we drove as carefully as we could. We finally got there with snow all over the ground. Thankfully, our car hauler and everything was there, and the cars were already in the garage.

There was nobody else at the track except us and Alan Kulwicki's crew. It was freezing with winds blowing like crazy.

I'll never forget this. Alan had his crew out trying to reset the bump steer on his car. Alan just stood there with his helmet on because it was so bitterly cold. Thankfully, NASCAR postponed the race.

We had to leave our cars there and come back the next week.

We returned believing Atlanta could be our first win. Jeff and I had won there before, and we were good at Atlanta that day. A lot of people thought we had to pit for fuel, but Michael Landis was spot-on with his fuel strategy.

We knew exactly how much fuel went into the car based on the weight of the fuel can before and after the pit stop. We had worked on our fuel cell. We knew exactly how much it would pick up. From those numbers we knew how many laps we could run. I could always count on intel I got from Michael Landis, Brian Whitesell, and our tire guy at that time, Billy Chandler.

We made our last pit stop, and I was confident we were good on fuel. Then, sure enough, Jeff felt a vibration and damned if we didn't have a loose wheel, forcing him to pit early.

This threw us out of our pit cycle. We ended up having to re-pit, giving up the lead.

We placed fourth. We had to put it in perspective. We had a rookie crew and Atlanta was our fourth race together. We had a loose wheel. Simple as that.

After that we started a streak of crashing cars like you wouldn't believe.

At Darlington, we crashed into one of Richard Petty's cars. He wrecked at Bristol. Then our car crashed and caught fire at North Wilkesboro.

We wrecked at Talladega, too. (Which is really all we ever seemed to do at Talladega.) At Sonoma, during practice, Jeff was driving our road race car when all of a sudden, he came on the radio and said, "I just turned this bitch over!"

"Excuse me, what?" I asked.

"I wrecked!"

We flipped the car back over. However, there was too much damage, so we switched to the backup—our rebuilt North Wilkesboro car. We only had one road racing car with us, so we had to use a short-track car. We ended up finishing eleventh.

People knew we were wrecking a lot of stuff, but we had also nailed down some legitimate top-five finishes in between crashes.

Then came the Coke 600.

The 600 is not only a big event—it's in our hometown. Rick Hendrick's hometown, too. We knew how important it was to him.

He wouldn't say anything directly to us. He just mentioned in passing in front of the group, "Got a lot of dealership people coming to that race."

That's all he had to say. We got it.

We had a pretty good record at Charlotte. Jeff and I had only worked together twice before at Charlotte and won both times. We nearly triumphed this time, too. Instead, we came in second to Dale Earnhardt.

You'd have thought that might have been one of those "pinch me" moments, coming in second to Earnhardt in front of the boss and the hometown crowd—coming this close to beating one of your heroes.

Instead, we were thinking, "Damn it! We should have done this or that and we could have beat 'em."

Second was never fun for us. Never. We figured if we could run second, we should have won.

Now, I think if you look at Jeff Gordon's record, you'll see a decent number of firsts and probably thirds, fourths, and fifths. Not a lot of seconds.

Because if Jeff could get to second, he could find a way to win.

———

So far, we didn't have any points race trophies to show for our efforts, but we came close a few times. And we were damn competitive for being a true rookie team.

Yet here we were busting off these top fives and second-place finishes. We had our share of scars from the mistakes we'd made; however, we were getting seasoned quickly because we kept our eyes on the prize.

We got to Michigan in June and wound up wrecking the car during qualifying. Jeff tried to run a wide-open lap and crashed. That meant we had to go to a backup. I remember Michael Waltrip remarking on the quality of our cars. "Most people don't carry a spare car as good as their race car. Gordon crashes one and they just roll another out of the truck and run second with it."

That was standard operating procedure for us: every race, two competitive cars. Most teams brought a backup that was barely usable, with no motor in it. Our guys could get our backup car out, plugged in, and it'd be ready to go. We could crash a car or endure some other problem early in practice and have the backup out and on the track before practice ended. That's another standard we set early in the nineties. People still talk about it.

I'm proud of the preparation and efficiencies we were developing. We practiced changing car parts and made components that could be changed out faster. We also made contributions to NASCAR with our systems and some of the safety technology we developed for Jeff.

———

While we were making real strides with the team, I didn't feel the same about my progress on the home front. Things were wearing on me due to my anger over Ray J.'s condition. I didn't see him getting better. I'm sure as hell not proud of this now; I was conflicted.

Career-wise, great things were happening. It was exciting on the road. The contrast between that and my homelife was night and day.

Then one day, after an intense conversation with Mary, I realized I wasn't who she married. I had to get back to being that person.

Mary's a tough woman and she told me straight up, "Hey, look. You get your act together or I'm gone. That's the bottom line."

I needed to be called out and she did it. Every once in a while, you need the people who really love you, who care about you, to call bullshit on you.

Once I had that epiphany, things changed for the better. Attitude is a powerful force. Life at home began improving. Ray J. still had his leukemia struggles. But Mary and I were working more closely than we had in years. I removed the distractions. I prioritized my real responsibilities and the people who mattered most. I also started listening to my better angels. Ultimately, you know if what you're doing isn't right, no matter what excuse you use to disguise it. If you don't feel good about something initially, you'll never feel good about it. You must figure out how to change. It doesn't matter how much money you have in the bank, how many trophies line your shelves, or how many times you read in the paper how great you are. The only way you'll ever feel good about your accomplishments is if you feel good about yourself.

One of our main team goals going into the '93 season was to win Rookie of the Year. We did it. Still, we were disappointed we didn't win a race that counted. It was cool we won the 125, but it wasn't a points-paying race. We had the chance to win some races and we didn't.

I felt like we should have.

Something else happened during that season, and it wasn't anything on the track. Jeff had been secretly dating Miss Winston model Brooke Sealey. Only problem? There was a rule that Miss Winston could not date a driver.

So they had to do it in secret.

Although I didn't notice it, apparently their connection started in February, when they made eye contact in Victory Lane as Jeff celebrated his Daytona 125 qualifier win. Jeff kept their budding romance on the down-low, slipping out the side doors of restaurants, staggering their entrances and exits from hotels.

Honestly, I can't tell you if it affected his performance in a good or a bad way. The one thing I can say about Jeff Gordon is no matter what happened to him during the week, no matter what he had on his mind, in all the races we ran together, I can count on two fingers the times he didn't give me 100 percent of his attention from Friday to Sunday.

As far as I'm concerned, dating Brooke had absolutely zero effect on his performance at the racetrack.

Still, Brooke's occasional visits did affect at least one team member. We had a guy working for us named Joel. He was funny. I think I fired him seventeen times because he kept screwing off or showing up late.

Brooke was showing up more often.

After a while, she'd hang out by the car. Joel thought for sure Brooke had the hots for him. He'd say stuff like, "Miss Winston is always over here talking to me and smiling."

I was thinking, "No, she's just watching as you put stuff in Jeff's car. She's smiling at Jeff, you idiot."

Still, Joel swore it was him. It turned into a big joke, especially when the other guys found out. Joel gave us some laughs. He ended up being a spotter for Greg Biffle.

I liked Brooke. But I didn't care for some of the things she did when she and Jeff were going through their divorce. I know divorce is hard. It can be costly, too. I've been there. And sadly, there's always collateral damage.

Toward the end, I think Brooke overstepped some boundaries as far as her job and mine. And I think she introduced some people and some ideas into Jeff's business that weren't team oriented.

———

There was little arguing between us. There were stern talks like a father to son, and there were times when he had to call me out. "Wake up, Ray, what are you thinking about?" It doesn't mean we were arguing.

Still, in '93 we did have a little blowout in the hauler.

But it wasn't due to a conflict between us. It was carbon monoxide. When carbon monoxide built up in the car, it caused a change in Jeff's personality and temperament.

He got angry. One time, he pulled out of the pits and hit a car on Pit Road. It bothered me because it almost hurt the crew members. He yelled at us all day long, and we just didn't have a good day.

At that point, we had no idea it was carbon monoxide.

Jeff came in. Ricky Craven was in our hauler. Jeff looked at Ricky and made some crack about how I was just pissed at him for hitting the No. 8 car.

I spun around, putting my finger in Jeff's chest. "No, I'm not pissed at you for hitting the eight car. I'm pissed about how you talk to me and the guys on the radio! Nobody feels any worse than I do when our car isn't good. And those guys bust their asses for you week after week. The next time you yell at us like that on the radio, you can put your own fuel in and put on your own damn tires because there won't be anybody on Pit Road waiting for you."

I'll never forget the look of shock on his face.

Then his expression went from surprise to apologetic. He hadn't even realized what he'd done. It took us all a little while to figure out what was going on. Short tracks like Martinsville and Bristol were the worst places for the in-car buildup of carbon monoxide.

At the same time, we heard from other teams about drivers getting headaches. The effects of carbon monoxide are relative to body mass. Jeff was 142 pounds and had a low body fat percentage. So as the race went on, the carbon monoxide buildup would cause intense headaches, even causing a change in Jeff's voice.

We got permission from NASCAR to run tests using these balloon-like devices in the car. Sure enough, the particles per million were high enough to cause carbon monoxide poisoning. Right away, Gary Aker, one of our engineers at Hendrick, invented a little carbon monoxide scrubber that purified the air flowing into Jeff's helmet.

Instantly, our performance on the short tracks improved. Even though Jeff had fewer headaches, at one point he still took oxygen before and after the short-track races.

Once we fixed the carbon monoxide problem, he won a gazillion Martinsville races in a row.

Whether it was working for the Penske organization as part of IROC, or my experience with other drivers, in retrospect I feel I brought an analytical, mechanical, and "can do" mentality to my job as crew chief. I also maintained the philosophy that just because it wasn't possible yesterday, doesn't mean it won't be possible tomorrow. Technology, designs, and materials were evolving so rapidly, nothing was ever off the table when it came to improving performance. I believed the No. 24 team and Hendrick were further ahead than most teams in NASCAR at that time. Even so, I was glad our rookie year would soon be behind us.

By the end of the season, I knew one thing for sure: I didn't know as much as I thought I did.

We needed better cars, and I needed to be better prepared as a leader. I had to find a way to get my own shit together. I was responsible for the race team and our results. I had to improve my skills at motivating people if I ever hoped they'd get more efficient at their jobs. I needed to set a better example.

We had rookie guys who needed a more experienced leader, so I had to be faster on my learning curve than they were on theirs. Especially because I could see Jeff Gordon was much faster on his learning curve than all of us.

As for Jeff and me, we've always had a relationship unique from any I have had with anyone else on the planet. It's based on trust, honesty, and respect. Maybe we haven't been honest with each other 100 percent of the time, but at least 98 percent.

I've felt that bond ever since the first day we met at that hotel in Charlotte in 1990. We clicked instantly, and it's never changed. That trust and respect has never wavered.

At the end of '93, I could see how fast his star was rising and I had to catch up. Job one for me was to ensure he could be all he could be. As a coach or a crew chief, when you're given one of the greatest athletes in a sport, it's your responsibility to make sure that person reaches their full potential.

I felt that way right up until the day I left Jeff in 1999.

Our first Cup win was at Charlotte in 1994. Left to right: Mr. H, Jeff, and me.
Ray Evernham Enterprises Archives

CHAPTER 14

WORK SMARTER AND HARDER

Designing Tricks for Our Trade: 1994

"Two tires!"

Going into the 1994 season, I started to feel like we belonged in Cup racing. We'd won the 125 at Daytona the year before, we'd come close to winning a couple other races, Jeff was Rookie of the Year, I understood the inspection process, and we had a better grasp of what we didn't know.

We learned how races worked at each track since we'd raced them all twice. (One of the things that makes the NASCAR Cup Series unique is how tracks present different challenges depending on whether you're racing in spring or fall.) Race setups for tracks like Daytona and Martinsville aren't even close. To be competitive, your car's setups must be specifically tailored to the track you're racing on. We had to learn these things the hard way: through experience. Nowadays, team's setup choices are assisted by computers and simulators.

I wouldn't say I felt confident we were going to go win the championship, but I felt good about our chances to be more competitive because we were better prepared. We had hundreds, if not thousands, of hours of preparation from all the testing and racing that first year. (I'd been at the racetrack more in 1993 than in my whole driving career.)

At home, Ray J. was still sick. I continued to struggle with the guilt I felt over what I believed I should be doing with him and Mary; I was torn between them and my responsibilities as a crew chief. At least we were living in the same house now.

I've always said, I made my career working half days, seven to seven, twelve hours a day. And truth be told, there was still a part of me that regretted the fact my own driving career was effectively over. I admit I had a little case of jealousy, thinking, "God almighty, why couldn't I have been born with that kind of talent?" Yet the more time I spent around guys like Jeff Gordon, Dale Earnhardt, or Rusty Wallace, I realized I had to let it go.

It was all still overwhelming. In less than three years, I'd gone from IROC to trying to jumpstart my own driving career to moving to a different state and becoming a NASCAR crew chief. For a guy who developed a reputation as a planner and perfectionist, I hadn't planned any of it.

———

In our rookie season, we learned enough about what we didn't know to realize there was plenty more we didn't know. At least we weren't going into the '94 season blind. For one thing, we'd learned winning NASCAR races took a helluva lot more than just having a fast car.

A strong team culture was essential. *The Winner Within*, a book by famed basketball coach Pat Riley, has been—and remains—one of my favorite reads on leadership and fostering a constructive organization. Pat Riley was an incredible coach, and his book covers team building and team destruction. My team management philosophy is based on principles outlined in the book.

In short, it was a game changer for us.

On the wall in the No. 24 shop, I posted Coach Riley's success checklist. We were so proud we could check off a few items. The lines read:

"From nobody to upstart."

"From upstart to contender."

"From contender to winner."

"From winner to champion."

The fifth and final line:

"From champion to dynasty."

It was incredible to see how far we had come so fast. Winning the 125 at Daytona and taking second to Dale Earnhardt in the Coke 600 allowed us to put check marks beside "From nobody to upstart" and "From upstart to contender." We had no idea at the time, but later in 1994, we'd mark "From contender to winner" off our list.

I started putting up motivational signs all over the shop, on most of the machines, and even on the bathroom door. Short, powerful,

144

inspiring quotes, they made a difference in our day-to-day attitudes. Those sayings, plus having a goal posted right in front of you, can help you reframe your mindset to stay positive.

Every year we'd choose a new motivational saying that expressed our goal. I created what I called a commitment sign, and everyone was invited to put their name to it in one of our team meetings. It was like signing a contract to make a commitment to the team. If you didn't sign it, chances were you weren't going to be on the team long. I did this annually with my own team, and I'd do it again with any other I put together in the future.

Some might think all this is corny, but making that commitment before your teammates is powerful. Every time you see your signature on that sign it's a reminder to hold yourself accountable to the team.

When a team of people truly work together, they can accomplish things they never thought possible on their own. I was lucky enough to have a core group of Rainbow Warriors who exemplified what it meant to be a team. They punched above their weight, and their collective IQ and racing ability was through the roof.

It's amazing to think in 1993 we were rookies who didn't know shit. By 1994, we were like a golden retriever puppy stumbling around with energetic potential.

Team members came and went, but the nucleus stayed together. Even today, I'm particular about who I work with. If I discover you aren't fully committed to the team or the mission, if you're just around for the paycheck, you'll find your toolbox pushed outside pretty quickly.

That's just how it is.

It's how you keep your good people together. You can't accept less from someone else and say it's okay. If you want your team to be like a special ops squad, you can't accept below-average performances. You need everyone to be fully committed and performing at their best.

———

We were really looking forward to the Daytona 500. But in the days before the big race, we were reminded once again about how risky and dangerous our sport can be.

NASCAR legend Neil Bonnett was set to compete in that year's Daytona 500. He was happy to be back in the car again after sitting out awhile recovering from an injury. Neil and I had known each other since our days at IROC. He always called me "buddy." He was a member of NASCAR's famed "Alabama Gang," a real character off the track but a tough competitor on the track. He was just a great guy.

Neil had racked up eighteen Cup wins in his twenty-year driving career. What's so remarkable is that he won all those races, including two back-to-back Coke 600s, by competing in only five full-time seasons.

Neil had a smooth Southern voice and a charm that made him a media and fan favorite. He appeared in the 1983 movie *Stroker Ace* and the 1990 film, *Days of Thunder*. He also did television race commentary for CBS, TBS, and TNN.

On Friday, February 11, Neil and I were in the garage at Daytona. He was anxious to get on the track for practice. We were just shootin' the shit about our old IROC days, how well the No. 24 team had done our rookie year, and the upcoming 500. When Neil spoke to you, he made you feel like he was truly interested in you. That meant a lot to me.

"Well, buddy, I'll see you later," he said as he headed to his car for the start of practice.

Only about fifteen minutes into the practice session, Neil's car slammed head-on into the outside wall, killing him instantly. He was just forty-seven years old. I was devastated.

As shocked and as sad as I was, I knew I had to focus on getting ready for the Busch Clash, which was only two days away.

The Busch Clash was an exhibition race exclusively for the 1993 pole winners. Jeff, who was competing in his first Clash, started in sixth place. Despite leading only two laps, he won the race, beating out Brett Bodine, Dale Earnhardt, and Ernie Irvan.

Not bad for a young team of short-track racers and a sprint car driver. We beat legends that day. It was crazy. I mean, holy shit, the Busch Clash is for the best of the best, and we won it on our first try.

Then the next day, as many were preparing to leave the track and fly to Hueytown, Alabama, to attend Neil's funeral, Rodney Orr, who was attempting to qualify for his very first Winston Cup race, was killed when his family-owned Ford Thunderbird hit the wall coming out of Turn Two during a morning practice run.

For the second time in four days, a Cup driver was killed in a single-car accident.

But once again, we had to compartmentalize the tragedies and get our heads in the game for the 500.

We wound up finishing fourth. We were frustrated because we felt like we could have won. Then again, it was only our second Daytona 500, and we came away in both with top-five finishes.

It's a tough race to win. Even Dale Earnhardt, who I consider one of the greatest speedway drivers of all time, won it only once. All in all, it was a very good weekend, but due to the tragedies we just wanted to get home.

The next weekend, we took third at Richmond. After that race, we had a pretty ugly six-week stretch where we did no better than fifteenth, and we failed three times to crack the top thirty.

Then we went to Atlanta, where we normally ran well, but I brought the wrong car. We tried to run a speedway car because everybody told me Atlanta's almost like a speedway track. I learned you can't beat downforce. We ran so bad that day I told my crew, "If I ever suggest this again, hit me in the head with a hammer."

Darlington, Bristol, North Wilkesboro, Martinsville, and Talladega were not our best showings. These were tracks where experience mattered. And Talladega—holy shit—if there was a wreck at Talladega, we were in it.

But our fortunes turned for the better when we returned to Charlotte for the Coke 600.

———

My hope was that the Coke 600 could serve as a chance for us to make up for our previous shortcomings. We'd constructed a brand-new ride specifically for the race. The beauty of being a part of Hendrick was that we could go from tubing rack to racetrack in just three weeks, an impressive turnaround.

We debuted the new car at the Winston Select race weekend. The Winston Select was a special, invitation-only exhibition race that took place one week before the Coke 600. Since it was a non-points race, many teams used it as a warm-up for the 600.

Since we had not yet won a points race, we had to compete in the Winston Select Open. Our new car was fast. We won both the pole and the race, qualifying us for the Winston Select. The winner of the Winston Select Open would be positioned at the back of the Winston Select field. We had just beat the rest, now we were going to race the best.

Jeff drove from the back to the front. I felt we had a real shot at winning. Instead, we got caught up in a wreck with Dale Earnhardt and Rusty Wallace. Even though we beat the rest, turns out we wrecked with the best

We raced the Winston Select on Saturday night, and we had to be back at the racetrack on Wednesday. We had only three days to fix our car, and they were long days. We worked around the clock, fixing the body and repairing the chassis.

We completed the repairs in time for Wednesday's pole qualifying. Sure enough, Jeff set a new track record with his qualifying lap, capturing the pole for the Coke 600.

————

Going into NASCAR's longest race, I put a lot of focus on strategy and preparation.

One of the things I studied was the impact of two-tire pit stops. I was aware that cautions often happened toward the end of the race, and we needed to be prepared for any situation. I assigned my engineer Brian Whitesell the task of researching the last five years of Coke 600 races to determine the average time when cautions occurred.

Armed with Brian's data, we came up with a plan, but it was only going to work under green-flag pit stops.

We figured a pit stop for four tires took an average of seventeen seconds. I knew our guys could change two tires in about nine seconds. I also figured that having two fresh tires rather than four would slow us down by two-tenths of a second.

So, if we were only two-tenths of a second slower, with a gain of eight seconds due to our faster pit, there would be no way they could catch us if there were twenty laps or less to go in the race.

But our lead wouldn't last forever. My fear was the caution flag. With four tires, you'd be able to maintain speed longer, but I was prepared to roll the dice.

Although we started from the pole, the lead changed hands twenty-five times in that race. It was crazy.

We fought back and forth the whole race. We had a good car, but Rusty Wallace's was better. Both Rusty and Geoff Bodine were driving Fords. We felt like we were the best Chevy out there, even better than Earnhardt.

We were running third, with Rusty ahead of us by a decent lead of three or four seconds. And then, cars started to pit. I kept waiting to see what our competitors would do because I wanted to pit once we were inside that twenty-lap window.

Rusty pitted with around twenty-two or twenty-three laps to go. He took four tires. Before pitting, Rusty had a three- or four-second lead on us. His pit stop was seventeen seconds.

To speed up our pit stop, I knew we could do just the two new tires with adding only enough fuel to get us to the end of the race.

I thought, "Okay, Rusty's pit stop was seventeen seconds with a four-second lead on us. That gives us thirteen seconds. We can do this pit stop in about seven seconds and come out with a six-second lead. If we're only losing two- to three-tenths of a second per lap to Rusty, with only eighteen laps to go there's no way he can catch us before the race ends unless there's a caution."

I keyed my radio, telling Jeff and the crew, "All right, guys. Two! Two! Two!"

Mr. Hendrick, seated beside me on the pit box, glanced at me with a concerned look. "You sure you wanna do that?"

I had a plan, and I was confident. "Yeah, we're goin' with two." He nodded at me and said, "Okay."

Jeff came down Pit Road and the guys executed the pit stop perfectly. We put a splash of gas in, two tires, and he came right back out.

Now, we had about a five-second lead on Rusty.

Still, I expected him to catch us little by little as he had four new tires. Looking at my stopwatch, I thought, "Shit, not only is he not catching us, Jeff's pulling away."

With fewer than eighteen laps left, I couldn't believe it, we were winning!

Then, inside ten laps to go, I heard Richard Petty, who was doing TV commentating, second-guess my pit decision. "Gordon takin' just two tires might've been a mistake."

If a caution had come out, he would have been right.

I didn't blame The King for questioning my decision. Throughout my career, I was often questioned because we won several races taking just two tires. They didn't understand the strategy behind it. They just couldn't figure out how we did it.

Depending on the circumstance, we'd either put on new lefts or rights, but the real secret was in tire pressure. People back then seemed to overlook the importance of tire pressure. Having worked closely with Goodyear Engineering on radial tire development during my IROC days, I had a good understanding of just how important correct tire pressure was to the radial tire.

I also spent time at Penske Shock, where I learned how critical shock tuning is to the radial tire. A shock designed for a radial tire varies from one meant for a bias ply tire. Our cars always had better tire wear than our competitors because we paid attention to these details.

Besides only taking two tires in the 600, we also didn't fill our gas tank all the way up. We only put enough in to finish the race, making our car lighter and faster.

As we'd hoped, there was no caution flag. The race stayed green, and Jeff collected his first NASCAR Cup points-race checkered flag.

Our first win was a combination of Jeff's driving talent and simple math.

That Charlotte victory is forever etched in my memory, not just because it was our first, but also because of Jeff's tearful reaction. He was just a kid, and it was his dream to be a successful race car driver. It meant so much to win.

When we won our first Busch race at Atlanta, he cried then, too, and I began to understand him better. It was a sign of his passion—how much it meant to him.

When Jeff cried after winning his first Cup race at Charlotte, it hit me hard. I felt it.

I could see how far he'd come, how much he'd achieved. The sacrifices his stepdad, John, and his mom, Carol, had made to get him there, and the relentless pursuit of his dream—it was all there in that moment. It was a dream he'd nurtured for years, and to see it finally come to fruition was a beautiful thing.

To know I was part of it, and that our hard work had paid off, was an incredible feeling. I was proud and humbled to be part of something that meant so much to a friend.

The win made my head spin. I had so much going on, my mind was whirling like a tornado. I was trying to organize everything but at the same time, realizing all we had accomplished. It was a lot to take in.

I still joke today with Rick Hendrick about my call for two tires in the Coke 600 race. He was so nervous, he nearly wore the soles off his shoes from pacing around the pit area those last few laps. But I know this about Rick. If it had turned out to be the wrong call, he's not a guy who would have said, "Told you so."

Instead, he would have put his arm around me and told me we'd get it next time.

The next morning, as I drove past Charlotte Motor Speedway on my way to the shop, it hit me again. "Holy shit. We won the race last night."

When I got to the shop, I was by myself for a bit and had time to reflect. We had won a prestigious NASCAR Cup race, and no one could take that away from us. It was a great accomplishment, and even if we never won again, we had that one.

This photo from Victory Lane at Indy in 1994 says it all.
Ray Evernham Enterprises Archives

CHAPTER 15

HITTING THE BRICKS

1994 Inaugural Brickyard 400

"I may not be driving, but I'm racing at Indianapolis today."

T he 1994 inaugural Brickyard 400 race at the Indianapolis Motor
Speedway was a major turning point for the No. 24 team. It was a
huge deal for everyone involved.

With our new engineering and car-building staffs in place, I felt like
we had an advantage going to a new track for the first time.

In reality, we couldn't have tried any harder to win at Indy than we
tried at Martinsville. We didn't try harder to win at Daytona than we
did at Rockingham, either. We worked our hardest to win every race.
The only limitation is the amount of time you have to prepare, and we
were fortunate enough to have had extra time to prepare for Indy.

We did get to test at Indy, which was great. At the time, the Hendrick
teams had a mix of Laughlin, Hutch, and Hendrick cars. I wanted to
take a Hendrick chassis and get a win for Mr. H. We took one of our first
Hendrick chassis and rebuilt it with trick things, designed specifically
for Indianapolis.

Where other teams were doing their regular stock car modifications—comparing Indy to Pocono, for instance—I spent a lot of time on
the phone with Poncho Carter, Wayne Leary, and A. J. Foyt, all smart
Indy car guys, gathering their insights. Wayne had been crew chief for
Dan Gurney and Bobby Unser. He and I hit it off well.

I spoke with A. J. Foyt a good bit about front-end settings. I felt like
I already knew a little bit about Indianapolis Motor Speedway as far as

weather and track changes because of my time at IROC-Penske and my original goal of becoming an Indy car driver.

No one had ever run at Indy in a stock car. It leveled the playing field. When racing on NASCAR tracks, we were going up against teams and guys who had raced on them multiple times, so they had notebooks that were inches thick.

Nobody had a notebook for Indy.

Meanwhile, during practice, people were fighting loose in, tight off. A. J. advised me to change the caster in the front of the car. Normally with a Cup car, you run more positive caster on the right front than the left front. Instead, we ran more positive caster on the left front. This meant the car wouldn't lead Jeff down into the corner, and the further he turned the wheel, the more camber it would gain to help the car cut on exit.

Bingo! It worked.

We also ran a left-front spring stiffer rather than a right-front spring, and they were both soft. This was the opposite of what we did everywhere else we raced. It was Wayne Leary who told me to run a much bigger front sway bar and softer front springs. He said it would help keep the car from rolling too much and keep it flat.

Underneath the car, we put in brake ducts to cool the brakes. We added pans under the front with NACA ducts, which sucked the car's nose down to the racetrack. We also installed a rear sway bar, unheard of in NASCAR.

I theorized that as Jeff went down into the corner, the rear sway bar would keep the car up in the air on the right rear, holding the spoiler up and the nose down. Much better for aerodynamics, but possibly worse for mechanical grip. It was a big risk. Had I shown my chassis sheet to some, they might have laughed. Even some of my Hendrick teammates didn't believe our setup. But I was convinced it was our best shot at winning, and I was willing to take that chance.

When we got to Indy, there were certain parts of the day when the track was going to be nothing like it would be during the race. Clouds, sun, temperature—they all required crazy adjustments. If you corrected your car based on the last practice, you were going to suck in the race. We chose not to run in the final practice because of that, and it was the talk of the garage.

We got beat for the pole in qualifying by Rick Mast, and we started third. Rick was one of the nicest guys in NASCAR, so it was hard for us to begrudge his getting the pole.

I knew our car was strong in the long run. Between our setup and the intel I'd learned from talking to Poncho, Wayne, and A. J., I was confident going into the race.

————

Indy holds a special place in my heart. It always will. Whenever I go there, just like Daytona, I feel energy from ghosts of the greats who raced there before. It's a hallowed space. I'd always wanted to be an Indy car driver; that's probably why it's so special to me.

On race day, the team was as focused as I'd ever seen them. At our standard prerace meeting, I talked about our fuel and tire strategy, reminding everyone this pit road was narrow. I made sure not to say things like "This is a really important race" or "We have to win this one." I also didn't tell the pit crew they needed to be on their toes; they were professionals and they knew what to do. Saying stuff like that would only have made them nervous.

As I've said before, avoid making mistakes during races was priority one. There are plenty of things that can happen. Even though Jeff and I won forty-seven Cup races together, we didn't always have the fastest car. Instead, we won some races because we remained vigilant and took advantage of other people's blunders.

Don't get me wrong. Most races we had a solid car, an excellent driver, and a fantastic pit crew. Those things make a great team in my book. Even if we were in third or fourth place, we didn't worry about why we weren't winning. We just kept our focus on not making errors because we knew the other teams may slip up, giving us the chance to take that win.

On race morning we wanted our car to be first on the line. Normally, the cars were lined up on Pit Road. But for the Brickyard, they were lining the cars up on the track like they do for the Indy 500. I wanted the No. 24 car's bright rainbow paint scheme to be the first on that straightaway in front of Jeff's hometown crowd.

When we pushed the car out to the starting grid, I looked around and was awed by the massive crowd: 350,000 to 400,000 people. More than I'd ever seen in any place in my life. It was overwhelming. Then I looked up and saw the number 24 on the historic Indianapolis Motor Speedway scoring pylon, and it hit me; *I'm racing at Indy.* It took my breath away. I may not be driving, but I'm racing at Indy today. It was surreal. I'm so glad I stopped to take it in.

But then I had to shake it off, get my uniform on, and prepare.

It was an intense race with lots of passing and several crashes. At one point Jeff was trying to pit and Brett Bodine just came right up on him and put a big ol' donut in the door and almost crashed both cars.

Back then, I used to get really heated on the radio, calling folks all kinds of names. I probably owe a blanket apology to the many people I cussed out that day.

Not surprisingly, our pit crew was absolutely killing it. They were flawless. As we neared the end of the race, it turned into a nail-biting game of cat and mouse between Jeff and Ernie Irvan. They were both good at getting each other aero loose. It was like watching the old Daytona draft days with Petty and Pearson—whoever was the last guy drafting would win.

As the laps wound down, I was on the edge of my seat. Both Jeff and Ernie were running nose-to-tail, pulling away from the rest of the field. On lap 145, Jeff finally slipped past Ernie. But Ernie didn't give up. He made a move in Turn Four on lap 150 and passed Jeff.

It was a moment of pure excitement and adrenaline.

Then as fast as it happened, Ernie's right-front tire went down on the backstretch. Maybe it was too much camber, low pressure, or just a puncture, but he got a flat. He slid high in Turn One then disappeared. Jeff made his move, diving under Ernie's car for the twenty-first lead change of the race.

"Listen to this crowd in Indiana as they cheer for their boy, Jeff Gordon!" shouted Bob Jenkins. Bob and Benny Parsons were calling the race on TV.

Bob was right. It was nearly deafening.

With two laps to go, the entire team was standing on pit wall, but they weren't cheering. I had a rule about not celebrating until the checkered flag falls. If you did, you weren't allowed into my pit again.

They damn sure cheered as Jeff crossed the yard of bricks just 0.53 seconds ahead of Brett Bodine.

The whole crew exploded when we saw Jeff take the checkered flag. It was pandemonium. Everyone was jumping, hugging, high-fiving, and throwing Gatorade. The noise was deafening with 350,000 people cheering.

Winning at Indy was one of the craziest, most memorable moments in my life. The pageantry is like nothing else in racing. When we pulled into Victory Lane, they raised us up on a platform. The crowd was cheering so loudly I couldn't hear myself think.

It was overwhelming. There's even a picture of me standing in the background looking stunned. But that's just how it is at Indy. People in Speedway, Indiana, really love their sport, and they hold you in high regard if you're part of it.

To this day, I can walk into the Speedway and people recognize me. They treat me like someone special. It's one of my favorite cities to visit because of how passionate the people are. You feel like somebody when you walk into Indy.

Following the celebration, I tucked the rulebook under my arm and headed for the postrace inspection. I was not looking forward to it. I knew I'd have to explain everything I'd done to the car. I also knew much of it was stuff they'd never seen before. The car passed inspection with no problem, but our secrets were no longer secrets. Then I just hung out with the guys and celebrated our big win with the champagne we'd taken from Victory Lane.

We had accomplished something huge, and it was important the guys took time to acknowledge it. We'd all set a goal to build a car that could do what we needed it to do, and we did just that. We spent tons of hours practicing and perfecting our pit stops, and it paid off. The next time I asked them to push harder or do something extra to win another race, they could look back on that moment and know the effort was worth it.

I wanted to make sure they understood the importance of the process and how it led to our success. I wanted the guys to know our win wasn't just luck. It was because we followed a process, planned, practiced, and followed through. I also wanted them to feel proud of what we had accomplished and, more importantly, to keep striving for further greatness.

For me, winning the Brickyard was a huge confidence builder. We'd just beat some of the greatest NASCAR teams. We had what it took to be champions.

The win also meant I was going to be driving one sweet ride. The day before the Coke 600 at Charlotte, Rick Hendrick rolled up in this incredible looking car. I thought, "Damn! What is that? It looked like a Ferrari."

He told me all about it. He said it was a 1991 Acura NSX. Then I asked him how much it cost. He said around $70,000 to $80,000. I said, "Well, I'm going to get one of those someday."

"I'll tell you what," he said. "If you win two races this year, I'll give you that car as a bonus."

Sure enough, the next day we won the Coke 600 and I started imagining driving that car.

As Jeff crossed the finish line for the Brickyard, I grinned at Mr. Hendrick, "Driving my NSX tomorrow, pal."

I still have that car to this day. The license plate on it is BRKYRD1. It's my trophy.

That's not the only drivable bonus I've received from Mr. Hendrick. I also have a '96 Viper GTS with license plate 1CUP95, a Prowler with license plate 1CUP97, and a Harley-Davidson motorcycle with license plate 1CUP98. Those are all bonuses from Mr. H for wins, championships, and more.

––––––––

When we started at Hendrick, we were inexperienced rookies. We were so different; the veterans really didn't really understand us at first. We had to work hard to prove ourselves, but after the Brickyard win, they started believing in our way of thinking.

We'd earned our place in the Hendrick family.

Though we were competitive with each other, we still respected our Hendrick teammates. When they won, we were happy for them. Of course, we didn't like it when they won and we finished second. But on the days when we couldn't win, we definitely cheered them on.

We were on one team, and we all wanted to see each other succeed.

Ken Howes, Kenny Schrader's crew chief at the time, was one of the best teammates I ever had. Even after he stopped working on the No. 25 car, he still helped me out behind the scenes during the '97 and '98 seasons. We had two of our winningest seasons and championships with him by our side. I owe Ken a lot for his support and guidance.

As for Jeff, he was becoming more successful and mature. I had known Jeff since he was a kid, and it was amazing to watch him grow into an incredible driver and become one of the sport's biggest stars.

––––––––

We ended the '94 season in eighth place in points standings. I was satisfied with making it into the top ten, but we were inconsistent as hell. There were certain tracks we just couldn't get right, like Phoenix. Phoenix was my Achilles heel.

At one point we had a chance to make it into the top five. We were in sixth, but we had a few weeks where we wrecked, dropping us down to eighth. Despite that setback, Jeff was still going to be on stage at the NASCAR year-end awards ceremony in New York, a great accomplishment.

Even though we didn't win more races in 1994 after the Brickyard, there were moments during certain races where we showed potential. That kept me optimistic, even when we made mistakes in the pits, wrecked the car, or I didn't make a good call. I could see we were better than our record showed.

We just needed to work on the things that were holding us back.

I was also excited about the new Monte Carlo that was coming the next season. It was going to be a great race car. I don't feel we ever figured the Lumina out. As a matter of fact, I think the only guy that ever ran worth a shit in the Lumina was Dale Earnhardt. And that's just because RCR was a great team and Dale was an incredible driver.

I was encouraged by what I saw at the season's end. The whole Hendrick organization was making big strides to improve our equipment. I knew if we could just get better in certain areas, we could take our team to the next level.

We weren't a fluke anymore; we had built a solid foundation, one we would continue to build on.

While I couldn't predict the future, I had a good feeling about where we were headed. We were making progress, and it was clear we were on the right track. We had improved a lot from the '93 to '94 seasons, and I was confident we would continue making big improvements heading into '95. I can't claim I had any sort of premonition of winning a championship, but I knew we were going to fight like hell.

Breaking out the Refuse to Lose T-shirts after a win at Rockingham in 1995.

CHAPTER 16

NO DISTRACTIONS, NO EXCUSES

Building the Monte Carlo: 1995

"Refuse to Lose!"

Even with the Coke 600 and Brickyard wins in 1994, we still had a lot to learn.

By the end of the season, we'd started to develop the 1995 Monte Carlo. We also started having more fun. For a couple of tests, we painted the car flat black and put a big skull and crossbones on the hood. No number 24 in sight. We also replaced the American flags on the trucks with pirate flags.

Earnhardt's No. 3 car was black. So was Rusty's No. 2. So we thought, "The hell with it, we're just painting this bitch black."

We didn't want to show up as the "good guys" with the rainbow car. Hell, we didn't even shave. We thought we were badasses. We nick-named our new test car "Blacker," and it was fast.

I loved the Monte Carlo's overall shape.

The nose on the car led nicely up into the windshield. The windshield laid back and the greenhouse narrowed, putting air on the rear spoiler. (The greenhouse of a vehicle is the "glassed" area above the fender line. This comprises the windshield, rear and side windows, and any pillars separating them.) The car was way more aerodynamic than the Lumina.

The only flaw on the car was the narrow tail. It needed to be wider, so we redesigned it. The hurdle was getting NASCAR to sign off on it. This is where Rick Hendrick's "car salesman" talents came into play.

We had three different tail designs. There was the one already on the stock model. Then we had our preferred tail we'd crafted, which was wider, squarer, and very sharp so it would direct the air to break off the back of the car cleaner, creating even more downforce and reducing drag. Finally, at Mr. Hendrick's request, we made an even more extreme-looking version. I wondered why he'd want that even though we knew it may be worse performance wise and NASCAR would never approve it.

Rick asked me, "Which one do you want?"

"We want the one we made, it's the best aerodynamically."

"Okay, then put the wild one on the car."

"What? We're not gonna get that approved."

He said, "Trust me, Ray. Put that one on for the inspection."

We did what he said and slapped the more extreme version of the tail on the car. Then in walked Bill France, Mike Helton, and some other NASCAR officials.

They all looked the car over. Checked it against the templates. (Back then the car had to fit the street-car parameters. So NASCAR brought in templates copied off of a production Monte Carlo.)

Certain things were negotiable with NASCAR, but there were other things that were not. It was all in the interest of creating equal competition. But the problem was, as bad as they wanted equal competition, all the manufacturers, whether it was Ford, Chevrolet, or Pontiac at that time, were playing whatever games they could with their cars to gain an advantage.

Mr. France got to the tail. "Geez, what the heck is this?"

Rick jumped in. "Look, we really gotta have a little help back there to make this thing competitive. The car's pretty good otherwise."

"Well, we can't approve that tail. We just can't."

Knowing this wouldn't be approved, Rick said, "Look, we gotta have a little help."

Mr. France asked if we might have another design they could consider as a compromise.

"Well, we've got this one." Rick pointed to the design we preferred. "But it's not as good. We'd really like to have the one on the car."

Mr. France quickly glanced at his colleagues, looking for signals. "All right, you can't have the one that's on the car, but you can have our approval of the second design."

Holy shit. Rick just snookered those guys.

That was the car salesman in him.

Going into the '95 season, we were getting the cars built how we wanted them. We made a front-end geometry change on all our No. 24 cars, along with the modification to the tail of the new Monte Carlo. I felt like we had what we needed. If we were missing anything, it was because we didn't know we needed it yet. Overall, I believed we were prepared.

Despite my confidence, we had a discouraging start to the season.

We should have won the Daytona 500. We had a fast car, and we were dialed in. Instead, our jack man Andy Papathanassiou, hurt his back and we had to bring in a backup.

We were leading the race when Jeff came in for a pit stop. The backup jack man dropped the jack before the left-front tire was on. Jeff started to pull out and the tire came off, damaging the fender. We tried to repair it on Pit Road but didn't get the proper clearance. Metal from the damaged fender rubbed through the new tire on the banking, giving him a flat.

That screwed the day.

Despite the chaotic pit stop and our twenty-second place finish, it was still a big day for us as a team. Instead of Jeff yelling on the radio, which given the circumstances he had the right to do, he said, "Look, guys, don't worry about it. We'll get it next week. There's gonna be another race."

Right there and then, his maturity and leadership pulled the team together. It was a huge moment for me and for the team.

Everybody thought, "Okay, that's our leader. We're gonna kick ass next week." And we did.

Coming off the disappointing Daytona finish, I wanted to do something that would unite and motivate the team and let Jeff know we were done screwing up. That's when we came up with our "Refuse to Lose!" T-shirts.

The next race was Rockingham, the first time we all wore our "Refuse to Lose!" T-shirts.

Everybody wore them under their fire suits and uniforms. Since Jeff couldn't wear a T-shirt under his fire suit, we just drew "Refuse to Lose" on his fireproof underwear with a Sharpie.

We won the race, and in Victory Lane we exposed our "Refuse to Lose!" T-shirts. The TV coverage caught the eye of University of Massachusetts basketball coach John Calipari. As much as I'd have loved to believe we came up with the slogan, turns out *Refuse to Lose* was the title of his book, and he'd trademarked it.

He called us up. "Hey, really cool you guys are using this. But now you're selling T-shirts. I own that logo. Let's be partners."

That meant we had to pay him a licensing fee. But the coach is a great guy, and his dad was a Jeff Gordon fan, so it all worked out.

Beyond the T-shirts, I was constantly dreaming up ways to motivate the team, to keep them focused on improving the car and their performance. Again, that's why I had so many motivational signs hanging in the shop. They needed to see it to believe it. We went to Rockingham focused on "Refuse to Lose" instead of thinking about repeating the shitty Daytona pit stop. We won the pole and the race at Rockingham. We refused to lose.

———

Two weeks later we won again at Atlanta. That was extra special because it was still the old Atlanta track where Jeff and I won our first Busch Grand National race together and made our first Cup start.

We ran the same car we did at Rockingham: "Blacker." It was fast and balanced. I thought, "Okay man, we're on a roll."

Heck, we'd won two of the first four races of the season and we could have won the Daytona 500. While a championship never entered my mind, it was encouraging we'd already won as many races that early in the season as we'd won in our first two years.

The credit goes to the '95 Monte Carlo and our maturing as a team. Jeff and I now had two years of Cup racing under our belts and a taste of winning. Hendrick had stepped up, too. Their research and development and engineering were unmatched. They approached the new Monte Carlo like a potter with fresh clay.

The rule book was very thin back then. So there was plenty of opportunity for ingenuity. Of course, people accused us of cheating. We weren't. We were just leveraging clever engineering in areas like reducing unsprung weight, custom chassis construction, unconventional placement of bars for strength, and the use of various metal alloys in engine design.

We also built cars with specific frame rails, body placement, and offset for particular racetracks. Hendrick was so far ahead of every other team in their craftsmanship. We had experience, we knew what we wanted. We were entering a new era with a new car. We had ten or twelve Monte Carlos, each custom built to meet specific maneuverable goals.

Something else that took shape that season was the start of the Earnhardt/Gordon rivalry. Dale was razzing Jeff every chance he could.

It started when Dale won the Brickyard, and said he was "the first man to win it."

That didn't have any real negative effects on us. It was an honor to race him. Even better? We were starting to beat him. Consistently.

We were going to Victory Lane. We had the most wins, the most poles. We were leading in points. As reigning champion, Earnhardt's car got the first garage stall. While we hadn't taken that spot yet, we'd become his neighbor.

Yet from day one, we knew if we were ever going to become NASCAR champions, we had to go through the No. 3 car. There was no way around it.

Like Hendrick, Richard Childress's organization was strong, and Dale Earnhardt was one of the best. I was then, and still am now, a huge Dale Earnhardt fan. I worked with him several times at IROC.

Earnhardt would tease the shit out of you. That's just who he was. And his "rivalry" with Jeff was just for show, never personal, hurtful, or nasty. Hell, they even became business partners down the line.

Don't get me wrong. When it came to basic competition, they'd wreck each other for a dollar. It was all about the winning for those two. Each of them had to win. They'd do whatever it took to prevent the other from beating them.

And it wasn't for the money, either.

It was more than that. Bragging rights meant more to them than money. Just like two stallions fighting over which one leads the herd, only true champions like Jeff and Dale understand that level of competitive instinct.

Dale and Jeff used to run at each other so hard in practice, they even wrecked a couple times in Michigan. Finally, Richard Childress and I agreed to keep them separated.

Jeff and Dale knew if they played up this rivalry, along with winning, they could outsell everybody else with T-shirts. That's where the money was. It wasn't in driving the car, it was in merchandise.

Most of Dale's fans were awesome. But there were those who didn't understand it was all in fun. They made it personal. I didn't like that.

I couldn't get why some fans literally hated us and said the cruel things they did. Sometimes they'd take it too far. Our truck would routinely suffer from people pelting it with bottles and rocks, kicking it, and hitting it with coolers and stuff.

People would throw beer at us too, or they'd say hateful things like, "Crash and die, Gordon."

There was the incident at Indianapolis toward the end of my career with Jeff. It might have been 1998 or '99. As we pushed the car through a crowd of people, some drunk asshole jumped out from behind the barriers.

He leaned down, yelling, "Fuck you, Jeff Gordon!"

He was also grabbing and sticking his crotch in Jeff's window. Jeff had his helmet off and the window net was down. I was on the left-rear quarter panel of the car. I ran up pushing the guy away.

He spun around, thrusting his middle finger in my face, screaming, "Fuck you, Ray Evernham! Fuck you!"

And I lost it. I grabbed his middle finger, twisting it back as hard as I could. Then I punched him right in the face. He grabbed me, and we went tumbling ass over head into the crowd. My radio went flying. And we're fighting like hell in this sea of fans.

My crew was desperately trying to break us up.

All of a sudden, I feel a hand grabbing the back of my neck. I balled up my fist as I turned to see who it was.

Damned if it wasn't Les Richter, former vice president of competition for NASCAR. Les dragged me into the NASCAR hauler, sat me down, and asked what the hell I thought I was doing.

I explained how I thought the guy was going to damage the car, or worse, Jeff. I was just defending us. He gave me a friendly warning and I headed back to the pit, never to hear another word about it.

Les was the coolest guy.

I'm sure he wasn't thrilled about the brawl. But I can only assume he's the one who covered it up. He made that thing go away. I could've easily been suspended. Probably should've been. I think the fan was so drunk he most likely got thrown out. He was lucky he didn't get arrested. But I'll tell you what: two things that guy got from me were a sore finger and a black eye.

It felt like a Saturday night at Wall Stadium.

————

We were starting to generate significant media interest, which I saw as a major distraction. Consequently, I didn't have the greatest reputation among the press, or with Jeff's PR reps. I chased more reporters and press people out of our garage than I can count.

My thinking was, when I'm working, that's not the time to interview me or bother us for a picture. (One time in our pit at Bristol, a camera operator got his foot tangled in an air hose during our pit stop, causing us to lose several positions. I've always believed that cost us the win.)

My theory was, if I acted like an asshole all the time, the press would be too afraid to bother me. And I did not want to be bothered at the racetrack.

Being a crew chief during a Winston Cup race back then was a lot like playing a game of chess on fifteen different levels. Today, a lot of the data to make decisions is supplied by a computer and two to three other engineers. To do it without that support took a lot of preparation and concentration. I didn't have time to chat.

What I didn't consider was my standoffish attitude would result in certain press members being a little harder on me at various points in my career.

No doubt I deserved it, but I did what I had to do.

I was completely focused on performance, and our winning percentage and accomplishments in that brief period proved it. I wanted Jeff and the team to know nothing was more important than what we're doing at the track.

I did not want any distractions—none at all. Not for Jeff, not for the crew, and not for me.

The T-shirt says it all.
Nigel Kinrade

CHAPTER 17

BENDING RULES AND BURNING RUBBER

The 1995 Season

"We got past the three, in only three."

We were feeling like Jeff was the man to beat every week, and since we were called the Rainbow Warriors, we thought it would be cool to paint his helmet to resemble a Native American headdress.

For one prominent tribe in Loudon, New Hampshire, we had stepped over the line.

It turns out, the term "Rainbow Warrior" was in a prophecy from a Lakota tribe elder named Standing Bear.

In his prophecy, Standing Bear describes the devastation of nature due to "man's greed and disrespect for Mother Earth." It goes on to say that "great leaders, warriors, and shamans of many nations will be born to be Pathfinders, and they . . . will cleanse the earth for rebirth. . . . The Storytellers, Warriors, and Planters will live in the way of the Great Spirit and teach ways to keep Mother of the Ground sacred forevermore . . . they will be called Rainbow Warriors, for they will bring together the four races of man to live in peace."

The tribe's Chief Lessard reached out to us and very respectfully explained why calling ourselves "Rainbow Warriors" and co-opting the headdress design was offensive to Native Americans.

I explained to the Chief that offending Native Americans was the last thing we would want to do. On a personal level, according to my dad, my grandmother was part Cherokee, although I've never had a DNA test to verify it.

The Chief and I ended up becoming good friends. He and his family visited us several times at the racetrack.

Years later, when I took on the Dodge project, he called to say he was coming to Charlotte and wanted to come to the shop to bring me into the tribe.

I was so honored. He presented me with a ceremonial feather as well as a bow and arrow. Then he bestowed a native name on me, Megaso, which means "eagle," inspired by how I sit perched on the pit box and watch what goes on around me.

The Chief, his wife, and another tribesman staged their ceremony in the center of our fabrication shop. They performed a ceremonial dance to the sound of their beating drums. As honored as I was, the whole time I was hoping the ceremony didn't involve cutting me for some kind of blood oath.

Kidding aside, I was deeply honored by the Chief's thoughtful gesture. I've long held a great respect for Native American cultures and embraced many of their values as my own. My belief centers around the connection between humans, animals, and the Earth—a profound bond that ties everything together in a meaningful way.

To this day, I rely on the wisdom Chief Lessard shared with me during our friendship.

———

After our early win at Atlanta, we headed to Darlington.

They'd paved Darlington so the track was frigging fast. We sat on the pole, and I thought we could win it. But the groove was narrow, and they used to let all the lap cars line up on the inside of the lead lap cars.

We led a bunch of laps, but on a restart going into Turn One, a lap car just bashed into Jeff, and we crashed. Man, I was pissed.

The Monte Carlos were so good that day that NASCAR had them impounded. Ford was starting to complain. Thank God our car got wrecked so they could not take it to the wind tunnel, or they might have found out why ours was so fast.

Regardless, we were ready for Bristol the next week with a new car we had prepared specifically for that track. Beyond having a great car and driver, we won that race on tire wear. It was a long green run. We'd been working on shock absorbers and unsprung weight. (This slowed tire wear.)

That day, Mark Martin had a faster car and led most of the race, but he wore his tires out and we didn't.

Now we were rolling.

We ran great at North Wilkesboro, a track I loved, except we couldn't win. We sat on the pole, but Dale Earnhardt beat us. Dale was just that good.

Every time we lost a race, we would knuckle down, study why we didn't win, then get back to work. That was especially true if we came in second.

We would spend a shit ton of time trying to figure out why we didn't win. Most teams are happy with a second-place finish. Not us. We'd ask, "What stopped us if we were that close to winning?"

Jeff dominated at Charlotte, winning all three stages in the annual Winston Select All-Star race. Then he won the pole for the 600 with a speed that was more than 1.1 miles per hour faster than anyone else.

But less than a quarter of the way through the 600, one of our hubs snapped and the right front-wheel came off. Fortunately, it didn't go soaring into the grandstands. Jeff came in and we fixed what we could as fast as we could, but we ended up finishing an abysmal thirty-third.

Given my well-earned reputation for bending—but not breaking—the rules, accusations started flying about how we used titanium hubs or drilled holes in our hubs to lighten them up. It was all bullshit.

What I did do was buy a set of hubs that were lighter.

At that time there was no official list of approved or unapproved parts. The tricky thing was that NASCAR could fine you for having what they arbitrarily deemed an unapproved part.

After putting the lighter hubs on the car, we'd take a piece of sheet metal and TIG weld it to the back so it looked thicker. Typically, we only used those hubs for qualifying or for short races. They weren't suited for the longer races.

I had a couple of new guys on the crew for this race. One of them put the hubs on for qualifying and MIG welded them instead of TIG welding them. The difference is in the way the heat transfers into the metal when it's melting the two pieces together and the wire that's used to create the weld. (MIG welding was faster but not the correct process for the billet steel hubs.)

So, two things happened. The mechanic MIG welded it instead of TIG welding it, which led to a stress fracture in the hub. Then he assumed that we generally raced with those hubs and left them on the car. Of course, as crew chief, I take full responsibility.

Jeff came on the radio and said he felt a vibration. He pitted, but we couldn't figure out the cause. Without X-ray vision, we couldn't see that the hub was cracking. So we sent him back out and the next thing we knew, the right-front wheel came off the car.

Thank God it didn't fly off and injure people in the grandstand. I was prepared to take responsibility and figured we would end up with a $1,500 fine. However, what I didn't anticipate was being hit with a major violation called "actions detrimental to the sport," and a mammoth fine of $50,000, which was the largest in NASCAR history at that time. Plus, they wanted me suspended for a week.

It felt personal because, at that that time, I'd had an ongoing feud with Gary Nelson, the Winston Cup Series director. I just figured they decided to make an example out of me so that I'd stop bending the rules.

To his credit, Rick Hendrick called Bill France directly to plead the case and throw us at the mercy of the court. "What can we do, Bill, so Ray doesn't have to miss a week?"

Bill France, being the benevolent dictator that he was, took the one-week suspension off the table, but raised the fine to $60,000 and put me on probation. As a matter of fact, I think I'm still on probation. I don't think I've ever officially come off probation.

I also had to promise Bill I'd never do anything that could poten-tially put my driver or the fans in jeopardy.

Rick Hendrick would never tolerate cheating, but he and Jeff didn't mind me pushing the rules. But I think NASCAR had had enough of me doing that. At the time, the rule book was pamphlet-thin, and I was really good at finding the loopholes. Now, you need an attorney to interpret the rule book. That hub was probably one of the dumbest engineering mistakes I made.

Mr. France told me, "Look, you screw around a little bit with the template, I get it. You're playing games with pit stops. I get that, too. But here's what you won't do. You won't run a big motor, put anything on the tires, put anything in the fuel, or do anything that tinkers with the safety of the sport. You stick to those rules, and we'll get along just fine."

That was a wake-up call for me; those rules were put in place for a reason. We dodged a bullet. It could have been a terrible tragedy. I could have hurt the fans. I could have hurt Jeff. That wheel coming off that car is one of my biggest regrets in racing. That one left a scar.

Right then and there, I decided to quit screwing around with the rule book and instead, focus more on aerodynamics and horsepower.

We got another pole at Dover. But we missed the race setup. Kyle Petty was on his game and just beat everybody. Kyle did well in Dover, Rockingham, and places like that. I kept thinking, "Is there something we can do to make Jeff's cars more like Kyle's?"

Then we went to Pocono.

We were running great. But after leading 124 laps, Jeff missed a shift on a late restart and hurt the motor, putting us in sixteenth place.

Yes, we suffered some bad finishes, but we didn't run like crap anywhere. It was because we either wrecked, blew a motor, or had some other issue.

Summertime arrived and we were leading in points.

Then came Michigan. That particular race caused me to draw a line in the sand I may not have had the right to do.

In 1995, Hendrick was building motors for Joe Gibbs Racing. Their driver was Bobby Labonte, and he had beaten us a couple of times that season. Here we were getting beat by our own motors. It really pissed me off.

This inspired one of those conversations with Rick Hendrick I later regretted. "Mr. Hendrick," I began. "We want to win races. We want to win this championship. But we're getting beat by our own stuff."

Then I said Bobby's motor was a little bit better than ours that day.

I'll never forget the look on Rick's face. I obviously was not seeing the big picture. I came off like a spoiled little kid. Instead, I should have taken responsibility for improving Jeff's car.

In hindsight, gear choice beat us.

We were shooting for fuel mileage. Bobby was a little bit better off the corner. So, it came down to something I could have controlled rather than shoving blame on the motor. My mouthing off in our post-race meeting caused controversy and some hard feelings. I think that's when Joe Gibbs became motivated to build his own motors.

Looking back, I wished I'd have kept my mouth shut that day. Honestly, at that time, I didn't care about anything else but winning.

———

By mid-season, we had added two more victories, five top-five finishes, and landed outside the top ten only twice. We were contenders. In just two years, we proved we deserved to race alongside seasoned drivers like Dale Earnhardt, Rusty Wallace, Mark Martin, Terry Labonte, and Dale Jarrett. We had broken into the rarified class of consistent Cup winners.

In July, we won our very first restrictor plate race at Daytona, the Pepsi 400. Racing at Daytona comes down to handling and strategy.

I felt restrictor plate racing was a weakness of mine as a crew chief so that was a big win for us. It made me feel like we could build a solid speedway car. (There were four speedway races, and they pay a lot of points. We needed to run good in them.)

Then at Loudon, New Hampshire, Jeff crashed into the wall during qualifying. Fortunately, there was a second qualifying round, and we fixed the car and came back the next day. The fastest second-round driver would start twenty-first. That's where we wound up.

I needed a strategy to gain track position fast. I decided when we pitted under green, we would take four tires while most everyone else got two. However, under caution we would take two tires when most everyone else got four. My reasoning was that even though we would lose time under green flag conditions by taking four tires, we would lose fewer positions because the cars are more spread out. Taking two tires under caution while most everyone else took four would allow us to gain positions because the cars were bunched together.

We settled on taking two right-side tires under caution and four under green. Left-side tires would go two fuel stops versus the right sides which would only go one fuel stop.

Now, given that the Loudon race was only three hundred miles, you could almost run the entire race by changing left-side tires just once. The strategy worked perfectly, and by the end of the race we moved the car into the lead and won. That day Jeff drove his butt off. We gave him a good car, did the math, and came up with a great race strategy.

Two weeks later, we were back at Indy for the '95 Brickyard 400. While we didn't repeat our win from the previous year, we did create some excitement. During qualifying, Jeff turned completely sideways off of Turn Four, leaving black marks on the front straightaway, but he still took pole position after setting a new one-lap track record.

It lit the fans up! I'd never seen anything like it. Fans thought Jeff was frigging amazing.

That's one of my favorite memories of that year's Brickyard. That, and Earnhardt's victory. If it couldn't have been a Hendrick car, I was glad it was Dale.

It always bothered me how even up to that point Earnhardt had not won the Daytona 500, when he should have ten times. I knew winning the Brickyard 400 meant a lot to Dale and his fans, which I count myself among. The big difference between me and them? I was the only Earnhardt fan who didn't chuck beer cans at the No. 24 car.

Two weeks later we were back in Michigan, and Bobby Labonte trounced us again with a Hendrick motor. I hated that we didn't win that race, but I didn't bitch about the motor this time.

The night race at Bristol was next, and it was also disappointing. I felt like we should have won. For some reason, I never could get the night setup as good as the day. Bristol in the spring during daytime was nothing like Bristol in August at night. We won four spring races in a row and never a night race at Bristol.

The nuances of the racetracks themselves were part of the competition. Tracks like Bristol would throw you curves, literally and figuratively. A unique challenge to racing at Bristol was the need for steering boxes with a quicker ratio. Jeff kept describing the car as being too tight in the middle (what we call "pushing").

We realized he couldn't turn it fast enough. The track is so small, the cars are running fifteen-second laps at over 120 miles per hour. Drivers must be on the throttle. It's like they come off the back straightaway and they're in the air when entering Turn Three. The car lands onto the banking, then they just mash the gas and go. It's violent. Those guys are hauling ass like crazy. It's like being whipped around on a wildly fast roller coaster, but instead of being on rails, you have to drive it.

To compensate, I designed the front end with what we call bump steer. As the front suspension compressed going into the corner, both front wheels would turn left. As the suspension rebounded on the straightaway, the wheels would straighten.

That meant whenever Jeff would go in the corner, the car would just turn. It worked! We won four races with that trick. I was only able to figure out things like that because of how thoroughly Jeff could describe what he felt behind the wheel.

I didn't realize I was capable of doing half the things I did with a car until I had to. Even then, I didn't think it was any big deal. I didn't think I'd made any great discovery. I was just doing my job, finding ways to win. And sometimes things I thought were just common sense, others didn't see. Like taking two tires that day at Charlotte to win the race.

Many of my decisions were unorthodox, but Jeff supported me and so did my team. It worked, and we won races.

———

Next up was Darlington. It is the oldest and toughest track on the circuit. Period. It requires the most pit stops for tires, and you must be prepared for every possible thing NASCAR racing can throw at you.

We went there that September and won our first Southern 500. Again, we should have swept that year, but we got in a wreck with the lap car in the spring.

It's hot as shit there in September. The race is five hours of just treacherous conditions. The car must handle perfectly. The driver must also be in tremendous physical condition. Everybody must execute their job flawlessly.

The Southern 500 is a race you win as a team.

I could be wrong, but I believe if you were points leader at the Southern 500 and you won, you were considered the favorite to be going all the way.

Guys like Dale Earnhardt, Bill Elliott, Cale Yarborough, David Pearson, and Richard Petty had done it. So, we were in good company.

Then we went to Dover. This time we had figured out the concrete plus the tire pressure, and we smoked their asses that day. Again, we couldn't manage it in the spring, but we figured it out in the fall and won.

At that time, we didn't bring extra crew guys, so I used to have a job during the pit stop. I'd get off the pit box to catch the first empty fuel can tossed by the gas man while he was being handed the second. My routine was to catch the can, wait for the pit stop to finish, then radio Jeff to go.

So, during one race, I was standing there waiting to catch the can when I became distracted by the left-rear tire changer who was having difficulties.

When I looked back for the empty can, *wham!* The can hit me in the face. I used to wear Ray-Ban sunglasses. Thank God I had them on or it would have cut me even worse than it did.

It about knocked me out.

I stumbled back, trying to get my bearings. They dropped the jack and Jeff waited a second or two until somebody finally signaled him to go.

He radioed, "Whoa, what happened there?"

Since we were under caution, I could take the time to tell him what happened and we had a pretty good laugh about it.

Jeff and I had an appearance scheduled at DuPont headquarters the next day. The cut across my nose and two black eyes became the talk of the appearance.

From there we went to Martinsville. We sat on the pole but finished seventh.

Back at Charlotte, Ricky Rudd got the pole and Mark Martin won. We broke a gear and hobbled under the checkered in thirtieth place.

After the race it dawned on me. I was being too conservative. I had chosen a gear that would take a little bit of rpm out of the motor. It was a small difference, maybe only a hundred or 200 rpm, but I felt the gear choice would take stress off the engine without hurting the handling.

I mistakenly chose a gear that was not as durable as the gear we should have run. The pinion gear we went with was a bit thinner. It wouldn't have mattered, except for one thing. At Charlotte the pit stalls are concrete, which gives more traction. After finishing a pit stop, the jackman dropped the jack, Jeff dumped the clutch, and the car had so much forward bite it broke the pinion gear.

That took us out of the race. Had that not happened, I feel like we could have won. Either way, it took a big chunk out of our points lead.

To protect our lead, I started being more careful with strategies. We'd become more concerned about the championship than winning races. We'd gotten this far this fast through bold, sometimes risky ingenuity. I should have realized we were making mistakes because we weren't being ourselves.

We went back to Rockingham, where again, we'd won the spring race, but we didn't run well in the fall. Still, we kept learning from our mistakes.

Then we traveled to Phoenix. God Almighty, I could never figure out Phoenix worth a damn. I just could not get the car where we needed it to be. Still, we finished fifth that day, about average for us in that challenging city.

We left Phoenix with a top five and headed to Atlanta. We had the championship all but sewn up. Jeff had to come in no better than forty-first, but there was a point in the race when even that position was in doubt.

I don't know what the hell happened.

Other than the fact we'd taken a different car instead of our favorite car, Blacker, I can't really say to this day why we sucked so badly in that race. God, we were awful, just awful. I feel like it may have been aerodynamically loose and mechanically chassis tight. Either way, I couldn't fix it. So, Jeff was basically running around like he was on two wheels.

Even though we looked worse than we ever had in our rookie year, we were able to pick up additional points for leading some laps when the other cars pitted. That locked up the championship for us.

Although we had wrapped up the championship, the team was still in a funk because we were running so badly. I could not allow our season to end on such a low note. So I got a crazy idea.

I keyed my radio mic. "Listen up! Everybody who has never been over the wall on a pit stop this season, raise your hand."

Hands went up. Rick Hendrick, Ed Guzzo, and several others.

"Shit, we're laps down. We're not gonna win. But we've won the championship. So, anybody who has ever wanted to go over the wall and do a pit stop, you're welcome to."

Then, I radioed Jeff. "Hey, man, we're gonna pit."

Jeff came down Pit Road, and our ragtag wannabe pit crew jumped over the wall to meet him.

Ed Guzzo jacked the car up. I tried changing a tire. Rick Hendrick wiped the windshield—well, actually just the driver's side.

As Jeff headed back on the track, he came on the radio, "Hey, was that Rick washing the windshield?"

Some NASCAR people ripped me over that little stunt.

Whatever. It meant something to my guys. It snapped them out of their funk and reframed their attitudes. Instead of dwelling on losing the last race of the season, they were able to let the 1995 Winston Cup championship win sink in.

Given we'd locked up the championship, you may be wondering why the team was upset by our performance in that single race. But that's exactly why we were champions.

When we got to the last few laps in the race, and the championship was becoming a reality, I thought about all the people who had influenced me along the way. Starting with my mom and my dad, my Uncle Nick, the Bayshore gang, John and Jim Bauma, Jay Signore, Roger Penske, Bill Davis, and Rick Hendrick, along with so many others who, whether they knew it or not, pushed me forward in my journey.

Winning that championship was validation I hadn't let them down. I hadn't wasted their time, and they could know they were a part of it.

Still, I cannot help but wonder: If any one of those people had not shown up in my life, would I have made it?

Once the checkered flag fell, it was all a blur.

Smiles. Tears. Hugs. High fives. Champagne. I do recall the guys picking me up and carrying me to Victory Lane.

I knew it wasn't a dream. But I no longer had to wonder what it would be like to be a champion. I was a champion. It was done and in the record books.

And in just three years.

The first of our three Winston Cup Championships. *Ray Evernham Enterprises Archives*

CHAPTER 18

ON THE WORLD STAGE

A Championship Year

"You're gonna need a good suit."

I heard a lot of Jeff Gordon interviews covering the 1995 championship season, probably more than anyone alive. Practically all included a variation of this question: "How do you feel about your championship season?"

Jeff answered this in different ways at different times, but one answer stands out. He said, "Everything was happening at the speed of light."

He wasn't talking about his pace on the track, although we could have sworn he broke the sound barrier occasionally. He meant how his life was changing—and mine, too. In fact, I couldn't stop thinking about just how much my fortunes had shifted in just a few short years.

Think about it.

We were 1995 NASCAR champions just two years after our rookie season. But it goes beyond the short time we'd been in NASCAR—my life was unrecognizable from where I was in 1992. Thinking about that year has kept me humble ever since. It all revolves around me driving a pickup truck south toward an unknown future, leaving my wife and baby son back in New Jersey.

I wasn't in a great place back then.

During that lonely trip away from my young family and toward uncertainty, I recall hearing a financial advice radio show. The host asked a caller, "What's your plan for the next five years?"

While the caller droned on about their career goals and so forth, I considered my own life. I thought to myself, "Gosh Almighty! Five years from now? I don't know where I'll be in five months!"

I think you can understand. If you teleported through time and spoke to the Ray driving that truck and told him he'd be crew chief for the 1995 NASCAR Winston Cup Series championship team, he'd look you square in the eyes and say, "You need to get your head examined."

———

Jeff and I achieved massive success in NASCAR fast, but you can't call either of us an overnight success. Jeff busted his ass for years racing anything with four wheels. I'd also spent considerable time building and racing cars of all types. There was a lot of blood, sweat, and tears being put in—and then boom—we got our break and success happened quickly.

With success came money, and I had no idea how to handle it.

I didn't come from money. My family and everyone I knew were New Jersey clamdiggers struggling to get by. I had no concept of wealth. Being rich to me meant not owing anyone and paying cash.

Now suddenly, I was earning an amazing salary. Bonuses were flying in faster than I could count, but I knew I couldn't spend my time count-ing money. I was 100 percent focused on the race car, my team, and my driver. I decided I'd worry about that when I stopped racing. Just like the awards and trophies, I mentally put the money in a room, one I'd sort through when I was done.

The truth is, I was very conservative with my earnings and still am. I remembered how it was growing up back in New Jersey. I also remember seeing the movie about Jake LaMotta, *Raging Bull*. In one scene, he's popping jewels off his championship belt so he could pawn them just to get by.

No matter what, I wasn't going to end up like that.

I didn't require much. Hendrick provided practically everything for free, including sunglasses. I only needed a supply of T-shirts, under-wear, and socks. The things I did splurge on were for my family.

That started with Ray J.

With the very first bonus I received from Rick Hendrick, I went out and bought my son the fanciest swing set I could find. It was a big wooden structure from Rainbow Play Systems and worth every penny for all the time Ray J. and his friends put on it.

Of course, I had to do something for Mary to recognize everything she'd done for us through thick and thin. I bought her a Rolex, which is something she would never have bought for herself. We also splurged on a jukebox because Mary loved them.

We made smart decisions with money even though we weren't used to having it. We paid off debts and our mortgage before buying more property. It was a struggle as a car guy to not go out and buy every vehicle in sight, but I always applied the same mindset to buying vehicles I used when I didn't have money.

Every car or motorcycle I ever looked at, I thought about selling it before buying it. This resulted in two questions:

1. Can I make money selling this vehicle?
2. If I'm going to lose money on this deal, how much fun will I have with it?

In '95 the only vehicle that got through this process was a hotshot motorcycle, a custom Harley-Davidson that my boss Rick Hendrick hated. He believed motorcycles were just too dangerous. So I eventually caved and got rid of the bike, and yeah . . . I sold it for a profit.

My conservative nature served me well.

The money was coming in thick and fast, but it wasn't phasing me. I kept my mind where it belonged: on the race car, not on luxury living and a fleet of fancy cars.

Still, old habits die hard. Later in life I sold my race team for more money than I could ever have imagined, and my big splurge was buying two pairs of designer sunglasses. (It was a "buy one, get one 50 percent off deal," something I wasn't going to pass up.)

At the end of the '95 season, I had something on my mind besides race cars and tracks for once. I knew we were approaching the annual awards banquet, and I was nervous as hell.

NASCAR banquets can be tortuous affairs running up to five hours. They're awful if you aren't the championship team up on the stage because you're spending the evening watching somebody else sitting in the place you wish you were sitting and listening to people ramble on about how great they did all year long.

But now that it was my opportunity to sit on that stage, I worried about how to present myself and what to say. What I didn't realize at the time is that someone who did know these things was thinking about me.

I got a phone call from the Charlotte Motor Speedway offices. The office manager on the other end told me, "Ray, Humpy Wheeler wants you to come up to his office and see him."

"Okay" was my simple reply, but my mind was racing. What the hell does Humpy want to see me for?

Humpy was president of Charlotte Motor Speedway and right-hand man to NASCAR Hall of Famer, racetrack owner, and promotional genius, Bruton Smith. Many folks don't know he was with Firestone long before taking the reins in Charlotte. His career spanned back to the mid-sixties in Indianapolis. Like Smith, he was a showman with a vision for what stock car racing could become.

He saw in Jeff and me the same thing Colonel Tom Parker saw in Elvis. When he saw us, he thought, "These guys are different. They have something special going on, and they can take it to the next level."

That's exactly why he called me into his office that day.

Entering, I thought he might want to discuss the upcoming season. Instead, he got down to business. "Ray, you have an opportunity at this banquet to show people you are more than just a mechanic, that you're bigger than the pit box. I've seen a lot of people get in front of a crowd on national TV and be unprofessional, and I think you can do better."

Looking back, what he said was obvious, but you don't know what you don't know. He tried to instill in me the mindset that I could make a statement by being more than a Jersey redneck turned crew chief, but I was lost on the details.

"Thanks Humpy, your confidence in me means a lot, but I have no clue what to do or where to start."

This wasn't Humpy's first rodeo. "You're gonna need a good suit. Do you have a good suit?"

I nodded. "I have a suit."

He looked at me knowingly. "You don't have a good suit, so you're going to my tailor. You're gonna buy yourself some good shoes, and you're going to make sure they're polished before the banquet."

Humpy was talking my language, rattling off specific steps like I might instruct my crew. He then turned his attention to my speech. "When you get up there, I want you to open with a great quote from someone. That'll get their attention."

"Like a great racer?"

"Think bigger than NASCAR, Ray. Find a quote from a great mind that will knock their socks off, and they'll be on the edge of the seat for the rest of your speech."

I had my marching orders.

I had some clothes shopping to do and some serious speechwriting to start. Looking back, it's clear that meeting changed my career. Humpy showed me I could have my own personal brand and be much more than a crew chief.

Whenever I was asked to do a TV spot or speak to a crowd in the following years, I'd always think of Humpy and how he got me going.

———

Before long, it was time for the banquet in New York City.

What a wild, amazing time. This was Rick Hendrick's first championship, and he celebrated it in style. Rick rented a jumbo jet and flew all Hendrick Motorsports employees up for the event.

He must have dropped a million bucks putting up his full operation in the Waldorf Astoria Hotel. Hell, I grew up right across the water in Jersey, but I'd never been there once—not even as a sightseer.

Now I was ordering room service.

When it was my turn to speak, I think the crowd expected this crew chief to get up to the mic and start rattling off a bunch of random "Thank you's."

They didn't know that I'd recently graduated from the Humpy Wheeler school of public speaking.

Wearing my nice new suit, I approached the podium and said, "'If I have been able to see further than others, it is because I have stood on the shoulders of giants.' That's a quote from Sir Isaac Newton."

Suddenly, everyone was on the edge of their seat, just as Humpy said they'd be. They were all thinking, "Holy shit, this guy's serious." My speech was about all those who helped me get to that championship podium.

Of course, I thanked Rick Hendrick and the team at Hendrick Motorsports. The Rainbow Warriors had taken over the balcony and cheered wildly. My crew chief buddies, Andy Petree, Tony Glover, and Jimmy Fennig, also made a ruckus—they had a part in putting me on that stage.

Some of the people I thanked were more personal. I made sure to recognize Jay and Barbara Signore, who had secured a spot at one of the front tables. I mentioned how Jay took me out of the dirt pits at Wall Stadium and let me drive IROC cars. He taught me an incredible amount about race cars and invested considerable time in me. There's no way I would have been on that podium without the Signores, and I made sure the world knew it.

Barbara was a strong, resilient woman, who guarded her emotions. So I was surprised when she hugged me afterward. "You don't know how much this means to us," she said. "Given all the people Jay and I helped, we've rarely been recognized for it." I loved Barbara and Jay. They were almost like a second set of parents to me, and I'm so grateful they were able to experience that moment with me and hear my appreciation for them.

My parents and siblings were there, and I spoke about them, too. I've had ups and downs with my parents, but they sacrificed for me and got me started. When I was trying to build race cars on my driveway in a bitterly cold New Jersey winter, they mortgaged their house to construct me a garage.

Some parents pay for their children's college education. Mine financed my garage. I'm glad they got to see it was money well spent. It was also important that my siblings experienced my championship, too. They'd battled their own personal demons, so I wanted them to see we were more than just Jersey Shore folk.

We were on a world stage now.

When I finished, there was a second or two where you could hear a pin drop, then a rousing applause broke out. I looked around the banquet hall trying to make eye contact with all the important people from my life and career.

Jeff and Rick were proudly applauding. Humpy looked pleased. Dale Earnhardt tipped his wine glass and gave me an approving nod as if to say, "Good job, kid." Even the people we battled on the track were applauding.

The '95 banquet was my transition from being a crew chief and mechanic into something more. The number of interview requests I got from the media shot up immediately, and that only grew over time.

It was such a wonderful night; I was almost tempted to start thinking about what I might say if we came back as champions the following season.

Entertaining that thought even for a moment might have been a bad idea.

The smiles of '95 soon
became the stress of '96.
Nigel Kinrade

CHAPTER 19

STRETCHED THIN

The 1996 Season

"You can't ride two horses with one ass."

In the offseason, the racing press doesn't have much to report on. Between the 1995 and '96 seasons, they seemed preoccupied with speculating if the No. 24 team would score back-to-back championships.

It's an incredibly difficult feat. As of this book, only eight drivers in all of NASCAR Cup history ever pulled it off. We were determined to give it our best shot.

Clinching our first championship after just two years of racing at the Cup level only served to distort my perspective. The saying success doesn't necessarily teach you anything rang true. In retrospect, my overconfidence heading into the 1996 season is almost embarrassing, considering the hard lessons in store for me that year.

At the time, though, given our achievements, I had legit reasons to be so confident.

We were at the pinnacle. It wasn't just the No. 24 team, either. Rick had made tremendous investments in engineering and tooling along with creating real depth in Hendrick Motorsports. With the resources all three teams had, I thought we ought to finish first, second, third every race in 1996, with the No. 24 team taking most firsts, of course!

Plus, I knew our crew would outbuild and outwork every other team. Jeff Gordon would outrace every other driver. What I didn't know? Within the next twelve months, I'd be looking in the mirror knowing I wasn't as smart as I thought I was.

Not long after the '95 championship banquet, Rick came to me with a question. "Ray, the twenty-five team is unwinding on us. Do you think you can help me fix it?"

The champagne from the banquet was out of my system, but the euphoria of winning wasn't. I told Rick yes right away. Part of the reason I jumped on it was because I wanted to help Rick. Another part was the pride I had in the organization.

My thinking was, "We're Hendrick Motorsports, we're gonna be dominant." But there was a personal piece, too.

I was thinking about what had happened over the past three years. Shit, yes, I can do this. Hell, I built the No. 24 team from nothing to a championship. I can keep that team going and fix the No. 25 team and Hendrick Motorsports will fill the podium weekly.

So I set out to be Jeff's crew chief while also managing the No. 25 team. The changes began with the personnel. I moved some of the No. 24 team over because I thought building the No. 24 team "part 2" was the answer. Although the No. 25 team had some good runs, I felt I let them down. A lot of that was due to treating the crew like it was the exact same group as the Rainbow Warriors, but it had its own culture.

I also treated driver Kenny Schrader just like Jeff Gordon.

I'm not saying Jeff was better—they were just different drivers as well as different types of people. They contrasted in their level of seriousness and preparation. Kenny was older and a racing veteran. While Jeff's sole focus was on Winston Cup cars, Kenny raced cars in other series besides Cup. He also didn't believe in physical conditioning the way Jeff did.

I should have respected Kenny's needs as an individual, but I was trying to mold both him and the team into a carbon copy of the No. 24 team. That was a mistake—one that was really hurting my own team and Jeff.

One of my personnel moves was to put Phil Hammer from the No. 24 team on the No. 25 team's box as crew chief. I couldn't be two places at once on race day, so Phil took the reins. I guess I should add an asterisk there.

He took the reins, but he had me talking in his ear during the races.

Phil is a great guy and a good friend, but I put him in a bad spot. I underestimated how much actual management the crew chief needed to do.

Hell, I had only been doing it for a few years myself. Phil had a great race team mentality, but he didn't have enough experience in people management, which is what the job is all about.

It might have looked to outsiders like he didn't do as good a job as he should, but that isn't true. He gave it his all—but he didn't have the help he needed.

The plan I came up with for race days worked perfectly in my head but not in real life. While I was on my radio with the No. 24 team, I had a second radio to communicate with Phil.

During races I was like a half-assed crew chief. I tried to give Phil advice while directing the Rainbow Warriors at the same time, ultimately confusing both teams.

I quickly learned you can't make decisions from the sidelines. If you aren't right there on the box with the team, you can't read the situation and make the right call, so all I was really accomplishing was screwing two teams up at the same time. My distraction from total focus on the No. 24 car was having a negative impact on performance. I learned the hard way that the old expression, "You can't ride two horses with one ass" was true.

As usual, the season started with the Daytona 500. As I juggled radios to guide the No. 25 team along with my own team, nothing was going the way we wanted. Eventually, the No. 24 car wrecked, breaking the fuel pump.

We got it back to the garage with hopes of replacing it, but the chassis was bent too badly to get a new one in. We were done for the day. "Son of a bitch!" is the politest thing I said in the garage that day.

The next race was at Rockingham. We blew up, which was something we rarely did with Hendrick engines.

So, the defending champs started out the 1996 season with two utter failures and a top result of . . . forty-second place. Jeff knew there was a problem.

After five or six races, things weren't improving. I was saying to myself, "Man, I've turned this into a shit show, now how do I fix it?"

I knew what I had to do: put all my focus on Jeff and the Rainbow Warriors to get the season back on track.

But I didn't like admitting I couldn't handle both teams. This wasn't an ego thing; I just didn't want to let Rick down after everything he'd done for me. Despite this feeling, one day I walked down to his office to break the news.

I got right to the point. "Rick, I've been trying to manage both teams, and it's not working. I need to refocus completely on the twenty-four team moving forward."

Rick smiled. "I know you do. I've reached the same conclusion myself."

I was surprised, but I shouldn't have been. Rick has described his management style as passive, but I would call it patient. When you work for Rick, you're learning something daily.

He isn't running around giving orders and micromanaging. Rick would always ask questions about why I was doing something a particular way, but this is one of many examples of a time where I had a problem and I thought I had discovered an answer—only to realize he already had the answer and was waiting for me to catch up.

So, I handed off the No. 25 team to Phil, confident he could take it from there. With that out of my mind, I dedicated my attention and energy to turning around the No. 24 team's season. We saw immediate progress and a huge change from those first two miserable defeats.

We won at Bristol. We won at Richmond. We ran good at Atlanta. We added Darlington and the second race at Talladega to the win list.

Talladega has always been a wild card. It's the only track where I've ever feared for the safety of Jeff and the other drivers. I don't know if you can blame the Native American burial ground nearby or what, but bad shit has happened at Talladega.

We've lost a lot of drivers on that track. Davey Allison's helicopter crash happened there. When I think back to the 1996 DieHard 500, what comes to mind is the awful Earnhardt wreck that happened right in front of me. Even before Jeff's win, I recall how relieved I was to see Dale give the crowd a thumbs-up, broken sternum and all.

Still, the season was looking up on many fronts. We were about to reach the point where we were consistently finishing top three in short-track races. Everything was trending the right way and we were winning races, but one of the most personally rewarding experiences of my career happened about as far away from a racetrack as you can get—on an Ivy League campus.

———

Jeff and I were invited to lecture a freshman engineering class at Princeton University. Princeton and NASCAR were not words you'd put in the same sentence back in 1996, although I bet you would now. Our visit occurred on the Thursday before the MBNA 500 at the nearby Dover Downs International Speedway. I felt like a fish out of water.

Here you have a clamdigger who grew up just forty miles away at the Jersey Shore but had never dreamt he'd ever visit Princeton and a California boy who went to high school in Indiana, walking onto the campus of one of the top American universities. It was awe-inspiring for both of us.

I kept thinking: "Holy shit, what am I doing here?"

I've long been fascinated by Albert Einstein. That Princeton visit brought me a little closer to the great man. I got to see the house Einstein lived in on campus. Someone was living in the house at the time, and I remember standing there wondering what it must be like to live in Einstein's house. Would it make me any smarter?

Touring the engineering building, I grew nervous about speaking to the class. I was convinced one of the kids was gonna ask a question about astrophysics and I was gonna have no clue what they were talking about.

In the end, I didn't have anything to worry about.

The session took place in an outdoor courtyard jammed with freshman engineering students. I asked how many had watched a NASCAR race. To my surprise, about 90 percent of the students held up their hands.

After that, I spoke to them about what we did with our race cars and how it involved a lot of engineering and physics. The whole group listened attentively as we spoke. I'd love to know where those students are today—did any get into racing? Did they go on to other great things?

After we spoke, the session turned into a Q&A. The first question was for Jeff. A young lady asked, "Are you single?"

It was the most common question Jeff ever got. Both on that campus and just about everywhere else.

———

In the end, we lost the 1996 championship to Terry Labonte by a few measly points. Let me tell you, coming in second by a few points stings worse than coming in tenth. I could blame an engine failure or lap cars crashing us in the spring race at Darlington, but I hold myself responsible. We lost more points early in the season when my attention was divided between the No. 24 and No. 25 teams than we lost the championship by at the end.

It was my responsibility to lead, and I knew it. I sensed the team questioned my priorities when we struggled in the standings and weren't performing well on the track. The team was confused about my focus because, by taking on both teams, I sent a confusing message. I've always emphasized commitment, but in this situation, I muddled the message. Ultimately, that's my responsibility.

The bright spot? Terry Labonte was our Hendrick Motorsports teammate. So we were happy Terry brought Rick the championship.

Everyone knows Terry's a great driver. But near the season's close, Terry also proved himself to be a tough son of a bitch. He broke his hand in a crash during practice at Phoenix with two races to go. I was incredibly impressed with how he powered through those final crucial races with his hand in a cast.

Terry and crew chief Gary DeHart beat us when they needed to. Even though we won ten races, they had the consistency to gain the most points. I felt good about Hendrick Motorsports winning the championship. I also felt like we played a big part in their win because the No. 5 team started building their cars like the No. 24 team did.

After the season I had to clear my head. I turned to an unlikely source of inspiration—the drag strip. I had driven drag cars before, but only up to 90 miles per hour. That's standing still in drag terms. One day I was talking to Bill Simpson, another one of my great advisors. He said, "Why don't you get your ass out to the drag strip and learn a little bit about what those guys are doing?"

That sounded like a great idea, so Bill hooked me up with Frank Hawley, who ran a three-day drag racing school in Florida. I broke the 200-mph barrier on the drag strip, passed the class, and got my top alcohol license.

While there, a pro stock car champion named Jim Yates was also present doing some testing. Jim's a great guy and I wore him out asking questions and getting his perspective on performance. My conversations with him directly affected my approach to our speedway racing strategy.

Jim was telling me about friction and metal coatings, and I realized his mindset differed from mine. I was looking at tenths of seconds, and guys like Jim were concerned about thousandths of a second in their adjustments. I took his attitude of micro efficiency and began imagining how we could apply it to our speedway program. I knew we could get more exact on our bodies and drivetrains. I also knew I could use this approach to counteract the restrictor plates cutting down on our horsepower. Shaving a little aerodynamic drag, using a lightweight oil, and reducing friction—all these little modifications could really pay off.

The 1997 Daytona 500 would be the test of my new micro-efficiency attitude. Besides, I thought we couldn't do any worse than how we started '96.

T-Rex misses the pits in qualifying, comes from last to first, and then gets outlawed at the 1997 Winston in Charlotte. *Ray Evernham Enterprises Archives*

CHAPTER 20

WHIPLASH

The 1997 Season

"Don't stink up my show!"

The Championship banquet was coming up, and I didn't even feel much of a sting losing to Terry Labonte and our teammates on the No. 5 car.

In fact, I was feeling good. But there was a problem: Rick just wasn't being Rick.

He should have been thrilled heading into the event. Between the No. 5 car and the No. 24 car, we won practically everything there was to win. Rick had back-to-back championships for Hendrick Motorsports, but I could tell he wasn't feeling it the way he should have.

This left me wondering what was going on.

After checking in at the Waldorf Astoria, I wanted to spend some time with Rick.

Like the crew chief I was, I spent the walk to his suite organizing my thoughts, thinking of all the things that might be wrong. Did we lose a sponsor? A key crew member quit? Something bizarre going on with NASCAR?

I walked into the room to see Rick beside his wife, Linda.

As soon as I said, "Hey Rick, I want to talk to you for a bit," I could tell he was troubled. Still, I started a few lines I'd rehearsed. "Look, I know you're down. We didn't win the championship, but I want you to know we love you and we believe in you. I don't know what's bothering you, but I know I want to help."

Instantly, Linda broke down.

Rick looked like he was using every ounce of his power to not join her in tears. I didn't understand what was happening. I could only think to myself, "What the hell is going on here?"

Rick looked me straight in the eye and said, "I've been diagnosed with leukemia."

I was stunned. Holy shit!

The boss has leukemia after he helped my family get through the same disease. It was all I could do to pull myself together and say, "Okay, what can I do to help?"

I can't tell you how long I was in that suite with them sharing the pain they were hiding. I was sworn to secrecy because Rick wanted Terry Labonte and the No. 5 team to enjoy their victory without a dark cloud over their head. I couldn't even tell Mary, and it was a heavy burden to carry through that banquet.

It is extremely hard to share such emotional pain and uncertainty with people you love. I wish devastating news like that was a once-in-a-lifetime experience. Unfortunately, I would be sitting with Rick and Linda again after the terrible plane crash in 2004.

I knew one way I could help Rick was to have the best season possible with Jeff, so I set out to make it happen.

———

Heading into Daytona to start the season, Jeff and I were both focused on improvement. For me, that meant giving him a better car. For him, it meant mastering the art of restrictor plate racing.

There have been many crew chief–driver combinations where the crew chief thought, "I'm giving him a great car, he needs to race better," while the driver thought, "I'm pretty damn good at restrictor plate racing, I need a better car." That wasn't us. Jeff and I would each focus on our areas, knowing we could both get better. Going into Daytona, our confidence was high.

In fact, I was so confident in our team, I brought a film crew with us to document the whole experience. I told the team we were going to win the race and we were going to get it all on film. In reality, I had no idea if we were going to win or not. I gambled looking like a total idiot if we had a lousy race, but my gut told me that wouldn't happen.

We videoed the whole thing without any permission from the track or NASCAR. It would never fly today—but somehow, we got away with it. We didn't even get the guys the proper credentials to film on-site. In those pre-internet days, we were able to pull this off because track officials assumed it was just something we'd show at the team's Christmas party. Instead, we documented an unbelievable race. Twenty years later when Fox Sports learned I had the footage, they took it and produced their documentary, *Refuse to Lose*.

———

We kicked off the week by winning the Busch Clash.

Later in the week, we ran well in the Gatorade 125-mile qualifying race, serving notice we had a car that could contend for the 500 win.

Jeff was running first or second in the 500 when he came on the radio with some bad news. "I have a flat."

Before I could even swear at the bad luck, he whipped the car off the track onto Pit Road yelling on the radio, "I think it's the right rear!" Jeff identifying the specific tire and getting to the pits quickly saved us from losing a lap to the field.

Jeff was able to get back out on the track ahead of Mark Martin, who was now leading the race and towing a pack of cars. Jeff did a great job of keeping Mark and the other leaders behind him.

A few laps later, the caution flag came out and everyone pitted, including us. We were the last car on the lead lap and had to start at the rear of the pack. When the green flag flew, Jeff drove through the entire field like a madman, catching Earnhardt, Dale Jarrett, and Ernie Irvan. With ten laps to go, Jeff dove under Earnhardt and the air from our car pushed Dale up into the wall.

The wreck took out DJ and Ernie, too. Shit was hitting the fan, the caution flag came out, and everybody had to pit.

Earnhardt's car had completely rolled over, landing back on its wheels. He drove that crumpled car down Pit Road to massive applause. As he passed us, he flipped his middle finger at me. He was mad and wanted to let me know he was still gonna race despite his car looking like it was held together by duct tape. It was the damnedest thing I'd ever seen, but there was still a race brewing I needed to pay attention to. We finished our pit stop and went back out.

When the green flag dropped, Bill Elliott, one of the few drivers who stayed out, was trying to hold off our teammate Terry Labonte for the lead. Bill went high to block Terry, and Jeff drove under both. No sooner had we grabbed the lead than there was a wreck behind us. The caution came and there weren't laps left to go back to green. The race was effectively over—and the Hendrick cars finished first, second, third, with Jeff taking the checkered flag as the youngest ever to win the Daytona 500.

And we had it all on video, too!

In Victory Lane, Hendrick general manager Jimmy Johnson handed Jeff a phone so he could speak to Rick immediately. A first, second, third finish at the Daytona 500 must have done wonders for Rick's morale, and he got to share it with Jeff over the phone.

Also, since the three Hendrick cars carried the National Bone Marrow Registry telephone number, 1-800-MARROW-2, in honor of Rick Hendrick's battle with leukemia, the TV exposure caused so much traffic, it crashed the sign-up website. Since that day, the partnership between Hendrick Motorsports and the National Bone Marrow Registry has matched thousands of needed donors with patients.

———

Winning the Daytona 500 kicked off an amazing season.

Prior to the Winston race, Rick Hendrick gathered lead engineer Rex Stump and all the HMS crew chiefs and asked us to pool our ideas for a next-generation race car. His plan was to put all the bold ideas into a single experimental chassis.

We started by focusing on the basics. We worked on lightening up our driveline components and worked really hard on shock absorbers. We designed a new front-end geometry and made the chassis stiffer. We paid attention to things like unsprung weight and center of gravity.

We focused on underbody aerodynamics by raising the floor pan and dropping the frame rails to create a vacuum under the car.

When the car was finished, we took it to the Charlotte racetrack to test it.

Jeff took it out for a few laps, and it ran about a half second off our favorite car Blacker's average lap times.

That's when I got an idea. I said, "Let's try something crazy." At that time, we ran a 1,200-pounds-per-inch spring on the left front, a 1,900 on the right front, a 400 on the right rear, and a 350 on the left rear. I suggested we put a pair of 1,400s on the front. Then I added the biggest sway bar we could get and jammed a pair of 450s on the back.

Everybody looked at me like I was crazy. "'Don't get him hurt," some of my crew warned, "He's going to hit the wall with that setup."

I told Jeff just to drive carefully for a lap or two because I had no idea what this thing was going to do.

As he drove by, I clicked my stopwatch. He had picked up one full second, which made the new test car a half second faster than Blacker.

Jeff came in with a big smile on his face. "What was that?"

I shrugged my shoulders, replying, "I have no idea."

What we know now is that we dropped the front and got the under-body aerodynamics to work.

We brought the car to The Winston at Charlotte Motor Speedway. It was sponsored by the *Jurassic Park* film. We nicknamed the car "T-Rex" because of the dinosaur head decal on the hood and because Hendrick engineer Rex Stump did the design work on the car.

Starting position in The Winston was determined by the total time it took to do a lap, followed by a pit stop, and one more lap to the checkered. Jeff logged one of the fastest first laps but overshot pit lane. Consequently, he had to start the race from the back. It didn't matter. He drove right through the field and took home the $200,000 prize.

As the car was going through post-race inspection, an official walked up to me and said, "Mr. France would like to see you." I thought Bill was just going to offer me a beer and we'd sit and talk about the race.

I walked into the NASCAR hauler and Bill was sitting next to a beige-colored telephone that we used to call the "Bat phone." There weren't many cell phones at the track in those days, so NASCAR always had a dedicated landline. Expecting a "Congratulations," instead I got, "Ray, you see that phone?"

"Yes, sir."

"You need to pick it up and call your boss and tell him that car's illegal."

I was stunned. "What? No! It passed inspection. It's good. It fits all of the rules and it's legal."

He looked at me, deadpan, and said, "It won't be tomorrow."

NASCAR rewrote a ton of rules based on the T-Rex. We tried to fix the car, following their new rules, but it never really ran the same.

By that time, everybody caught up to us anyway. That wouldn't be our only run-in with Mr. France during the 1997 season.

———

We'd won nine races, including a couple back-to-back, by the time we pulled into Darlington at the end of August. It was an amazing streak. In fact, it might have been a little too amazing for some.

The night before the race, I had an encounter outside of Darlington Raceway that helped me understand why NASCAR was becoming such a dominant sport.

Walking across the hotel parking lot, I saw two of racing's main movers and shakers holding court, T. Wayne Robertson, the man responsible for R. J. Reynolds's sponsorship of the Winston Cup we sought to win, and next to him Bill France Jr., NASCAR CEO and one of the greatest motorsports entertainment showmen in the world.

Bill waved me over. "Hey, come here."

I'm thinking to myself, "Why does the head of NASCAR want to talk to me?"

He answered my nervousness with a smile. "I hear you're pretty good here, you got a fast car." Then he asked me kind of a strange question. "You know what all the flags mean, right? Green means go, and the yellow flag is the caution flag."

I nodded along, thinking, "Where's this going?" But Bill wasn't done yet. "What about the black flag. What's that one mean?" he asked.

I went straight into crew chief mode. "It means you have three laps to come in for a consultation."

His smile turned serious. "Naw, it means you're disqualified. To hell with your three laps! Don't give me that crew chief answer." He gave me an appraising look before continuing, "You know, I got one of those black flags. And I bet as fast as you are, you could lap the whole damn field tomorrow. But I'm gonna tell you, if you don't want to see my black flag, don't stink up my show!"

It took me a second to figure out what he meant by "stink up his show," but I figured it out as he continued. "You know what looks good on TV? About a two-second lead. A two-second lead is all you boys need tomorrow. Keep it nice and close, and it's good for everyone."

He continued, "With a nice close race, the other teams ain't gonna hate you. They won't think you're cheating, just working hard like everyone else." As he spoke, I was wondering what other teams had gotten this speech at some point in their career. Certainly Earnhardt, Bill Elliott, Rusty Wallace—everyone of that caliber had probably heard Bill's speech before.

Bill wasn't telling me to cheat or shave points or do anything illegal. He just wanted to give the people a show.

As he put it, "If we don't put on a good show, the people won't come. Then we're back to being a bunch of bootleggers running in a field. The people need a show, not a ten-second lead. They need a good guy and a bad guy, and they need people passing."

Bill then gave me some of the best advice I ever got in racing. "Ray, you guys are inconsistent. You won ten races last year and you didn't win the championship. You know why? Because you run so fucking hard, you're crashing your shit or you're blowing it up. Think about it. Slow it down a bit. If you got that much of a margin, why do you gotta go as fast as you can every lap?"

Bill was warning us not to stink up the show, but he was really arming us with the secret to success. Consistency would bring more popularity, more winning, and more TV ratings—which was good for NASCAR and our team.

The next day, we were running for the Winston Million at the Southern 500. We started on the pole and the whole team was focused on winning that million-dollar prize. There was just one problem— the car wasn't cooperating like it had been. We quickly fell back outside the top five.

Everything we did to that car seemed to move us backward another step.

It was miserably hot that day and Jeff hit the wall a few times, crushing the right side and causing fumes to come in, giving him a headache. The car itself was a headache, and we pitted sixteen times trying every change we could think of.

In the end, we had to borrow tires from our teammates because we ran out. In fact, my whole box of tricks had been empty for the last one hundred miles. We were scrambling to find an answer to get the car to handle better when out of nowhere, the track started to change and came to us. The No. 24 car came alive, and Jeff drove to the front.

Suddenly, Jeff was leading the race with five laps to go.

I thought to myself, "Wow! Shit, we're leading this race in a car with the whole right side wiped out." But our luck hadn't completely changed. Jeff Burton came up like he was shot out of a cannon. *Oh my God, he's gonna catch Jeff!* Sure enough, Burton caught Jeff on the last lap. I was thinking, "Did we go through hell for nothing?"

But JG had a different idea.

Jeff ran Burton right down into the apron. I can't recall another time I saw Jeff block someone in a race without restrictor plates, but he impeded the hell out of Burton, who was gentleman enough not to spin both of them out. Jeff crowded him for a million bucks, which he acknowledged in Victory Lane, telling TV cameras, "Burton, I'm sorry buddy. A million bucks, man. A million bucks. I had to do it."

It took us a while to put Mr. France's advice into practice. I made sure to alert Jeff when he had a two-second lead, but that lead quickly became larger. I got on the radio and said, "Hey, uh, you are leading by about three seconds. Oh, now four seconds."

Jeff yelled back, "Man, I'm going as slow as I can! I'm slowing down and going faster!"

"Well, what the hell does that tell you?"

We realized Mr. France had given us some pretty good advice. Why should we beat the car to death? Why should we beat Jeff to death? All we had to do was stay toward the front and race hard at the end.

At some racetracks we realized we could go faster by going slower.

———

The '97 season contained so many stories it could probably be its own book, but it all came down to the NAPA 500 at Atlanta Motor Speedway. We knew if Dale Jarrett won the race, we had to come in at least seventeenth to win the championship. Murphy's Law was the only thing that applied during practice and qualifying day. Anything that could go wrong, did.

Jeff crashed our brand-new car leaving Pit Road during practice. Then we overfilled the backup car with oil, leading to poor qualifying. Late in the race, running about fifteenth, Jeff came on the radio. "I gotta pit! I gotta pit!"

I quickly replied, "You gotta hold. If you pit and that caution comes out, you ain't the champ this year."

Jeff had a bad tire vibration and came barreling down Pit Road. We put on four tires, and luckily the race stayed green. Dale Jarrett didn't win the race, and we ended up winning the championship by just eleven points. I was so mentally and physically exhausted I didn't even celebrate. I just went back to the hauler. The marketing folks had to come find me, saying, "Hey, we just won the championship!" and they brought me out to the stage.

All I could think is, "I don't wanna go."

That's not how a movie would go, but that was real life. The pressure was high in '97 because we were supposed to win and then almost lost it. I told Jeff I just wanted to win one where we weren't squeaking through the season. Jeff replied with an easy grin, saying, "Then we'll do it."

And damned if we didn't! In '98, we stunk up Bill's show something awful.

Hoisting the championship trophy after a record-breaking season in 1998. *Nigel Kinrade*

CHAPTER 21

FEELING THE PRESSURE

Fighting Tension and the Taurus: 1998

"A year like no other."

Have you ever heard of imposter syndrome? It's when people doubt their skills, talents, or accomplishments—sometimes accompanied by a fear of being called out as a fraud. Despite all the evidence, a person with this malady doesn't believe they deserve their success or their luck.

That's how I felt after winning the championship in '95, more like some lightweight boxer who'd landed a lucky punch, knocking out Ali. To me, the No. 24 team was like a bunch of kids that had somehow upset NASCAR's natural order.

Despite our dominance in '96, our teammate Terry Labonte won the championship. That year, I felt we deserved to win. Hell, we were supposed to win. We had the best car. The best driver. The best pit crew. We won the most races. We led the most laps. And won the most poles. But we didn't close the deal.

Going into the 1997 season, we had a big chip on our shoulders. We were committed and wanted to prove we were worthy. And that commitment paid off with another championship ring, no lucky punches this time.

In the offseason leading into 1998, Mary and I were still trying to figure out Ray J.'s (then undiagnosed) autism. Our poor kid bounced around from doctor to doctor, from psychiatrists to psychologists to counselors, from school to school, and from drug to drug. He was so high functioning, which complicated his diagnosis.

Now, I'm a fixer. I wanted to believe it was a simple behavior issue and I'd find a way to fix it. I was going to buy him a baseball glove and a go-kart and we'd just hang out and everything would be fine.

Rather than bringing Mary and me closer together, the struggle for a diagnosis kept us apart. Mostly because my mind was always somewhere else.

To Mary's credit, or fault, she was extremely supportive. People say, "Oh man, you paid a lot of money in that divorce." She deserved every single penny. Without her, there'd be no Ray Evernham. Her support was unselfish, but it also allowed us to drift apart. There were times I should've been called on the carpet. Still, she supported me, letting me build my career unrestrained.

But it came at a price.

———

As Pat Riley wrote in *The Winner Within*, "Upping the ante turns mastery into unbeatable excellence." Going into '98, we did just that. I was determined not to let it be a repeat of the previous season, racing to a stressful nail-biter of a finish.

During the 1998 preseason, Jeff and I dove into the statistics from our previous seasons and noticed an anomaly. We realized around August each year, our performance dipped. We figured it was because by that point in the season we started to get worn down physically and mentally. Jeff and I committed to getting the team and ourselves some breaks during the summer months. We did not want to win another championship just squeaking by. We wanted a knockout.

Around then, Jeff had become a bona fide NASCAR superstar. He was even cast to star in Pepsi's Super Bowl commercial that was designed specifically around Jeff and the No. 24 car. The commercial featured Jeff in a race, driving crazy as he was trying to grab a Pepsi can that had gotten loose, rolling around the inside of the car. I was in the commercial, too. I even had a couple of lines: "Oh, that's gotta hurt," and "We gotta get him a cup holder." It was a cool experience for the both of us.

I had other chances to appear with Jeff in various things, but I turned down most. My job wasn't to be the face of the No. 24 team. That's not to say I didn't want credit for things I was doing, I did. I just didn't think I needed to be in every commercial or appearance. Jeff was the star. My job was to support him and lead the team.

Nothing was off the table. We reexamined our speedway program, short-track strategy, pit stop protocols, and every nut and bolt in our cars.

Sometimes, I'd say to the guys in our morning meeting, "By the end of the day, I want everybody to give me a list of five things to make our cars better."

To their credit, the whole No. 24 team stepped it up. They came together and worked unselfishly. You don't get to be part of something like that often.

By the time the 1998 Daytona 500 rolled around, we had a car good enough to win, and we were in the mix most of the race. Running third close to the end, Jeff lost a cylinder, and dropped back to finish sixteenth.

As good as our car was going into that race, had we finished without motor trouble, Dale Earnhardt might not have won. The only thing that cushioned that loss was seeing Dale finally take the checkered flag in the 500.

A long time coming, he should have won that thing ten times, but the racing gods never smiled on him until that day. I had tremendous respect for Dale, still do. He was one of NASCAR's greatest champions, and I'm grateful I got to know him. I still get goosebumps recalling how every man from every crew lined up on Pit Road to show their respect and congratulate him, me included, as he drove by, collecting high fives on his way to Victory Lane.

———

By 1998, Ford had unleashed a new Taurus. They took the stock car, stretched it, and made it into a race car. It was the first time NASCAR let an auto manufacturer build a car that didn't fit the streetcar template. (Our Monte Carlo still fit all the templates and it was a great race car.)

This new Taurus caught us all asleep.

We went to Rockingham, where we'd already won a couple of times. Dale Jarrett in his Ford Taurus led us for much of the race and probably should have beat us. Then he came in for the last pit stop, put on fresh tires, and fueled up his car. I'm thinking, "Why? Filling the tank is going to take more time and make the car heavier."

So we pitted Jeff, giving him only four fresh tires, but we didn't add a drop of fuel, saving time and weight. Getting off Pit Road first and having our car a hundred pounds lighter than his, we ended up beating Jarrett.

I thought, "Okay, we were good, the Taurus isn't that great."

Then we went to Vegas, where aerodynamics are crucial. We got our butts kicked by every Taurus. The No. 24 car ran like twelfth, and it was all Fords in front. We realized: "Shit, we've got a problem."

We needed to catch up aerodynamically.

So, I returned to the drawing board. While the car was in primer, we laid the long template on and traced it with a black Sharpie. Then we laid the cross templates on and again traced the lines with the Sharpie. We took those templates off, and we were left with a gray car with template grids on it. I told my body guys, "We've got to work in between those lines to make this car better."

Then we went to Atlanta, where we got our butts kicked again. This time by Bobby Labonte in his Pontiac. We couldn't even run with Pontiacs at that point. Afterward, we went to Darlington. We considered Darlington our place. We always ran well there. But damned if Dale Jarrett didn't beat us again. We realized the new Taurus *was* a formidable competitor.

Next was Bristol. It's a short track where body and aero aren't a factor. Mechanical grip matters, driver matters, pit stops matter. And boom, we won Bristol.

Then we went to Texas and again it was Fords out front. We crashed. (We always seemed to crash at Texas.) Texas was like our Talladega without a restrictor plate. If something was going to happen there, we'd find a way to be in the middle of it—or run into it.

By the time we reached Fontana, I thought, "Okay, we've got a handle on this now." We had won the inaugural Fontana race the previous year. Our car was fast, and we sat on the pole, but the car was so trimmed out aerodynamically that the longer we ran, the more the Fords had an opportunity to beat us with more downforce. They just kept getting better as the race went on.

We had closed the aero gap between the Fords and Chevys somewhat, but not enough. It drove me crazy.

Our body guys back at the No. 24 shop worked 24/7 cutting and remolding the cars, just trying to give us an edge. One of the hardest things in car design is aerodynamics. It's not like changing a spring or a shock, which produces an immediate result. You go to the wind tunnel, you test it, you come back, you cut the body more here or there, you try again. Back then, there was no CFD (computational fluid dynamics), so it was a lot of cut and try. It took time, and you still had to live within NASCAR's templates and spoiler sizes. We were forever behind trying to catch up to the Taurus.

In May, we rolled into Charlotte for the Winston, and it was one of the worst performances of my life.

We were kicking ass. I knew we had the field beat. Just like Rockingham, I had everything figured out down to the last ounce of fuel.

Then somebody jumped the restart and officials called the field back for a second restart. They never called back restarts, but they did that day. It required everyone to take another three laps to get back into position. Extra laps I hadn't accounted for.

Imagine: We're comfortably leading the race.

Then the white flag came out.

On the last lap, Jeff calls over the radio, "I think I'm outta gas."

I was like, "There's no way he's out of gas."

Sure as shit, he had run out because we planned to finish with virtually no fuel in the tank to lighten the car and give us more speed.

I missed it by a gallon.

I walked out of the pits with my head hanging low. I cost us a victory and I felt horrible. It's a funny thing. As a crew chief you don't think about the races you won. You only think about those you lost.

Jeff was pissed, as he should've been. But he never really got on me that hard because he knew I took it harder than most, and there was no way for me to work any harder than I already was. That day I lost the Winston because I was so intent on beating those Fords and playing too close to the edge.

It was tough leaving the track. I remember walking out with Mary and some of the Rainbow Warriors. At some tracks, like Charlotte, we'd stay in a gang for safety because you'd have to walk through crowds and there were a couple hundred thousand present to watch The Winston. It would routinely take two or three hours to get home from Charlotte Motor Speedway, even though I lived fifteen minutes up the road.

Well, that particular night was wild.

People were screaming things. They were just awful, and they made it personal. They were yelling horrible things about Jeff, me, and the team.

That shit never bothered me. What pissed me off was when some jackass tossed his beer at me, and it splashed on Mary. That's when I felt the Jersey erupt.

Spotting some dudes laughing, I approached. "Who threw the beer?"

Silence.

"Who threw the beer?"

This short guy stepped up. Stinkin' drunk, he said, "I threw it."

"You're a pretty short guy acting like a big man," I said, towering over him. "Would you be this big if all these guys weren't with you?" Then I said, "Here's the deal. I'm going over to Hendrick Motorsports now: Forty-Four Hundred Papa Joe Hendrick Boulevard. Meet me over there in a little while and we'll talk about this."

He and his friends left. I'm sure Mary was thinking that guy was an idiot because she knew from experience I wasn't afraid to fight. Neither was Mary. She's a Jersey girl, after all. I have no doubt she'd have been in there swinging beside me.

After that, we walked to our car in silence.

Every time something like that happened, it was just more motivation for me to win and piss those people off.

The next week was the Coca Cola 600. Armed with our qualifying "bag of tricks" (all legal, of course), we were ready to redeem ourselves. We knew how to qualify well at Charlotte. It was our home track and Jeff was freakin' fearless. He could always get a little more out of the car when it came to qualifying. Sure enough, he logged the fastest time, capturing his sixteenth career pole.

In Friday's practice, the car was okay, but it wasn't great. For Saturday's practice, we installed a new race motor. We for sure needed the practice on Saturday morning, the day before the race, to make sure everything was all right.

On Saturday morning our time to go on track was nearing, but Jeff was nowhere to be found. That wasn't like him. He was always on time for practice. I finally asked his PR assistant Kimberly to find out where the hell he was. A few minutes later she told me he'd overslept but he was on his way.

"There's no way he's going to make it for practice," I thought. Pissed, I wondered what was going on because it was just not like him. We had been fighting these Fords, and the team had worked so hard to prepare for Charlotte.

Then this shit happens?

I knew I needed to test the new motor for mechanical problems. With only twenty minutes left in practice, Jeff still hadn't arrived. So I asked Terry Labonte to do me a favor and run a few laps to check the motor and give me his input.

Later, people accused me of doing that to get back at Jeff for being late. That's stupid. The last thing I'd have wanted to do was put somebody else in Jeff's car. But I was concerned that practice in the afternoon could get rained out or delayed. Then we'd be flying blind on race day and possibly blow a victory—all because of some mechanical issue we could have fixed.

So, I stuck Terry in the car. He was going down the straightaway and damned if he didn't run over a piece of lead or some other sharp object that dropped off another car. *Boom!* It blew the right-front tire out. The car slid into the wall, crunching the nose, damaging the right-front suspension.

This cannot be happening.

Returning to the garage, I spotted Jeff. He was running in just as the tow truck delivered the wrecked No. 24 car. There was no disguising my anger, but I wasn't ready to talk to him. I needed to figure out what to do. Do we bring in another car, which would cost us the pole, requiring us to start at the back of the pack, or do we patch this one up? We knew it was fast—before hitting the wall—the guts were still there, and the frame was not bent.

We decided to fix it.

We had to race six hundred miles the next day. There's no way we could have done it without the support of Hendrick Motorsports, which, fortunately, was close by.

I called Rick, told him what happened, and explained our decision to fix the car. In no time, the cavalry arrived. I shit you not, there had to have been twenty-five people working on that car. Guys arrived from the body shop, the chassis shop, and the engine shop. There were some from other teams—the No. 25 car, the No. 5 car—all helping rebuild it right there in the track garage area.

People, parts, and tools filled the garage. At one point we cut the whole right side off the car. The fender, the door, the quarter panel, and the deck lid, all gone. The motor was out and the right-side suspension off. It reminded me of the Scarecrow in *Wizard of Oz*, some of it was over here, some over there.

I was under the car slicing the rocker panel off with a zizz wheel, a thin abrasive material that cuts perfectly straight. But those things can break and if it happens while turning, it'll blast shrapnel.

Well, sure enough, it snapped. Thank God I was wearing my Ray-Bans because it hit right across them. It still cut my nose and under my eye.

As I sat holding a blood-spotted paper towel on the cut, I kept thinking this just wasn't a good day.

The other thing in need of major repair was the communication between Jeff and me. Things came to a head there in Charlotte. While we all benefitted from his superstar status, it also meant he was being pulled in a thousand directions. And not as often in my direction as he had been. So we got into it.

"Some of the non-racing folks around you are distracting you," I began.

"Well, I don't like the way the cars are handling," he shot back. "They don't seem like the same ones I drove last year."

"You're not the same driver from last year. So, if they're not the same cars and you're not the same driver, it's cause we're not working together."

Then and there we remembered our successes had been because we worked well together. We realized we were the only ones who could get us back on track. People always wondered what the secret was to our success. It was our communication. That was our magic, and that weekend marked our reset.

Thank goodness NASCAR gave us enough time to get our car back together for the afternoon practice. That never would have happened without the support of an organization like Hendrick Motorsports. Sometimes that gets overlooked because it becomes about the driver, or the crew chief, or the manufacturer. But when you look at the history of that company, whether it's Tim Richmond or Geoff Bodine or Darrell Waltrip or Jeff Gordon or Jimmie Johnson, the common denominator is Hendrick Motorsports and the way Rick quietly supported everybody.

On race day, we were okay, but we weren't great. Rusty Wallace, in the No. 2 Ford, was in the lead with about sixteen laps to go.

We were running fifth when the caution flag came out. When the leaders pitted, including Jeff, I saw Rusty and the others in the top four taking two tires. I said to the team, "Four tires."

"What?"

I repeated myself.

I knew the No. 24 pit crew were badass. They could change four tires damn near as fast—if not faster—than most other crews changed two. So they put on the four tires, Jeff went back on the track, and we didn't lose a spot. And I knew the other top-five drivers were sitting ducks.

They threw the green flag, and from fifth place on four fresh tires with about ten laps to go, "Gordo" went through these guys like they were parked.

Rusty had a million reasons to keep Jeff behind him. The Cup sponsor, Winston, offered $1-million-dollar bonuses called the No Bull Million for certain races at Daytona, Talladega, Charlotte, Darlington, and the Indianapolis Brickyard 400. Rusty was eligible for the Charlotte Million, so he was driving like hell.

But he could see that rainbow rising in his rearview mirror.

With nine laps left, Jeff rode Rusty's back bumper down the backstretch. He dropped down into Turn Three, passed Rusty on the inside, and held the lead all the way to the checkered flag. On TV, race announcer Ken Squier summed it up, "Like a bandit in the night. [Gordon] pickpocketing Wallace."

That win was a big moment. It proved what we realized from our heart-to-heart. We both needed to step it up, and we did. Putting that car back together and winning that race served notice that we were still going strong.

———

Even with renewed commitment and a Charlotte victory, we were still getting beat. Dale Jarrett beat us in his Ford at Dover. We went to Richmond and Terry Labonte, one of our guys, beat us. Then we got beat by Mark Martin at Michigan and Jeremy Mayfield at Pocono, both in Fords.

Halfway through the season, we'd only chalked up three wins. I was still focused on dialing in our aerodynamics to make us competitive against those Fords, but the next stop was Sonoma. At that track the edge is less about aerodynamics and more about driving ability and a great team.

Sure enough, Jeff got the pole and won the race.

But then we went to Loudon and damned if we didn't get beat by the Fords again. While that stung, we did come in third, so I could see we were making headway on aerodynamics.

We were finally starting to figure it out.

In previous years, we could get sluggish heading into summer. People are worn out. Parts are used up. It's brutally hot. Plus, Jeff used to have terrible allergies.

But this summer was different. We'd made a plan to get Jeff and the team some breaks, and we had extra support in place from Hendrick Motorsports. We were better prepared for those hard summer months and the second half of the season.

Suddenly, all the frustration, all the aerodynamic work, and the doubling down on our preparation paid off. We went to Pocono and boom!

We won. We went to Indy for the Brickyard, win! The Budweiser at Watkins Glen, win! The Pepsi 400 at Michigan, win! We'd only won three races the whole first half, then we nailed four races in five weeks.

We took fifth the following week at Bristol. But by the time we rolled into Loudon, New Hampshire, for the August 30, 1998, Farm Aid on CMT 300, we had won five of the last seven races. No one wanted to believe we were that good. Some thought we must be cheating. Little did we know that race would spark a legendary NASCAR scandal known as "Tiregate."

Jeff started on the pole, but Mark Martin had the best car early and was leading the race. Jeff was running comfortably with the lead pack when a late caution came out, sending the top contenders to their pits. We put just two tires on the No. 24, while Mark Martin and the others all took four. With just those two new tires, Jeff outran the field to lead the final sixty-seven laps and score his sixth victory in eight races. Mark Martin finished second to the No. 24 for the fifth time in the same six races.

Mark's team owner, Jack Roush, a NASCAR Hall of Famer and an automotive genius I'm proud to call a friend, couldn't take being beaten by the two-tire pit stop. Jack was convinced a car with only two new tires couldn't have a grip advantage over cars with four new tires.

He'd also received an anonymous package earlier that week containing a can and a bottle filled with liquids marked, "Tire Softener. Undetectable." The person who sent this claimed Roush's competitors were using the tire softener to gain an unfair advantage, a process called "soaking the tires." (Soaking refers to applying a chemical substance to the tire's surface causing the rubber to soften, creating more grip.) Jack assumed it had to be us. After the race, he accused me of soaking our tires.

As I was walking out of Victory Lane, a reporter approached me, "Hey, Jack Roush is over with ESPN saying you guys cheated."

Bullshit.

I confronted him in the middle of his live interview.

"Hey, Jack, you know me," I shouted. "I'm no cheater!"

He could tell I was steamed and told me to leave his interview. It almost looked staged because Jack's way shorter than me. I was pointing down at him. He was pointing back. Still, I argued, "It's air, Jack. Air!"

I worked closely with Goodyear developing their racing radial tires and knew how important tire pressure was to handling.

If a caution came out and there weren't many remaining laps, I knew I could get us out of the pit fast and first by taking two right-side tires instead of changing all four. I could also keep a good level of grip by raising the right-side tire pressure to better match the hot tires on the left side of the car. We won more than a few races by taking two tires and adjusting pressure.

I regret revealing our secret because everybody caught on, but I didn't want people thinking the No. 24 team were cheaters, especially a guy like Jack. He's successful because he's viciously competitive. He's also mechanically brilliant. Once he heard my two-tire strategy, he told everyone what a genius I was. We have a tremendous amount of mutual respect, and earning that from someone like him means everything to me.

Regardless of my revelation, after we won at Darlington the next week, NASCAR Winston Cup director Gary Nelson confiscated our tires and put them through a sophisticated chemical analysis. He referred to it as "a DNA test for tires."

Needless to say, we were exonerated in Tiregate.

———————

One of the things I love most about Jack is his sense of humor. He enjoys a good back and forth ribbing. After our blowout at Loudon, I thought it would be a good time to play a little joke on my friend.

Jack has famously worn a wide-brimmed straw hat for years. He has appeared in lots of pictures donning it. Naturally, I decided to put a $500 bounty on it.

It didn't take long for one of the crazy guys who worked at Hendrick Motorsports on the No. 25 car to make it his mission to capture Jack's hat. Apparently, during a race, Jack set his hat down just as our guy was lurking nearby. Once Jack turned his back, our guy grabbed it and brought it to the shop to collect his reward—which I happily paid.

At the No. 24 shop we had a large cigar store wooden Native American we affectionately called Chief Cranking Wedge. We put Jack's hat on it and took a bunch of pictures with our "Refuse to Lose" motto in the background.

Then we boxed up the hat and delivered it to one of Jack's crew chiefs who lived nearby.

At the championship dinner later that year, I went to the Winston people and said, "Hey, I need a favor."

They used to project all these pictures from the season on a big screen while folks ate their meals. I gave them our photo of the statue wearing Jack's hat for their slide show.

While everybody was busy eating dinner and watching the slide-show—what should appear? Up comes the photo of a wooden Native American sporting . . . Jack Roush's hat.

The whole room busted up.

Jack just looked over at me with a big grin before toasting me with his wine glass as if to say, "Touché."

———

After our win at Loudon, we won the next week at Darlington, putting us at number one in the points standing.

Then it was on to Richmond where we would've clinched three wins in a row if not for Rusty Wallace. With twenty-eight laps left, Rusty was struggling to hold Jeff off. So, he hit Jeff's car as he passed, sending it spinning into the Turn Two wall.

Pissed, I punched the pit box side so hard it folded in. I thought I'd broken my hand. Our crew member Steve Letarte tried calming me down. But that chickenshit stunt ended our night with a thirty-seventh-place showing, knocking us from first in points down to third.

Of course, Rusty loved hearing all the cheering from the Gordon-haters in the stands. Afterward, he claimed, "It was just a racing accident."

He used to call Jeff, "that little prick." He later told me, "I didn't wreck that little prick on purpose."

Truthfully, the year before at Bristol, Jeff gave Rusty a little nudge coming out of Turn Four then passed him 600 feet from the finish line.

Rusty and I had history. Rusty competed in the IROC series back in my IROC days. So we'd known each other forever and we're still good friends today.

For years, Rusty refused to admit that crashing Jeff was no accident. It wasn't until we were all out in Arizona at our friend Ron Pratte's annual get-together one year that Rusty confessed.

Ron's a great guy, a world-class car collector, and he owns all these cool sand cars (aka dune buggies). Yearly, he'd invite a bunch of us for a few days of racing the sand cars in the Arizona desert.

One night, Rusty, Jeff, and I were throwing back a few when Rusty blurted out, "Hell yeah, I wrecked ya." Finally, he admitted his "payback push" at Richmond was on purpose. It's just funny how after a few years and a few beers things like that are nothing more than a good laugh.

We were winning so much that the competition watched us like hawks. We were in the lead at Rockingham just three green laps after a pit stop when a caution came out.

Jeff came on the radio, "I got a flat tire."

Shit! We had to give up the lead. He came down Pit Road all by himself. We put on new tires and he got back out in the back of the pack. Suddenly, I looked down Pit Road and here came the whole field. What the hell?

Then it dawned on me, the other crew chiefs thought they needed tires just because we got 'em. Little did they know, we had no choice but to pit and they had just handed us the lead back.

We raced at Rockingham on Halloween weekend. We were screwing around in practice and decided that since the dayglow orange nose of the No. 24 car made the damn thing look like a pumpkin, we might as well make it really look like a Halloween pumpkin. So just before the practice session, we put pieces of black tape on the lower grille to resemble the missing teeth on a jack-o'-lantern.

I used to scan everybody's communication channels during practice, and I heard one of them say, "Hey, check out the twenty-four car. They must've found out something in the [wind] tunnel." And damned if the rest of the Monte Carlos didn't all put tape on their lower grilles. It was fun back then. There was a lot of monkey see, monkey do.

We won three of the last four races that season, with the last two back-to-back. We locked up the championship at Rockingham, the second-to-last race, but not without a little pit drama.

All we had to do was start the race to gain enough points to win the championship. When the green flag flew, the PR team broke out all the Winston Cup championship gear, giving hats to the crew.

They all started celebrating. I got hot and shouted, "Put that stuff away! We still have a race to win!"

Everybody quieted down and went back to work. I felt like a dick, but I wanted to put an exclamation point on the championship with a win.

We won that race, then it was on to the last race of the season at Atlanta. We'd built a new car with a whole new package, and it was a rocket ship.

We were in the lead when it started raining. Earnhardt and Jeff had vacation plans, and they didn't want to postpone to the next day. The championship was already decided, so everybody agreed to try to finish that night.

When the rain let up, we got back on the track, restarted the race, and damned if it didn't start raining again. It would be another six and a half hours before the race resumed. At some point past the halfway distance, NASCAR announced there would be only twenty-five laps remaining. They wanted the fans to get home at a safe hour.

Sure enough, with about twenty laps to go, a caution came out and all but a handful of drivers came down Pit Road to get fresh tires. Some guys took two, some took four.

Jeff was the first guy back out and lined up behind Morgan Shepherd and the others who stayed out. They threw the green flag with about fifteen laps left. Morgan and Jeff were headed for the corner when Jeff had to check up because Morgan was moving a lot slower. Sure enough, Mark Martin and Dale Jarrett flew around the outside and we lost the lead. Jeff was trying to get under Morgan. Morgan came down and Jeff accidentally spun him, sending Morgan into the wall and out came another caution.

Now we're sitting third and Jeff was feeling terrible because he just wrecked Morgan. I got on the radio, "He's fine. He's okay."

As Jeff drove by again he saw them put Morgan on the stretcher.

Jeff used to get concerned if he felt like he might have been reckless or caused a wreck. Still, I tried to calm him down. "Morgan's waving to the crowd. He's fine. Let's get back in the game."

Truth is, I never actually saw Morgan waving to the crowd. I just needed my driver to get his head back in the race.

They were about to restart the race. Jeff was in third. With just a few laps to go, he made a move that was pure Jeff Gordon.

They dropped the green flag. Dale Jarrett was leading and Mark was in second. Jeff was just barreling to catch them. As they were coming off Turn Four, Jeff keyed the radio.

All he said was, "Watch this."

Jeff drove up around the outside of Mark Martin, then turned straight down between Mark and under DJ to snatch the lead.

Holy cow! He came back around leading and went on to beat Dale Jarrett to the finish line by 0.739 of a second. Wow, friggin' Gordo called it. Not only were we champions, but we'd ended the season by nabbing two wins in a row.

The race finally ended at 11:07 p.m., and the crowd that stuck around to watch got a heck of a race. From a starting position of twenty-first, Jeff led 113 of the race's 221 laps. It was our thirteenth victory of the season, tying Richard Petty for the most wins by a driver in a single season.

We did everything we had set out to do.

In 1995, we had no idea what we were doing. In 1996, I felt like we should have won but didn't. In 1997, we were just relieved by the end of the season after we won. But in 1998, we were committed to winning in a big way and we did.

I didn't know how we could ever top that season. The best of everything that could happen happened. We won thirteen races and locked up the championship with two races to go.

Our second Daytona 500 win
with a million-dollar bonus.
Nigel Kinrade

CHAPTER 22

END OF AN ERA

Time to Fly

"Help me move on."

Whenever I'm asked the secret to the success Jeff and I experienced when we raced together, I point to our communication and friendship.

Simple as that.

Yet by the start of the 1999 season, some people in our lives were pulling us in opposite directions. Our ability to effectively communicate started to erode.

Had he been available, I'm convinced Mr. Hendrick could have helped us straighten out our issues. Mr. H was famous for the "cookies and milk summits" he staged to smooth over feuds between his drivers and crew chiefs.

Jeff and I both trusted Rick.

Because Rick was sidelined from Hendrick Motorsports due to his leukemia, we were unable to benefit from his wise and rational counsel.

We both had those in our circles who weren't behaving in the team's best interest. Though I had to act like I liked him, I didn't care for Jeff's business manager, Bob Brannan. I also didn't care for Brooke's involvement in the race team.

I felt Bob, Brooke, as well as my own agent at the time, were muddling our communication and steering Jeff and me in different directions.

One key person in Jeff's circle actually pulled me aside one day to tell me, "Hey, Brooke and Bob feel like you get too much credit."

That really pissed me off.

It was like watching two trains about to collide and not being able to do anything about it. Our impending train wreck was fueled by lack of communication and burnout.

Jeff's stardom transcended NASCAR, and he became a pro sports celebrity. He didn't need my coaching anymore. And due to the No. 24 team's success, I had pretty strong confidence in myself, too. At the same time, given the change in our dynamic, I felt lost. I didn't know what I wanted to do. That's when the thought of changing careers first entered my head.

It just might've been time.

I felt I'd given all I had to get that championship in '98, and I was happy to do it. But as we geared up for the 1999 season, I felt underappreciated. I kind of lost my fire.

In his book, *The Winner Within*, NBA coach Pat Riley describes what he calls "the disease of me," which is when people are more focused on themselves and self-interests than the good of the team.

Among the danger signs are inexperience in dealing with sudden success, chronic feelings of underappreciation, and a leadership vacuum. All seemed applicable to the No. 24 team.

The disease of me tears teams down. Even the crew started to look for other opportunities. Many on our team suffered from the disease of me.

In late '98, Bob Brannan told Jeff and me that Dodge was coming to NASCAR. Lou Patane from Dodge, who I ended up hiring, wore us out in his efforts to get us to commit. He was calling me nearly every day. I finally told him, "Look, don't call anymore. We have a championship to win. I'll talk with you in the offseason."

Despite winning championships, there was a lot of uncertainty in '99. In fact, the only reason I gave any consideration to a potential deal with Dodge was that Rick Hendrick's fate was unknown.

While I hoped the best for Rick, at that period, I didn't know who was going to be captain of the Hendrick ship.

Speaking for myself, I had no interest in working for Jimmy Johnson. And as much as I loved John Hendrick, I didn't get a strong impression John was interested in running Hendrick Motorsports for the long-term. He loved his brother, and he was managing things until Rick could return, but what he really wanted was to go back to running his dealerships. It was a strange time.

I found the Dodge deal intriguing because of the challenge it presented and the opportunity to carve out my own future.

Like every season, we kicked off 1999 with the Daytona 500. From the pole, Jeff won the race for the second time in three years, becoming the first Daytona 500 pole sitter to also take the checkered flag since Bill Elliott in 1987.

But as the expression goes, every mountain becomes a plateau.

People reacted like we were supposed to win. Now go home and rebuild the car and go win next week. While it was fantastic to clinch the second Daytona 500, this time Victory Lane didn't feel the same.

In the first dozen weeks, we racked up three wins, but then fell to thirty-ninth, followed by a thirty-first, a thirty-eighth, and a forty-third-place showing. Some of it was just bad luck, including blown engines, parts failure, and a crash. Some of it was due to new things we were trying.

We tried a transmission combination with a third and fourth gear really close together with an overdrive. It was faster. With new tires Jeff could pull away and shift just like an Indy car. We did it at Darlington and Indy. At Richmond I underestimated the transmission temperature for a short track, and it broke.

That frustrated Jeff, but we needed to experiment. We were losing our edge. I had to step it up. It was time to start pushing the envelope again.

We experimented all the time when we started the team, even when people told us we were crazy and what we were trying wouldn't work. Back then, we suffered through the naysayers and dominated the sport for the next four years.

It was time to push boundaries again. We won the Daytona 500 and the Fontana race with the craziest setup you ever saw in your life. It set a new standard.

In both races, we had a very soft left-front spring and a stiff shock that had a lot of rebound in it. We also included a big rear sway bar to hold up the right rear. It was a very tricky setup. As soon as Jeff was on the racetrack, the car would fall right over on the left front, put the air dam on the ground, and ride on a little piece of rubber.

The shock held it down.

It was some tricky stuff, and all legal, but it was hard to balance.

In some instances, it took away the mechanical grip and made the car hard to drive.

After you pitted with a full tank of fuel and new tires, the car would be incredibly loose for three, four, maybe five laps. You'd have to be careful. Jeff was good enough, patient enough. We'd fall back a little bit and then after five or so laps, he'd just come trucking through. He'd white knuckle it for the first few laps, then just take off.

There weren't too many drivers that could've driven that setup. Jeff could.

We were still missing our magic when we got to Pocono. Jeff called on the radio saying he felt a vibration and wanted to pit. I told him to wait and ride it out. Sure enough, the tire went down and he almost crashed. Thank God he didn't.

The next week, he and Brooke sat me down in the bus.

"Hey," Jeff began. "From now on if I have a tire issue, don't tell me to stay out. When I say I want to come in, it means I want to come in."

I looked at him, then at Brooke. That was a first.

While I admit he was justified in expressing his annoyance, I wished he hadn't done it in front of Brooke. I thought, "Man that's really different." Until that moment, every time Jeff and I wanted to talk about something, it was just us. Now I was in his bus with him and Brooke, and she expressed an opinion about my performance. It was disturbing. I had always been somebody Jeff could depend on, somebody he had confidence in. Apparently, that was changing.

It frightened me to think he was losing faith in me. It made me question myself, which undermined my effectiveness as a good crew chief. I started worrying more about what Jeff and Brooke might think than what I knew to be best for the car of the team. The biggest reason I worked so hard was because I felt he believed in me. Counted on me. When that appeared to change, I started to lose my drive.

As much as I'd like to believe I remained a good leader and kept my emotions and doubts in check, if I'm being honest, I know I was distracted with my concerns over Jeff's waning confidence and the shiny new opportunity with Dodge.

I thought I could block out all that noise. I've always felt a sense of duty when it came to my job. I was being paid to lead those guys. But just because you think you're 100 percent committed doesn't mean you are.

In some sense, Jeff and I and the entire team had become victims of our own success. We were, without question, the premier operation in NASCAR. Individually and collectively, we had lucrative offers thrown at us from other owners, from agents, from anybody and everybody who saw dollar signs and wanted a piece of our pie.

We just weren't in sync like we had been.

Jeff and Brooke's move from North Carolina to Highland Beach, Florida, at the close of 1998 only added to it. When Jeff went to Florida, we saw him a lot less.

In previous years our pit-road jawing sessions would end in a laugh, or at least a brotherly agreement that we both wanted what was best for the team. Things were different now—less constructive and more biting.

As crew chief, I had to talk to Jeff the only way I knew how to talk to him. I was never a crew chief before Jeff Gordon, and I certainly had no experience with champions or veteran drivers. By now we'd won all these races and three championships. He was a veteran and he didn't need my style of coaching, but I didn't have another style to fall back on. It was all I knew.

You coach somebody to get them to a certain level, and once they're there, you've got to coach them differently. If we'd talked about it, I could've done that. I really wanted to be Jeff's crew chief, but I knew that was coming to an end.

I was lost.

I thought, "Man, I just want to be Jeff's crew chief the way I used to be."

I didn't care for the dissension and frustration. I also didn't like the way Bob was running things at JG Inc. I believe he cared more about licensing, T-shirts, and endorsement deals than our racing.

Ultimately, I was afraid I wasn't going to be able to commit to a different position at Hendrick and I'd end up letting everyone down. I did a gut-check. Did I really think I could jump in and be a manager at Hendrick Motorsports long-term and maybe someday fill Rick Hendrick's shoes?

Ain't happening.

Meanwhile, the Dodge deal was still being dangled in front of me.

They kept saying, "What's it gonna take?" And one day, I thought, rather than spending my energy on the ending of something, Dodge would give me the chance to focus on the start of something new.

I'm a project guy. I started to look at the Dodge deal in a whole new light. It would be the ultimate challenge.

———

Dodge had been persistent in their pursuit of me. Before accepting their offer, they asked me to fly to England on the off weekend in the Cup schedule to meet with Adrian Reynard. He was overseeing the whole

Dodge NASCAR initiative. Adrian specialized in building Formula One and Indy cars.

Because the trip was a quick over-and-back, they booked me to fly on the Concorde. If nothing else came from the trip, the fact I flew on the Concorde would have been cool enough. To an engineering-based guy, it was an amazing experience flying on that engineering marvel. I will never forget when the pilot came over the loudspeaker to announce we were about to go supersonic. Then came the g-force that pushed me back into my seat. It felt like I was back in a dragster.

I met Adrian at his big facility outside of London. Then I turned right around and flew home the next day.

Adrian's a brilliant guy, but after our meeting, I realized Dodge wouldn't be successful if they tried managing their Cup effort from England. There was no way Adrian could come to America in a short period of time and do everything needed with NASCAR.

I realized they didn't know how much they didn't know, and that was going to be a problem.

Just in the way he talked about building cars and using computational fluid dynamics (CFD—a computerized method for doing wind tunneling) I could tell there was a lot about Cup cars he didn't understand.

At that time, I was thinking there's no way I could do this. I knew Adrian was a smart guy, but NASCAR is not Formula One. They were underestimating NASCAR, its people, and the competition.

It concerned me enough I told Dodge no deal.

As a fallback, I continued negotiating a possible transition into Hendrick management. Mostly I was trying to talk myself into it.

I was doing serious soul-searching, thinking about what I had accomplished so far and where I wanted to go in life.

At the time, I was working on the No. 24 and our Busch team because I wanted to be with Jeff, but I didn't believe I was doing a good job. I was just treading water and not making any progress in my career or personal life.

Three weeks went by. Dodge contacted me again.

They asked me what it would take to get me to run the program. I remember staying up late one night and writing down a list of things that seemed outrageous, like seed money, decision-making power in engineering, and a contract to distribute parts to all the Dodge teams.

I even asked for a Dodge dealership.

They gave me the whole thing. They said, "We'll put you in charge of everything. The design and building of the cars, the engine, and we'll throw in parts distribution." A Dodge dealership was the only thing they couldn't do legally. I knew right then it was a chance I couldn't pass up.

Then they surprised me with an amount of seed money so large, I could've retired on it. So, I decided to do it. It was a bold move, but I knew it was the right decision.

They gave me a ten-year contract with enough guaranteed funding to race two cars. They also allowed me to sell the sponsorships on the cars.

At the time, I had a big fear that if I stayed at Hendrick, I wouldn't be in control of my own future. I was working as a crew chief for Jeff, and I knew if he ever got tired of me, or his "staff" wanted a change, I'd probably get fired or moved to a different team.

Plus, I knew if I took a management position at Hendrick and didn't do a good job, I'd end up sitting in an office getting a big paycheck for doing nothing, which is really a testament to just how loyal I knew Rick could be. So, given the chance to take control of my career again, I took it.

I couldn't bear the thought of being crew chief for anyone else. My crew chief career began and ended with Jeff Gordon and Rick Hendrick. The day I got off the box in Dover, I swore I wouldn't be a crew chief again, and I've never been a crew chief since. That's the way it's going to stay. I was lucky enough to work with one of the greatest drivers and team owners of our time, and I didn't want to settle for anything less.

Even though the timing wasn't perfect, and I still had six and a half years left on my ten-year contract, Rick had always told me if I ever wanted to leave, he'd let me out.

After all Mr. H had done for me, I felt like Judas asking him for my release.

I talk a lot about trophies and scars. Well, not all of my scars are physical. Many are regrets over how I didn't handle something correctly. I don't care what people say, you can't fix those scars. Like the little parable we tell our children: if you hammer a nail in a fence then pull the nail out, the nail might be gone, but the hole is still there.

That's the way it is when you hurt somebody's feelings.

True to his word, Rick let me out of my contract, "I told you, I'd never hold you back." He even allowed me to take a couple of the guys from the No. 24 team.

I met with Jeff and told him I was leaving. He understood.

The only other request I made to both was, "Help me move on."

Then I headed home. I felt sick to my stomach. It was one of the hardest decisions of my life, and in its wake, I was afraid I'd lost two great friends whom I respected a lot. I don't think Jeff was happy with me at first, but I understood where he was coming from.

I wouldn't have been anywhere without those two guys.

Rick had done so much for me. He'd given me a great opportunity and taken care of my family. Part of me felt like I was being disloyal. Like it was all about the disease of me. But at the end of the day, it was a decision I had to make for me and for my family's future.

I knew leaving Hendrick Motorsports would be tough, that fans would criticize me for it, but players switch teams in sports all the time. I will always be grateful for the opportunities Rick and Jeff gave me, and I'm proud of the success we achieved together.

Me, LuAnn, and Willie at the 1995 Championship Awards Banquet. I'm not sure who the photo bomber is. *Ray Evernham Enterprises Archives*

Me, Ray J., Chad Knaus, and race driver Bobby Hillin watching Jeff beat the high score in the driving game at a birthday party in 1996. *Ray Evernham Enterprises Archives*

From fighting leukemia to Victory Lane. He was my miracle child. *Ray Evernham Enterprises Archives*

Me, Jeff, and John Hendrick at Rockingham in 1998. *Ray Evernham Enterprises Archives*

Adam Petty and I in 1998. *Ray Evernham Enterprises Archives*

Locking up
the 1998
Championship
with a win at
Rockingham.
Nigel Kinrade

I am so happy that my dad got to be a a part of my wins and Championships. Even though it wasn't "baseball," I was a pro. *Ray Evernham Enterprises Archives*

Posing with Papa Joe Hendrick in 1998. *Nigel Kinrade*

Mr. H and I discussing the amount of tape on the front of the No. 24 car before the start of the 1999 Daytona 500. *Nigel Kinrade*

The first two Dodge show cars, pictured in 1999. *Ray Evernham Enterprises Archives*

Left to Right: Ben Kennedy, Bill France Sr., Ray J., and me on Mr. France's boat in the early 2000s. *Ray Evernham Enterprises Archives*

My first win as a team owner in 2001 at Homestead-Miami. Left to right: Me, Mary, Bill, Cindy, Chase, and Mike Ford. *Ray Evernham Enterprises Archives*

At my buddy Billy Pauch's sprint car driving school 2002. Left to right: Billy Jr., Buffy Swanson, Billy, me, and Bill Elliott. *Ray Evernham Enterprises Archives*

Me, Ruth Bauma, and Jim Bauma in 2002. *Ray Evernham Enterprises Archives*

Left to right: Tommy Baldwin, my dad, Kasey Kahne, and me after Kasey's first Cup win. I am so happy my dad got to enjoy that win with us. *Ray Evernham Enterprises Archives*

They combined drivers into teams at the 2005 Prelude at Eldora. Left to right: Aric Almorda, Ricky Carmichael, Carl Edwards, me, Tony Kanan, Ken Schrader, and Denny Hamlin. *Wolf Photograghy*

Now dirt! In Ricky Grosso's No. 24 at New Egypt Speedway in 2005.
Ray Evernham Enterprises Archives

We were the first NASCAR team to test on the shuttle runway at Cape Canaveral.
Ray Evernham Enterprises Archives

Me and Scott Riggs after winning the pole for the All-Star Open. Scott was not afraid to stand on the gas. *Ray Evernham Enterprises Archives*

Before we were husband and wife, we were owner and driver. I definitely had more pull then. *Ray Evernham Enterprises Archives*

On dirt at New Egypt Speedway in 2008. Those little things were quick. *Jim Smith*

I won my last sprint car race with a last lap pass at Friendship Speedway in Elkin, North Carolina, in 2012. *Ray Evernham Enterprises Archives*

Ray J. holding Cate at her baptism. She was baptized in our race shop. We wanted her to start early. *Ray Evernham Enterprises Archives*

Me and Cate with Mario Andretti and Jim McGee at Indy. *Ray Evernham Enterprises Archives*

Erin, Cate, and I pose with a *Cars 3* display at the NASCAR Hall of Fame.
Ray Evernham Enterprises Archives

Me, Erin, Ray J., and Cate attending the *Cars 3* movie premiere. *Ray Evernham Enterprises Archives*

Patrick Donahue, Jeff Gordon, me, Steve Letarte, and Brian Whitesell.
It was great to have so many members of the No. 24 team at my Hall of Fame
induction in 2018. *Ray Evernham Enterprises Archives*

Posing with
the checkered
flag after our
win at Pikes
Peak. *Ray
Evernham
Enterprises
Archives*

Doing *Jay Leno's Garage* with my 1940 Ford moonshine car. *Ray Evernham Enterprises Archives*

Racing legend George Follmer, me, and Jay Signore at Amelia Island in 2019. *Ray Evernham Enterprises Archives*

With racing legends Walker Evans and Don Prudhomme in 2022. *Ray Evernham Enterprises Archives*

My first Daddy-Daughter dance with Cate in 2022. *Ray Evernham Enterprises Archives*

PART III

STARTING FRESH

1999–2017

My first win as a car owner was with Bill Elliott and future NASCAR Cup champion Chase Elliott. *Nigel Kinrade*

CHAPTER 23

FROM SCRATCH

The Early Dodge Years

"I don't like the look of that."

After making the gut-wrenching decision to leave Hendrick Motorsports I was filled with mixed emotions. Accepting the enormous challenge of bringing Dodge to NASCAR filled me with anxiety and excitement.

Put simply, I had a ton of work ahead of me.

Building the Dodge teams from scratch—in less than five hundred days—became a classic case of "Be careful what you wish for."

One of the first things I noticed? I didn't have suitable clothes to wear. Ninety percent of my wardrobe was made up of Hendrick Motorsports or DuPont logo wear. I needed new attire to tide me over until Dodge sent me some swag.

A small detail, but it reminded me just how much work I had ahead. The other challenge?

Navigating the 24 team's last race with me as crew chief. Brian Whitesell would become interim crew chief until Jeff and Rick chose my replacement. I thought the world of Brian. Still do.

I was happy to do what I could to mentor him. I let him take over the radio with Jeff. By that time, my voice wasn't all that effective because everyone knew I was leaving.

Plus, the other Hendrick crew chiefs certainly didn't want to share any information with me. The magic had died. It was all a bit surreal.

Another strange moment occurred at Dover when Dale Earnhardt pulled me aside. "You really gotta think this through," referring to

Dodge's interest in NASCAR, "These things can be a flash in the pan. They're up. They're down."

But I wasn't in the right frame of mind to take his warning to heart. Jeff's seventeenth-place finish that day marked my last race as crew chief of the No. 24 team.

Two days later, September 28, 1999, Hendrick "officially" announced my departure. Probably NASCAR's worst-kept secret.

The next day I had to clear out my stuff. It was probably one of the lowest moments of my life. I built that No. 24 shop; I was there all that time.

Now I was being escorted from the building with all my shit in a cardboard box. Literally. On my way out, I said, "Bye, Chief," as I patted the shoulder of our wooden Native American mascot we'd named Chief Cranking Wedge.

Driving toward the exit gate, I thought of so many people I wished I could stop and say goodbye to but didn't.

Everything positive in my world happened at the Hendrick complex: Rebounding from my disastrous experience with Alan Kulwicki. The support I received during Ray J.'s illness. Having stability and a chance to excel in something I love doing.

I still tell Rick Hendrick all this today. The best times of my life and career were in a Hendrick uniform. And as I drove out that gate, I realized I was leaving a family.

And I felt I was leaving almost in shame.

It was terrible. And though there was mutual respect among the team till the end, I knew those relationships would never be the same.

It's hard to be friends with somebody you compete against.

Heading home, I told myself: "Look you made the decision, accepted the challenge, and now you're going to get that job done."

I just had to man up and get on with it. Boy, it sucked.

It was incredibly hard, but I knew I wasn't doing anybody any good by staying.

———

Initially, I thought I should allow myself to decompress, to take a vacation. I tried to take time with Mary and Ray J. for normal family things here and there on a Sunday, but I couldn't. I was crawling out of my skin knowing there was a race going on.

Then Jeff goes and wins the next two races without me, Martinsville and Charlotte. I thought, "Just gimme a razor blade. I'm gonna end this right now." In my mind I thought I didn't really make a difference.

They're right. I sucked. I'm done.

I wasn't, of course; I knew I'd made a difference.

We worked so far in advance, I knew we got those two cars ready before I ever left Hendrick, but I was super happy for Brian Whitesell to get his first wins as a crew chief.

After winning those two races, Jeff and his team fell on hard times. Even so, I never took joy in Jeff not running well. I never cheered against him. Well, to be honest, except when my Dodge cars raced him for a spot.

I knew the only way to get my bearings was by getting back to work. First, I set up an office in my house. I was starting from scratch. The only thing I had when I walked out of Hendrick Motorsports was my Dodge contract.

Next, I had to source buildings that would house our entire operation. That was crucial, given we were launching two race teams and planned on building our own engines.

Since I owned the building housing the Gordon-Evernham Motorsports Busch team, I was able to convert it into our engine shop. In the very beginning, I led the development, design, and building of every aspect of our cars from two small buildings in Mooresville. I was constantly in either the body shop, the chassis shop, or the engine shop, and I went to every test.

I used to drive a red Dodge Durango the team called "the firetruck" because I was running up and down Route 77 going from shop to shop. There were weeks, if not months, where I worked from 7:00 a.m. till 11:00 p.m. or midnight every night. Seven days a week.

————

One of my smarter decisions was bringing in a great friend, Bill Elliott, as our lead driver. He was the perfect choice, given his huge fan base and his history for winning. Plus, I knew Bill well from my early days at IROC.

It just so happened that about that time Bill lost his sponsor and wasn't sure of his next move. So I was able to buy his buildings and equipment, which really jumpstarted building the foundation for the team. I knew Bill hadn't won in eight or nine years, but he was trying to be an owner-driver. So he had all the distractions that come with being an owner diminishing his driving focus. On top of that, Bill was living in Georgia and the team was based in North Carolina, so he couldn't supervise the day-to-day operations.

Bill was one of the first people I confided in about my plan to leave Hendrick.

We met at the Loudon race just before Dover in September 1999. Sitting in the lounge of his hauler, I laid out my proposal. "I don't have a lot of time. I'm leaving the twenty-four team to take the Dodge deal, and I want you to come drive for me."

He just looked at me. Didn't say a thing. Then one of his PR people walked up to remind Bill he had an interview.

Turning to me, he said, "All right, call me." That was it.

He walked out without another word. Nothing.

I was thinking, "Shit, he probably doesn't want to do this."

The next day he called. "Hey, hit me with that again."

I said, "Oh, I thought you weren't interested. You didn't say anything."

Bill replied in his thick, deep Georgia accent, "I was stunned! I didn't know what to say."

Then he asked me if I'd be interested in buying some of his shop equipment. I was happy to do so, because at that time I had nothing.

We made a deal, and Bill became my principal driver for the 2001 season. Talk about great timing. It was perfect all the way around, for Bill and for me.

I needed a superstar, and I had one in Bill.

Though he hadn't won in a while, he was still "Awesome Bill from Dawsonville." He wasn't winning because of his cars, not because of him. He didn't have the right team to support him. I knew how good of a driver he was.

One of my proudest moments as a car owner was bringing Bill back to Victory Lane. Bill was the perfect combination of driver, business partner, and friend. He was my compass for those early Dodge years. I really trusted him and admired his experience and integrity.

Something else special about that partnership? Being able to keep Bill in his No. 9 car. Back then, he and I discussed him ending his career in my car. But he began in the No. 9 and wished to end it that way.

I wanted to do that for him.

We made a deal with Mark Melling, a good guy, who had the rights to the No. 9 in Cup at the time. He knew why we wanted the number. I made him a reasonable offer and helped him with Dodge parts.

As Rick Hendrick always said, "A good deal is a deal that's good for everybody. Can't be great for one guy and not good for the other. It's got to be good for all."

And it was.

In addition to being my marquee driver, Bill served as mentor for the rookie I brought in, Casey Atwood. I didn't want two guys at the same level. We got Bill as our lead driver, so we can focus on him. Then Bill would mentor our rookie. As our rookie improved, the former wouldn't feel pressure. Bill was getting older. By the time he decided he wanted to do something else, we'd elevate Casey.

Casey was a good kid with big talent. What I didn't know right away was, as mature as he was behind the wheel, he lacked maturity outside of the car. I imagined if I'd have been Casey's crew chief, I could have helped him. But I was doing a thousand other things. We brought him on believing he already had a grasp of the business and possessed the commitment it takes to race at the Cup level. He didn't.

He had plenty of talent, but talent's not enough to make it in this sport. And it's a shame because I really liked him. Casey's a good guy. But as I said, when you get to this level, you've got to be more than talented.

Casey lasted through his rookie year before I placed him on a satellite team.

After two years I cut him. I paid him through his full three-year contract. It was the right thing to do. To this day, I believe he could have been great, but it was too late.

Some criticized me for bringing him up to Cup level too soon. They may have been right, but he knew what we expected. We gave him all the tools. We gave him everything to be successful. In the end, there's a certain amount of responsibility that falls on the athlete.

Casey and Bill were just one piece of the Dodge team. Like any new start-up, my biggest challenge was bringing on the right people. I had to put together a complete organization capable of going toe-to-toe with Hendrick, Gibbs, Roush, and Childress. That meant I needed fabricators, engineers, chassis specialists, pit crew members, and mechanics. I also had airplanes, so I needed pilots. I had to have a marketing and PR staff. I needed a sponsorship sales force and an administrative staff. I had to hire hundreds of people almost overnight, all while leading the development of our car and engine.

Fortunately, we worked closely with Richard Petty and his group. They were a huge help. Kyle Petty was our lead test driver while Bill finished out the 2000 season with Ford.

Kyle's son Adam would have become a driver for the Petty-Dodge team. Instead, he tragically died in a practice crash at Loudon, New

Hampshire, in May 2000. Just nineteen years old and a rising talent, his death devastated the Petty family. Losing Adam was a real blow to the morale of everybody on the Dodge program. He was going to be our shining star.

————

While building our teams, we were also responsible for distributing all the engine and body parts to the other teams. That meant, in addition to my race team, I had to build a whole other parts distribution business.

We did it and did it all in less than five hundred days.

And though we were running at breakneck speed during those five hundred days, we never hit a single snag. Sometimes I feared we'd have to cut corners or sacrifice quality to hit a deadline. But that never happened.

The bar was high, and we reached it. And when we showed up in Daytona, we looked sharp. Everyone had new uniforms, shiny new tractor trailers, brand-new pit equipment, and Dodge red everywhere. We looked like we'd been racing for five years.

The only thing that might even resemble a snag came during car development. NASCAR allowed Ford to build the Taurus. We told them we were going to race the Dodge Intrepid.

We made our own template. We built a frigging Batmobile. At least that's what Bill France called it. That prototype car was badass and way too good in the wind tunnel.

We wanted NASCAR to make templates off of it. Mr. France put his foot down. He was fed up with manufacturers and everybody fighting over templates. He decided he wanted to establish a common template.

Not surprisingly, NASCAR disallowed our first car. Just refused it. NASCAR felt the aero had gotten way out of control. That's when they implemented the common template. They told us to basically use the Ford Taurus template.

Dodge entering the sport marked the start of the homologation. Cars had to match aerodynamically. The Intrepid was much like the Ford Taurus with a few changes. So even though they outlawed our first car, they made it easier to build the next batch.

We went to the 2001 Daytona 500 and put all ten Dodge cars in the race, two of them being my Evernham Motorsports No. 9 and No. 19. We took up the whole front row with Bill in my No. 9 car on the pole and Stacy Compton in Mark Melling's No. 92 outside pole. The crew chief on that car was a young guy named Chad Knaus.

When the checkered flag fell, Bill Elliott scored an impressive fifth-place finish, but any positive emotion we felt by having a great day was soon overshadowed by the death of Dale Earnhardt.

Even though that was a very successful day for Dodge and for me, I still feel very numb at the thought of that last lap crash that took Dale.

Dodge went on to win three races that season. Ganassi won two and we won one. (By comparison, when Toyota came into NASCAR it took three years to get their first win.)

———————

While everything was coming together work-wise, my health was another story.

Three months before the Daytona 500, I went to my dentist for a routine checkup. He suddenly stopped what he was doing.

He had a concerned look on his face. "I want to show you something." He positioned his mirror over one of my teeth. "See that pink dot?"

"Yeah."

"See the one next to it?"

"Yeah. What's up?"

"I don't like the look of that. I'm going to make a phone call."

Returning, he said, "Hey, I'm going to send you to see another dentist. I want you to go right now and I'm going with you."

On our way to the next office, he explained his suspicions. "If it's what I think it is, it's a rare tooth disease called internal resorption. It's serious."

It starts from the root canal and destroys the surrounding tooth structure. The progressive loss of part—or parts—of the tooth are due to odontoclasts, a type of naturally occurring cell that's responsible for breaking down the roots of our baby teeth so they'll eventually fall out.

No sooner did we get to the next dentist's office, than I was right back in the exam chair. The diagnosis was confirmed. I'm thinking, "What the f—? Why now?"

Both dentists told me they had seen only one case in North Carolina before me but had never seen two infected teeth in the same mouth.

Now, beyond building the whole Dodge program, I had to deal with a serious tooth disease. To make matters worse, it'd already spread into my jaw. If it had gone undiagnosed, it could have gone into my nasal area and eventually killed me.

But the dentists laid out a plan that saved some of my teeth and possibly my life.

Those two were geniuses. Here's what they did over the course of the next fourteen months. (Fasten your seatbelt!) They cut out two pieces from my jaw. Then they bolted in the replacement pieces with screws, then added implants with more screws. There were times I'd be at the track with as many as eighty stitches in my mouth. There were several days I was in a dentist chair for six to eight hours. After that, there were a dozen more days where I spent two to three hours in the chair. By the time one particular procedure healed, it was time for the next.

In a word? Awful.

When all was said and done, I had over 220 different stitches in my mouth, as well as seven permanent screws.

I kept the whole thing a secret from everybody except Mary, my assistant Ann, and company manager Eddie D'Hondt.

No one else on the team or at Dodge knew what was happening to me.

Living on smoothies, my weight plummeted. It typically fluctuated between 182 and 186 pounds for most of my adult life. I was down to 171 pounds on my six-foot, two-inch frame. I was as skinny as I'd ever been.

Rumors were flying.

Unsurprisingly, people were saying things like, "Ray's working himself to death. He's in a bad mood. He never smiles.

Everybody just assumed I was being "typical Ray Evernham" working and not taking time to eat.

In reality, I was in a hell of a lot of pain.

I couldn't eat anything that wasn't blended. And I didn't smile because I was afraid people would see I didn't have my real teeth and probably detect the stitches. I went through the first few months of the season in that excruciating condition.

Since that time, other than having some porcelain teeth replaced with new material, everything has gone well. But if you saw my X-ray, you'd be like, "Holy shit!" These days, my mouth is nothing but screws and bolts.

It's a wonder I don't set off airport metal detectors.

———

Bill's pole and fifth-place finish at Daytona gave us the confidence that we could be competitive, but we weren't there to be competitive, we were there to win. We were able to pick up several top-ten and top-five finishes over the next few months, but we just couldn't seem to put a full race together to get that first win.

With only three races left on the schedule, we headed to Homestead, Florida, with one thing on our mind. Right out of the gates, we swept the front row in qualifying, with Bill Elliott on the pole and Casey Atwood on the outside pole. Between the two, they led nearly half the laps in the race, and when the checkered flag flew Bill was out front to capture our first win as a team.

If it weren't for Michael Waltrip getting by Casey right at the very end, we would have finished first and second, but it was still a huge day for all of us. It was Bill's first win in seven years. I was so happy to see him back in Victory Lane. It showed everyone how far we'd come as a new team. It was, in my mind, the only way we could properly thank Dodge and all the people who believed that we could build something from nothing and take it to Victory Lane. And that's exactly what we did that day. For me personally, it's right up there with the first Coke 600 victory with the number No. 24 car. There are several defining moments in my career, and that victory at Homestead is one of them.

At the risk of repeating myself, Indy has always been a very special place for me. It's a textbook track. Jeff and I had a lot of success there, so I've always been confident about my setup and race strategy going into the Brickyard 400.

Leading up to the 2002 Brickyard 400, our engineering team was at the top of their game with new suspension and aerodynamic formulas. We wanted to test the new setup out before the Brickyard, so we took it to Pocono, which was the week before. Bill Elliott won the pole and the race, so we knew we were on to something.

We loaded up and headed to Indy with our new setup validated and a ton of confidence. Bill Elliott started from the outside pole and dominated the race, leading more than half the laps. He passed Rusty Wallace with around twelve laps to go to take the lead and then the checkered. I was thrilled for a couple of reasons. First, it was one of the crown jewels of NASCAR that Bill didn't have in his trophy case. Winning at Indianapolis meant a great deal to him. Second, it validated how strong our engineering department was at Evernham Motorsports.

The racing world was starting to pay attention to the things we were doing. Dodge felt good because they want people to believe their cars are engineered better than the cars of other manufacturers. It's easy for a manufacturer to connect the dots from their racing programs to their passenger car programs. You know what they say, "Win on Sunday, sell on Monday."

Every time you go to Indy you feel a sense of responsibility—the need to have your best day, since only the best win at Indy. Our win meant we weren't just a one-off, we were legitimate contenders. People started looking at our team differently. As for me, it meant the racing world had to consider Ray Evernham in a significantly broader context than before.

Despite it being a significant win for Bill, unlike Jeff and me, Bill's not an emotional guy. You're not going to see Bill crying in Victory Lane. I could always tell what accomplishments meant a lot to him by his handshake and the direct look in the eye. If it was just another win, he'd give me a different look. That day after his Brickyard win, he firmly grabbed my hand and looked me straight in the eye with a big smile on his face. It was Bill's way of saying, "Thank you."

———

It wasn't long into my new partnership with Dodge that I realized how much the culture differed from Hendrick Motorsports. How much time it took to build a Hendrick-like culture was the biggest thing I'd underestimated.

You see, I'd been on a hiring frenzy. I needed people as fast as possible to make the Daytona 500 deadline. I didn't vet folks as well as I should've.

Some weren't loyal followers as much as they were just employees. They weren't as unselfish as those I'd worked with at Hendrick. My nucleus was good, but we were adding people so fast, we ended up with several that weren't great teammates.

I couldn't afford to cycle them out right away. We needed the bodies. Our desperation actually hurt us. The Penske culture, the Hendrick culture, the Jack Roush culture—all had taken years to build. I moved so fast; we had leaders in key positions that didn't believe in the same things I did.

I tried to bring the Lombardi and Pat Riley values into our team philosophy, but there were some who just thought it was goofy. Some had come from other places that weren't successful teams and weren't smart enough to figure out why they needed to change.

By and large, Dodge had great people who lived up to everything they promised. They honored contracts, but there were some in the organization who didn't believe in the program.

The same goes for my leadership team. I was fortunate to have a select group of trustworthy, loyal people at our core who believed in the mission. But we grew so fast, I just wasn't able to get enough quality people to believe in the culture I was trying construct. There were even some who had their own agendas that slowed our progress.

Still, my leadership team built a very successful operation, winning poles and races in the NASCAR Cup and Busch series, as well as the ARCA series.

———

Leaving Hendrick was emotionally difficult, but it made me stronger.

In the end, it was worth it. The Dodge deal was a success, proving I was more than a crew chief. When I eventually sold the business to a private equity group, it proved I wasn't a bad businessman, either.

Years later, Rick, Jeff, and I agreed my departure from the No. 24 team and from Hendrick to take the Dodge deal was good for all. Jeff Gordon and Hendrick Motorsports went on to win many races and championships. As Rick always says, a good deal is a deal that's good for all. And in this case, it truly was.

Doing the Dodge program helped me grow both personally and professionally. And I will be forever thankful for the opportunity.

I'm thinking race strategy and Erin is messing with the photographer.
Ray Evernham Enterprises Archives

CHAPTER 24

BREAKING BARRIERS

An Outlaw Sprinter Steps Up: 2004

"You gotta see this girl drive."

In 2004, Dodge introduced a NASCAR-targeted diversity and inclusion initiative. It made perfect sense for a company relying on the support of a varied group of customers and fans. They approached us with the idea of creating a driver development program specifically for minority and female drivers.

At that time, Kasey Kahne drove for me and was also involved in sprint car racing. His brother Kale told me about a female sprint car driver who impressed him named Erin Crocker.

"You've gotta see this girl drive. Believe it or not, she's racing in the World of Outlaws series and she's really good."

In October 2004, Erin became the first woman to win a World of Outlaws feature at the Thunderbowl Raceway in Tulare, California. She beat Steve Kinser, the king of sprint car racing.

Even today, there aren't many female sprint car drivers. It's been nearly twenty years since Erin claimed her World of Outlaws feature win, and she still holds that record.

Historically, in higher-level racing series, female drivers haven't been given many chances and have been largely ignored. That said, it is improving.

And while it's easier for them to get a shot on the more affordable short-track circuits, the sad truth is that there are still many male drivers who hold a grudge against women on the track. Rather than trying to outdrive them, they'll just bump them out of the way. Erin has had certain male drivers crash her along with themselves just because they couldn't accept a woman passing them.

Or worse yet, beating them.

Her winning that World of Outlaws race put her on my radar, particularly because I always had huge respect for drivers in that series. It's pure old school racing. Drivers traveling the country, running from track to track, trying to make a living. All for the love of racing. To me, the World of Outlaws series is basic to racing's DNA.

So I thought, "Geez, any woman who can compete at that level deserves a shot." Coincidentally, John Bickford knew her agent, Alan Miller, who also happened to be Jimmie Johnson's agent. John facilitated the introduction.

When I first met her, she was shy, and Alan did all the talking. I told him what my budget was and what we thought we could do for her.

I laid it all out. First, we'd go test. Then we'd run her in ARCA races. After that, we'd have her compete in truck races, then move her into Busch Grand National races, all with the idea of working toward either a full Busch Grand National or a truck series ride.

That was our step-by-step proposal.

————

You could test as often as you wanted at Kentucky back then, so we used to go once a week. Sometimes twice. The track is shaped much like Charlotte and Texas, and it was the perfect place for Erin's first test.

On the way to the track, we stopped for breakfast and Erin seemed really anxious.

She told me she could hardly sleep the night before, so I was glad we had Bill Elliott along to ease her nerves and coach her. Bill was also going to test his own car.

He did a great job coaching Erin. Bill's a gold mine of racing experience, and he generously shared his knowledge with her.

One of the things I remember most about that testing day was asking Erin a question I should've on day one.

"So, where have you driven on pavement and how many times?"

She looked at me kind of sheepishly. "I, uh, ran quarter midgets on pavement, like when I was five or six years old."

"What about the sprints, or midgets, or stock cars. . . anything?"

"No, I haven't really raced on pavement since I was a kid."

Okay. I'd just assumed because she had done so well in her sprint car that she would have had much more experience. Either way, it didn't matter. The point of the test was to evaluate her abilities.

Bill talked to her about how to drive the Cup car. She was careful and followed directions. For each session, we told her what speed we wanted her to run. She kept passing all these stages with flying colors. By the end of the day, we just let her go as fast as she wanted to go.

She didn't run as fast as Bill—but damn close.

Her performance was impressive. She seemed comfortable with every challenge. No signs of nervousness or intimidation. We made the decision to offer her a two-year driver development deal.

At the same time we hired Erin, we also brought on a young African American driver named Tommy Lane. Tommy had driven midgets and go-karts, and I knew his family well from New Jersey. I wanted to give Tommy a shot.

We started him and Erin both in late-model stock cars. Unfortunately, Tommy just didn't develop. He couldn't advance past the late model. We kept trying to get him up to speed, but he just couldn't do it. After the first year, even Tommy realized he wasn't cut out to be a driver. Thankfully, he ended up staying and working at our shop until I sold it.

———

In 2005, we built an ARCA team around Erin and sent her to a series of races. Our hope was to attract a sponsor for 2006, enabling her to run the truck series or Busch Grand National full-time.

Our first ARCA race was in Nashville, Tennessee. She annihilated the field and set a new track record in qualifying. At race time, I gave her explicit instructions. "This is not like your sprint car. Do not drive underneath somebody getting into the corner. And do not be side by side with another car in the middle of the corner because this car has a spoiler, not a wing. You will lose your downforce and spin out."

From the pole, she led most of the race until a late-race caution. Under caution, all but one or two cars headed for the pits.

We pitted for new tires and some fuel.

Erin jetted back out onto the track directly behind the cars that stayed out. There were probably twenty to twenty-five laps left in the race, so she had plenty of time. On the restart, she easily passed the first couple of cars. The next lap she caught the leader getting into Turn One and tried to pass him in the bottom lane. He moved down just enough to take the air off her car. She spun out, and I was pissed.

She did a good job keeping the car off the wall and was trying to get it restarted when I keyed the radio. "What did you learn? What did we talk about?"

I'm the coach. I talked to her the same way I did to Jeff in our rookie year. When I felt like Jeff made a mistake, I told him. I didn't say, "Oh, you idiot, you screwed up." I'd just say, "What'd you learn? I told you why you shouldn't do that. You did it and what happened?"

While it taught her a lesson, I also think it killed her confidence a bit. So, I was doubly pissed. Had she won that race, it would've rocked the racing world. I don't know that there's ever been a female ARCA winner.

Certainly not in their first start.

As time went on, while I didn't change what I said on the radio to Erin, I did have to change how I said it. During the race, when I'd talk to Jeff about the car and how fast he could make it go, sometimes I'd say, "Man, that bitch is hauling ass!"

During one of Erin's early races, I was on the radio to the crew. Erin was just flying on the track. I got caught up in how well the car was performing. I hit the talk button and said, "Guys, we're in good shape. That bitch is hauling ass!"

Everybody turned to look at me. Debby Robinson, my PR rep, turned white as a ghost. Several in my crew made it clear, saying, "Dude, you can't say that anymore! You can't talk like that!"

We all started laughing, including Erin.

Erin and another female driver, Shawna Robinson, share the ARCA record for most poles and top-five finishes. Erin did win the ARCA Speedway Championship, which was a combination of about eleven or twelve races. She beat Frank Kimmel, a legendary ARCA racer, for that title.

There are many steps along the way to get to the Cup or Indy car level. In NASCAR, some used what was referred to as the A-B-C path to success. ARCA to Busch to Cup. Then the truck series became popular and added another pro-racing option.

Success at racing's highest level requires a lot more than getting in a car and driving fast. You have to know how to communicate the car's performance clearly and accurately to your crew. You need to study the drivers you're competing against. You have to know the processes and procedures of the race series you're competing in. Each is different.

You must also learn to deal with owners and sponsors. (A sponsor backing you for a hundred thousand dollars differs greatly from one supporting you with multimillions.)

Time management is especially crucial with all you have to do—plus you still require time to train physically and to run your life. Then when you're on the track you have to stay out of your head and keep focus. This is especially difficult for new drivers. They've most likely only watched these drivers race on TV. Now they're racing against them.

It takes more than talent to become a great racer at a high level. And every racer thinks differently.

For example, we were in Dover and Erin qualified well. She was an excellent qualifier in the stock cars and the truck. She struggled a little bit racing, but that's typical for a rookie driver with speed.

Early in the race, another driver spun her out and they got into a major crash involving several cars.

After the race, we were loading everything up, and I saw her off to the side with the hood of her sweatshirt pulled over her head, almost covering her face. I learned early on whenever she put her hood up, she was not in a good place.

I could see she was crying.

I thought, "Wow, okay. The only time I saw Jeff cry was when we won."

This was different for me. He'd cry when we won. If we wrecked, he'd want to fight somebody.

I realized she was questioning herself. That meant I had to have pep talks at the ready. Outwardly, Erin could appear supremely confident, bordering on stubborn at times. Inwardly, she could be insecure.

When Jeff got wrecked, I'd say, "Look, man, don't worry about it. We'll fix it. Screw that guy. Next week, we'll kick his ass and put him in the frigging wall!"

But with Erin, it was a much different conversation.

———

Erin attracted attention.

There were skeptics who thought female drivers were a novelty. "The girl's just a little something for the press to feed on," they'd snidely say.

Then suddenly, this "girl" wins the pole by six- or seven-tenths a second. Those naysayers started wondering what was going on. People started to think maybe there was more to this twenty-four-year-old.

In late 2005, Erin and I were spending more and more time together testing and racing. I really felt she could be "the one" female racer to break through. It would be such a huge feather in my cap. I thought with the right training, she could legitimately knock the racing world off its axis. She could be a legitimate contender. She just needed to win one of the Busch or truck races.

We also discovered we had things in common. We enjoyed talking about racing and different types of race cars. We also shared a love of sprint car racing. We were always at sponsor dinners, or on the road, or going to appearances together.

Our relationship grew to where the more I got to know her, the more I realized how mature she was. When she was racing, she was all business. Then when I'd go to pick her up for an event, I noticed her makeup, hair, clothes. She was totally different. I'd be thinking, "Is that the same person?" I started developing feelings for her.

I faced a life-altering dilemma that ate at me for weeks, months: the hard-hitting realization it was probably time to leave my marriage. I kept this to myself, unable to confide in anyone.

The weight of it nearly suffocated me. There was no family support to turn to, and most of my friends were my employees, leaving me with no one to talk to about it. Even if I did have someone to confide in, I wouldn't have known how to open up about it.

I kept going back and forth in my mind, trying to make sense of it all, summoning the courage to make the best decision.

It was also obvious to me that Mary was growing increasingly frustrated with me. She knew I was deliberately spending time away from home, and I couldn't deny it. I was avoiding our issues. I didn't want to confront the reality of my personal life. It was so much easier to be on the road, at the shop, anywhere but home. I could get on my plane, escape into my celebrity status, just do whatever made me happy, whenever I wanted.

But at home, I had a son that I loved that I wasn't spending time with, a wife struggling to cope, and I had to come to terms with the reality that I wasn't the king of the world. I was part of a family unit, and I was failing to meet my responsibilities.

Thankfully, Erin wasn't pressuring me, but a conversation we had toward the end of 2005 was a wake-up call. We had an open and honest discussion, and it was clear I had to face the truth about my situation. I needed to be honest with myself and my family before we could even think about taking our relationship further.

We both knew it was going to be painful, that it would have a significant impact on our careers. Still, I knew what had to be done.

Mary and I had a series of conversations over four agonizing days. She wasn't trying to talk me out of it, not by then anyway.

Once, between conversations, I remember locking myself in the bathroom and breaking down in tears, trying to figure it all out. It's not something you ever plan for or want to have happen, but sometimes life takes you down gut-wrenchingly unexpected paths. Many people think about getting divorced and moving on, but it was never so simple for me.

Emotionally, I wasn't ready to just walk away.

I didn't hate Mary, and I loved my son more than anything in the world. It was just that something wasn't right, and I couldn't ignore the feeling that I was missing something in my life. I wasn't genuinely happy, and I was constantly searching for something more. If I'd been fulfilled and content with my life, I wouldn't have wandered.

I took the plunge and left home between Christmas and New Year's 2005. I moved into a nearby apartment, hoping to be close to Ray J. during this challenging time. It was a tough adjustment, but it was the right thing to do.

My biggest concern was Ray J.'s adjustment to the changes in our family dynamic. Mary and I both talked to Ray J. about me leaving, but I don't think he fully understood it all at that point. I mean, I was gone a lot anyway, so it wasn't a huge change in our routine.

Then, months later, people began posting stuff on the internet and Ray J. had a couple of friends who weren't nice about it. They were saying things they'd heard from their parents, and that upset him. But as they say, "The enemy of any lie is time," and, now that time has passed, Ray J. understands the difference between truth and rumors.

I didn't walk away out of regret or guilt, but rather, because I needed to figure out who I was and what I wanted from life. I wasn't happy, and I didn't know why. It took time and effort to unlock the pieces, but in the end, I realized I didn't have to be a guy who turned his back on his ex-wife and son. I could still be part of their lives—and be happy on my own.

———

For the 2006 season, General Mills came on board with their Betty Crocker brand to sponsor Erin "Crocker" (no relation) for the full Craftsman Truck Series season, as well as five Busch Grand National races and some ARCA events.

Erin had a busy race schedule that was made up of almost forty events, so we traveled a lot together. Racing that many events in front of so many people, it was impossible for people not to see there was more to our relationship than owner-driver. Erin and I talked a good bit about it; neither of us were naïve to the consequences.

Certain members of the press were relentless in trying to be the first to break the big story, and it got pretty chaotic.

The Dodge people expressed concern, and I also discussed it with our other sponsors. Most in the business knew that, career-wise, nothing good would emerge from the situation. Betty Crocker and General Mills didn't renew their sponsorships after 2006, which I understood.

It wasn't just my marital situation, either. Erin's truck team hadn't performed to our expectations. I don't have any hard feelings toward anyone who had to back off because of it.

———

Everything happens for a reason. That whole situation opened up paths for a lot of people to become who they wanted to be.

Mary was freed from whatever was holding her back due to me. She got to live her own life, and she's grown so much as a person. The same goes for Erin.

Erin loved being a race car driver. Yet deep down, her long-term goal was always to have her own family. She wanted to be a mom.

Since I left, I feel like I've been able to handle everything better. I've become a better father and a better friend to Mary than I ever was as her husband. It might sound crazy to some, but my relationship with Mary and Ray J. has improved tenfold since I left.

Mary could've easily told me go to hell, but she's such an amazing woman. Unfortunately, in 2022 Mary was diagnosed with cancer. Even in her cancer battle, she never complained or made a fuss. Instead, she's always focused on others, like Ray J.

Mary knows I still care about her, and she still cares about me, too. I never disliked her, but I wasn't the same person she married.

Eventually, she came to terms with it all and realized we could either spend our lives hating each other or choose to be friends. We had great times when we were married, but things changed. It's like what happened with Jeff and me. Our relationship was great until it wasn't. Now it is again. With Mary, we decided to be friends instead of enemies.

I'm so grateful to still have Mary and Ray J. in my life. We're close and do things as one big family. We even share Christmas Eve and New Year's Eve dinners together.

———

Any regrets I have about how it all went down boil down to things I said or did that caused emotional distress to others—whether it was Mary, Ray J., Erin, or our families. It's hard to anticipate how much collateral emotional damage you can cause when you make a change like that.

If I could do it again, I'd try to be more aware of that. But in many ways, I think I handled this situation better than some other things in my life that I'm not proud of. I was honest and upfront, and I can look my daughter, Cate, and son, Ray J., in the eye and say, "This is how it happened."

One day, we'll need to face Cate and explain what really happened. She's already asked us about it. I recall when she was just five, she said to Erin, something like, "You're my mommy," and then, "Ray J.'s my brother. But Mary is Ray J.'s mommy. So, what is Mary to me?" Cate and Mary are close. It's important to clear things up for her.

One thing that's always concerned me is the age difference between me and Erin. It still does. It's been tough for me, and I think about it a lot.

But Erin and I talked it over many times, and she said it didn't bother her at all. I can't help but wonder what her brothers and her mom must have thought. I'm sure there was talk in her family she hasn't told me about. We knew that if we went through with this, there'd be a whole lot of drama, and we'd both have to handle our own issues. It meant so much to me that Erin's family accepted me unconditionally and with open arms.

If you'd told me before that I'd be married to someone twenty-three years younger and become a father again at fifty-eight, I'd have thought you were crazy. The same drive that pushed us to make the decision to be together might be what's made us successful. So, who's to say what's right or wrong in this world—just because it's not the usual way things are done?

Erin and I before the start of the NASCAR truck race at Daytona in 2006. *Ray Evernham Enterprises Archives*

CHAPTER 25

BATTLING FOR WINS

Sprints and More: 2005–2010

"Can you get Erin to sign this?"

As I was caught up in sorting out my personal life, I didn't realize a work relationship was unraveling. In 2002, I signed Jeremy Mayfield to replace Casey Atwood. I believed I'd made a smart decision. In his first year, he had four top tens and finished twenty-sixth in points. He improved in 2003, winning the pole at the Aaron's 499 and posting twelve top tens, finishing nineteenth in points.

In 2004 and 2005, Jeremy was fantastic, and I was proud of him. He won at Richmond, making it into the inaugural Chase for the Winston Cup, which was amazing.

But soon after, even though he won a race in 2005, Jeremy's team started to be a revolving door of crew chiefs and chief mechanics. These folks weren't getting fired; they were quitting or asking to be moved. It made me wonder if they didn't believe in him or if Jeremy was tough to work with.

In my experience, if a crew chief loses faith in a driver, they want to go.

By the end of 2005, Kasey Kahne was hitting his stride.

It was also when Jeremy's crew chief at the time, Slugger Labbe, and his race engineer told me they didn't want to race with Jeremy another year. At the same time, Kasey Kahne's crew chief, Tommy Baldwin, decided to move on and start his own team. We also had made a deal with Valvoline to become a partner on a third Cup team with Scott Riggs as the driver. It was the perfect time to restructure, so I proposed a new team format for everyone headed into the 2006 season. We held a team meeting, and everyone agreed with the new team structures going forward.

We hit the ground running in 2006, and, overall, it was my best year as a car owner. Kasey Kahne and his crew chief, Kenny Francis, pretty much dominated all the mile-and-a-half tracks.

Among them were both the spring and fall races at Charlotte Motor Speedway. For those of us who live in this area, the Charlotte track is a special place. I had a ton of success there with Jeff Gordon, winning poles and races, but to go there with my own team and sweep both races in 2006 gave me an incredible sense of accomplishment. It even provoked a phone call from Mr. Hendrick, saying something like, "Hey man, great job. You gave us a whooping." That kind of acknowledgement coming from somebody I respect so much meant a lot.

Kasey's win at Texas was significant because I'd never won there before. As crew chief for Jeff Gordon, I'd only competed there three times and, unfortunately, we crashed all three times. At that time, Texas was the only racetrack Jeff and I hadn't won at while we were together. Kasey taking me to Victory Lane there was special.

Add in the wins at Michigan, Atlanta, and Fontana, it was a hell of a good year!

Scott Riggs was having the best year of his career. He had secured two pole positions, he almost won at Charlotte, and he had two or three top fives and eight top tens.

But Jeremy Mayfield's performance started to dip, and despite all my efforts to help him succeed, we couldn't get him back to the front.

In July of that year, I was with Erin, running a Friday night truck race in Kentucky while my Cup teams were practicing in Chicago. One of my PR people called me and told me Jeremy had held a press conference near the hauler and was suggesting his team was suffering because of my relationship with Erin.

Man, I was pissed. After the truck race, I hopped on my plane to sort it out with him.

Confronting Jeremy, he was completely apologetic and denied everything. The next day, he spoke with the press again, and did a complete reversal.

He denied saying anything disparaging about Erin and me. He even spoke about how supportive I was of him. I was wondering, "What the hell is going on with this guy?" Meanwhile, the press was mad because of the contradictions, and I was just confused and disappointed.

I'd done everything I could to help him, and he was my friend, yet still he said all that stuff.

We tried to move past it, but if you look at the race results, Jeremy's performance was not on par with my other drivers.

It all came to a head at the Brickyard 400 in Indianapolis in August.

Jeremy was having a bad day and had crashed his car early. We repaired it and sent him back on track. We argued back and forth, and I was getting irritated. It seemed there was nothing I could do to fix the situation.

NASCAR was on me about him not making minimum speed. Finally, I just said, "That's it. Park it." As far as I was concerned, we were done for the day.

So, he drove it back to the garage.

I was furious and probably should have dealt with it myself. Instead, the next day, I called the folks at Dodge and got their permission to pull Jeremy out of the car. Then I sent my CFO to deliver the news to Jeremy. I was still pissed, and I didn't want a screaming match with Jeremy over what he'd said about Erin or anything else. We took him out of the car, and then he sued us to get back in.

It was about the money we would have owed him had he finished his contract, and the whole thing got ugly. In the end, I wanted Jeremy to do well because I genuinely liked him. I paid him and we moved on.

Bottom line: 2006 was a banner year for us with the most wins. So, his claim that my involvement with Erin was killing the company just didn't line up with reality. Although I can say I never saw any indication of him abusing drugs or alcohol when we were together, ultimately, NASCAR revoked his license after he tested positive for substance abuse.

Jeremy and I eventually managed to repair our relationship some-what. I even invited him to an SRX race.

I wanted to give him a shot in an SRX car; I thought it'd be a great story. I introduced him to everyone, saying he deserved a chance. But I got pushback from partners, sponsors, and the TV network.

Even with the Jeremy drama, my relationship with Erin continued evolving. Our relationship was a roller coaster. Both of us have strong personalities, so we'd be on again and off again. We broke up several times. One breakup lasted for three or four months. There was a lot of pressure around getting married, dealing with our families, and other issues.

Though Erin and I were hot and cold as a couple, she still worked for me, and that added another layer of complexity. In 2007, when I sold the majority of the company, we were no longer employer-employee and free to do whatever we wanted.

Thankfully, Erin was someone I could confide in when I realized being an owner just wasn't for me and started to look at selling the team. Between the stress of our relationship, the whole Jeremy situation, the changes at Dodge, and the physical and emotional toll of running three Cup teams, a truck team, an ARCA team, and a Busch team, I was getting worn down. Also, the company had grown so quickly, and I had so many more sponsor and business commitments, I wasn't spending as much time with my engineering staff as I used to, and if anything hurt our performance, it was that.

We took on so much, especially writing our own simulation, our own aero program, and tire data. It was overwhelming. We just didn't hit our stride in 2007. We were fast, but we couldn't replicate the success we had in 2006.

We might not have won a race in 2007, but in 2008 we came back and won two or three. Kasey Kahne even won the Coca Cola 600 that year, which was great. Even though I was a minority owner at that time, I took a lot of pride in the turnaround.

In 2009, weirdly enough, Erin and I were in one of our "off again" periods when we made the decision to get married. I hadn't spoken to her in weeks, so I decided to give her a call, but it didn't go through. Turns out, she'd blocked my number. Most guys would have taken the hint. Not me.

I used my assistant Ann's phone to call her. She picked up. She told me she was in Canada, racing a sprint car at Ohsweken Speedway.

I asked if she would talk to me if I came up to see her, and she agreed to talk but couldn't guarantee she wouldn't punch me.

I flew to Canada, going directly to the speedway. I didn't have a pass, so I had to talk my way in. Fortunately, the guy at the booth knew me. He took one look at the bouquet of flowers in my hand and joked I must have done something terrible.

Erin came and got me on a golf cart, and I watched her race. She did well that night. We drove back to her home in Massachusetts and talked the whole way. We discussed getting married and I suggested we make a pact to go to Vegas and have a small wedding.

I told her since we were both strong-headed and kept breaking up, it might actually be a good idea if we got married. I know that may sound like strange logic. My thinking was, if we committed to marriage, it might be harder for us to walk away. The truth was, I'd fallen in love with her. Even though we'd broken up a few times, we always found our way back to each other. I realized I couldn't imagine life without her.

Oddly enough, my "logic" worked, and Erin said, "Yes."

We insisted on having a small wedding, just her and me, our siblings, and our parents. No cousins, no aunts, no uncles.

We had a beautiful wedding. Ray J. and my brother Willy were my "best men" and Erin's sisters, Terry and Becky, were her "maids of honor."

Our good friends Brendan and Michael Gaughan at the South Point Casino in Las Vegas made it an amazing experience for us, but it was a tiny affair. We joked that there were more people in the band than at the wedding itself.

Believe it or not, Erin and I spent our honeymoon weekend in Knoxville, Iowa, where Erin was scheduled to race a sprint car. We left the South Point Hotel in Las Vegas, where we were wearing swimsuits and shorts and sipping champagne, and hopped on a plane to Knoxville.

When we got there, it was a chilly fifty degrees so on our way to the track we had to go to the local Walmart and buy warmer clothes.

And of course, the first thing I did was lose my wedding ring while changing gears in her sprint car. I never found it. Actually, I lost my original ring *and* the replacement I bought. One fell off when I was changing gears, the other I left on a sink when I took it off to wash my hands at the track.

Yup, two rings gone in three weeks.

Accompanying Erin to the sprint races was humbling for me. She was like royalty, and I was just Erin Crocker's husband. I recall this one time after a race at Knoxville, Erin was standing at the back of the trailer with a line of twenty or thirty people waiting to get her autograph.

I was putting tires away or something and this kid, probably around twelve or thirteen years old, comes up and asks, "Hey, are you Ray Evernham?"

"Who's Ray Evernham?" I jokingly replied.

"You know? The guy that's married to Erin Crocker?"

I told the kid, "Yeah, I'm Ray Evernham."

"Cool. Can you get Erin to sign this?"

And that's when it hit me. I wasn't the NASCAR champion to these people. I was just the guy married to Erin Crocker.

Erin and I talked often about her wanting to be a mom and have a family.

We had been married for six years when we were finally blessed that it happened.

We found out our baby's sex through a gender reveal party. We had someone deliver a pink or blue Bundt cake and invited Ray J. to share in the moment. It was important to both of us for Ray J. to be involved and to know we were all one family. When we discovered it was pink for a girl, we were thrilled—Erin, Ray J., and me.

During the pregnancy, I would talk to Erin's belly and call the baby by the name we decided on, Cate. I'd also play oldies music like the Beach Boys and Beatles for our growing baby.

The instant Cate was born, they had to rush her away to clear some mucus from her throat. They let me into the room where they were taking care of her, and a nurse offered to take a picture of us together for the first time. I leaned over Cate and said her name, and she lifted her head, opened her eyes wide, and looked right at me. The nurse captured that special moment.

She said she had never seen anything like it before.

In that instant, I was completely wrapped around Cate's finger. Now all she has to do is look at me, and I'm done for.

I have felt for a long time that I could have been a better father to Ray J. but just didn't know how. I wanted to do better this time, but I was scared. Having a baby is one of those doors you can't close once opened. It's a lifelong commitment. It comes with much responsibility and no instructions.

Frankly, I was also nervous about being an older dad. I was fifty-eight when Cate was born. I wondered if I'd be an embarrassment to my child. I'd be the same age as all her friends' grandfathers.

Erin put things in perspective, reminding me none of us know how long we'll live. She lost her dad when she was only sixteen. She said all we can do is make the most of our time with our daughter and create wonderful memories.

Cate has become the glue for our extended family. She keeps Erin and me in line, especially given our battles, and has brought Ray J. ever closer to us. I think she's even given Mary some peace, knowing that Ray J. has a connection to a sibling. He adores his little sister.

Looking back on that time, it was more than the turmoil of Jeremy, Erin, and the divorce. Psychologically, emotionally, it felt like I was in a room with a hundred doors, and behind each one was something I had to handle. I'd learned to compartmentalize, almost too well. It was overwhelming, and I often think about how I could have done things differently.

I was exhausted by everything happening in my life and by all the uncertainties. To offer another analogy, it was like opening a series of Pandora's boxes, where once you open a door, you can't shut it and ignore it. What was behind some of those doors took me years to deal with.

The uncertainty and chaos of it all, along with facing new challenges and trying to maintain my perfectionist attitude, made it tough. I had to figure out the difference between who I wanted to be, who the world expected me to be, and what I believed to be right or wrong.

Navigating that period of my life was overwhelming. But looking back, I'm proud of how I managed to handle it all. I took on so much, it's amazing to think about how big everything got in such a short period of time. I still find myself taking on big projects but with much more caution.

I didn't walk away from any of those challenges, leaving them to someone else. I faced each one and tied up every loose end. I can't say I did it alone, I had plenty of help, but I didn't abandon my responsibilities.

In the end, I feel like the people I love the most—Erin, Cate, Ray J., and Mary—are in a good place. The fans who supported me for so many years still back me because I've been honest with them. The ones that hate me will keep hating, and that's okay, too.

Erin's Baja team on the gas with 1,000 miles to go.
Ray Evernham Enterprises Archives

CHAPTER 26

OUT OF OUR ELEMENT

The Baja 1000: 2007

"What in the hell have we gotten ourselves into?"

T he continent's oldest and most prestigious off-road race—the Baja 1000—had its fortieth anniversary in 2007. To commemorate the milestone, television and film producer Bud Brutsman collaborated with BF Goodrich Tires to build a unique race team and produce a feature-length documentary film about the event titled *Chasing Baja*. They wanted to include a female driver and asked Erin to test for it.

It was a whole new experience for her. She had never been to Mexico, and she had never been behind the wheel of the Baja buggy, the cool little car built specifically for the desert race.

The test was as bumpy as it gets. In one section, she flipped her buggy, but she was so fast, they invited her back to race the 1,296-mile punishing, yet picturesque Baja peninsula course.

Erin would compete with about 350 entrants representing forty states and fifteen countries across eighteen pro and sportsman classes for cars, trucks, and buggies, plus additional classes for motorcycles and ATVs.

Team BF Goodrich consisted of four drivers split into two teams. Erin was partnered with Tracy Jordan, a rock-crawling pioneer who holds several championship titles in that sport and was also an off-road racing veteran, competing in the Baja 1000 in 2004 and 2006.

Brutsman, the creator and executive producer for *Celebrity Rides* and *Hot Rod TV*, along with The Learning Channel's *Overhaulin'* and *Rides*, also had two previous Baja 1000 races to his credit. He shared driving duties with retired US Navy SEAL turned off-road enthusiast Bill

Weber, who worked as a consultant for several off-road motorsports-related companies, supporting vehicle development and training, and was a two-time class winner of the Baja 1000.

I joined Erin for the trip, but being a Goodyear guy, I wanted to stay behind the scenes. While Erin and her partner drove the buggy through the desert, I drove the chase truck on the roads to meet up with them at the designated checkpoints along the way.

Race officials advised me and the other chase truck drivers to pay attention and obey all the local speed limits. It didn't take long for me to learn that was all bullshit. Everybody was just going as fast as they needed to so they could keep up with the race car and not cause any delay.

We had to be really careful. In some ways it was just as dangerous to be flying down dark, narrow rural roads in the chase vehicle as it was to be racing the buggy in the desert. Especially the truck I was driving. It was a big old Ford Bronco with a huge engine, but the steering box had so much play that when you turned the wheel it didn't respond immediately. For the first half hour, I was all over the road.

Instead of chase trucks, some teams used helicopters. A helicopter chasing one of the cars, supposedly financed by a cartel, crashed. We heard the whole incident on the radio as it unfolded. We found out later, for some reason, someone didn't want anyone to know the pilot died in the crash, so they went to get the body from the morgue and ended up in a shootout.

What in the hell have we gotten ourselves into?

Like Erin, I had never raced Baja, so I didn't know what to expect. And I sure as hell didn't expect what happened to us in the very early hours of the first morning.

It was around 2:00 a.m. and I was hauling butt in the chase truck. The cameraman was in the back sleeping. The BF Goodrich guy was in the front passenger seat slumped against the door trying to nap. I was probably running close to a hundred miles an hour, wide awake just trying to keep the Bronco on the road, when suddenly, these big blinding lights glared right at me through the windshield.

Like a deer in headlights, I slowed and noticed an army Jeep parked across the road ahead with a 50-caliber machine gun mounted on it. Standing guard next to it were three guys shouldering automatic rifles. Keeping my eyes on the guys and their guns, I reached over and nudged the BF Goodrich guy.

"Hey, man, we've got a problem here." He straightened up, rubbed his eyes, looked out the windshield, and calmly reached into the glove box. He took out an envelope. I watched him flip through a stack of cash stuffed inside.

"Here," he said, "hand this to them."

I pulled up to the Jeep and nervously handed the envelope to one of the guys. He opened it and gave me a look that left me with the distinct impression he was not happy to see me. But then he climbed in the Jeep, pulled it out of the way, and we got the hell out of there. I thought, "Well, welcome to Mexico."

As crazy as it sounds, driving through rural Mexico in the middle of the night is an incredible experience. There's zero light pollution and the sky is breathtaking. You can see planets and the Milky Way, and the whole sky is densely packed with stars. It was like being on a different planet. It's a sight that makes you want to say, "Hey, thank you, God, that was pretty cool."

Besides the night sky, one of the coolest things I saw were the trophy trucks. They are impressive racing vehicles. Equipped with NASCAR-style engines and incredible suspensions, they are engineering marvels tearing through the desert at 120, 130 miles per hour and capable of jumping twenty feet in the air and landing like a marshmallow. I'd be waiting for Erin at a checkpoint in the middle of the night and hear the distinct roaring engine of a trophy truck. Then I'd see lights that looked like a UFO and one of those trucks would come flying through the air, land, and be out of sight in a heartbeat.

At one point, according to our plan, we were supposed to be about eleven minutes behind Erin's car. But after a night of me driving pretty quickly we both hit the checkpoint at the same time. Their original math was correct. We should have been eleven minutes behind if we had followed the speed limit.

The BF Goodrich rep looked at me and said, "Holy shit. How fast were you going?"

In addition to our chase truck, there were vans that carried a pit crew with fuel, tires, and parts. They would run ahead and set up pit areas. When the cars pulled in for a pit stop, they added fuel, repaired any damage, and changed drivers.

The race was all about how long it would take to travel from one city to another. Team BF Goodrich expected to finish in about twenty-four to twenty-six hours. However, Bill Webber and Bud Brutsman crashed while running in second place less than one hundred miles from the finish line. Luckily, nobody got seriously hurt, and they managed to fix the car in the desert and continue driving it to Cabo. As a result, our race lasted closer to thirty-two hours, and I was ready to get the hell out of there.

Looking back, it was a good experience. While Erin's team didn't have a great finish, they did a hell of a good job. Erin did a great job as well. She followed directions, she didn't overdrive the car or put it in danger, and she hit all the checkpoints on time.

I wish she could have gotten more opportunities like that in her driving career.

Personally, I thought participating in the race was an amazing experience, and I would have loved to have been one of the drivers. However, I have my doubts about ever going back to Baja. Besides, I'm not sure if my back and neck would survive driving one thousand miles through the desert.

Me tuning the engine on Erin's sprint car at Knoxville in 2010. *Ray Evernham Enterprises Archives*

CHAPTER 27

SHORT-TRACK SAGAS

World of Outlaws and More: 2010–2012

"I've always loved sprint cars."

I've had a longtime fascination with sprint car racing. In 2010, I started a sprint car team for Erin to race in some World of Outlaws events and take a shot at qualifying for the Knoxville Nationals. I also thought that would be a great time for me to finally get behind the wheel of a sprint car.

Sprint cars are beasts. There are three basic divisions of sprint cars. The entry level division has cars with 305-cubic-inch engines and about 500 horsepower. Next up are the cars with 360-cubic-inch engines and about 700 horsepower. The top-class cars have 410-cubic-inch engines with 850 horsepower. Erin, being a World of Outlaws sprint car driver, would race in the 410 division. Never having driven a sprint car, I was going to start out in the 305 class.

I traded one of my motorcycles for a used sprint car a few weeks before the start of the season. We had planned on testing and practicing so I could learn how to drive it. Unfortunately, the practice sessions got rained out. There wasn't enough time to reschedule before we left for Knoxville, Iowa, in June so my first time behind the wheel was going to be among the veteran drivers at Knoxville Raceway.

As luck would have it, I ran a few laps of practice on the track, my car burned a piston, and I was out for a while. My buddy Wayne Johnson talked another owner into letting me drive his car.

At that time, drivers drew for starting positions, and I drew the pole for the heat race. Just before the race started, the guy who had loaned me his car was chatting with Erin. "He's going to be okay, right?" he asked her.

"Well, we'll see," she replied.

His face shifted to a look of concern, "He's driven sprint cars a lot, right?"

Erin answered, "No. He hasn't."

His brow furrowed. "How many times has he raced in sprint?"

"This'll be his first," she responded, and the guy turned white as a ghost.

Despite his concern, I did fairly well and got to cross driving a sprint car off my bucket list. I had a lot of fun racing in the 305 series at Knoxville, but we were there to focus on Erin qualifying for the Knoxville Nationals, the biggest sprint car race in the country.

Sprint car racers come from all over the world for that race. There are normally around 150 cars, narrowed down to a field of twenty-four. The week before the main event, they run a race called the 360 Nationals for the 360-cubic-inch cars. Many drivers use this as a warm-up for the Knoxville Nationals. We entered Erin for the same reason.

At the start of her heat race, she broke an axle and took a horrible series of end-over-end flips, destroying the car and beating her up pretty badly. The car's axle broke going into the corner. It was not her fault.

Fortunately, we had three days for Erin to heal up and get ready for the big race. While she recovered, we built a brand-new car right there at the speedway. Brooke Tatnell, a well-known World of Outlaws driver, helped us get the car set up. We took it to a race on Monday night at a track in neighboring Oskaloosa, Iowa. Brooke ran fifth in the car and dialed it in for Erin.

At the Knoxville Nationals they have so many cars trying to qualify for the A-main that they have to split qualifying into multiple nights. First-round qualifying was scheduled for Wednesday and Thursday. On Friday night, they ran some support races then final qualifying. The big race was on Saturday.

I was Erin's crew chief and decided that we would make our qualifying attempt on Wednesday. Our crew consisted of my nephew Willie, Danny Bohn from my shop, and our only sprint car veteran mechanic, Ray Brooks. We also got some help from our engine builder Paul Kistler. Erin, being a great qualifier, turned a lap fast enough in single-car qualifying that she placed ninth out of 128 cars. That lap put us in a good position to run our qualifying heat race.

She finished in the top six in the heat race and then had a top-ten finish in her Wednesday night main event, earning enough points to lock us into the big show on Saturday. I was so proud of her. Erin is the only female driver ever to qualify for the Knoxville Nationals. She did it twice, once in 2004, when she was driving for someone else, and once in 2010, when she drove our car.

To put her accomplishment into context, to a stock car racer, there's the Daytona 500. To an Indy car racer, there's the Indianapolis 500. To road racers, there's the 24 Hours of Daytona. To sprint car racers, there is the Knoxville Nationals.

We went there on our own, with Erin driving a car that I was crew chiefing, and we did it in our first attempt. I look at it as one of our biggest accomplishments, and it is one of the jewels of my career.

As the season wound down, we participated in one more sprint car race. It was a 360-cubic-inch sprint race at Carolina Raceway in Gastonia, North Carolina.

It was the only time Erin and I got to race together, which was really cool. Even cooler was Erin won the race and I finished sixth. What wasn't so cool was on the last lap, Erin was lapping me as she crossed the start-finish line; she says she was giving me extra room, and I say she was waving to me. Either way, she hit the wall and her car tumbled into the air and out of the speedway. The racing headlines said, "Husband and Wife Crash at Start-Finish Line. Wife Wins." We laugh about it now, but it wasn't very funny then.

After making our successful sprint car debut in 2010, I got the itch to race some more in 2011. Erin decided that she was not going to race anymore because you cannot race at her level part-time and be competitive. She had already been through all the stages I was trying to go through. While it was new and fun for me, Erin had raced with the World of Outlaws and was the only woman ever to win a World of Outlaws main event. (That was in 2003 and no other woman has done it since.)

So, Erin and I decided we would go run my car up and down the East Coast. We planned to hit some tracks in New Jersey, Virginia, and Pennsylvania. I could get in some dirt racing, and we could see friends, family, and people I used to race with along the way. It was a lot of birds to hit with one stone, but we were going to have a blast.

We had hired a mechanic, Scott Fisher, to be the crew chief on our sprint cars. Primarily, he was hired to work on Erin's car, but for this trip he was going to be my crew chief.

Our first race was scheduled in New Jersey at New Egypt Speedway, but we were rained out. The next day: September 10, 2011. That's right, the date was nine, ten, eleven. I'll never forget it.

We pulled into a track in South Jersey called Bridgeport Speedway. The night's race lineup included dirt modifieds, dirt late models, and my class: the 305 sprint cars.

As we were unloading and setting up our work area, the evening had sort of an odd feel to it. I can't really explain it. It just seemed strange and disorganized.

The track announcer gave starting instructions over the loudspeaker, "Okay, you can't push off till five thirty p.m." (Sprint cars don't have starters; they have to be push started.) He also said that cars could only push off in one direction.

But then shortly after the announcement, I started hearing motors running and I saw cars crisscrossing behind my trailer. I thought, what in the hell? It was only around five o'clock. They weren't supposed to start for another thirty minutes.

Scott was down changing the left-rear tire when I walked up and stood by the left-front tire. I was trying to tell him we needed to drop the wing down because the track was big, and I wanted to have more straightaway speed. (Dropping the wing in the back would make the car go faster on the track's longer straightaways.)

Scott was standing there listening to me, when suddenly I heard an engine running and it was getting louder, like it might be headed in our direction.

Out of nowhere, an out-of-control sprint car was coming right at us with its motor racing.

Before I could get a single word out to warn him, the car hit him, crushing him between the two cars. The impact was so violent it flung our car into the air. In an instant, everything was gone. I watched as Scott was being dragged backward. His legs were caught underneath the front of the car, leaving his torso bouncing on the hood.

I chased after him, but the driver panicked and kept his foot on the throttle.

Finally, Scott rolled out from underneath the speeding car. I could see his legs were horribly mangled. "What the fuck was that?" he said as he looked up at me.

Blood was shooting out of Scott's mutilated legs, so I ran to get a tourniquet. I realized he may not live long enough for me to get to the truck and back.

I ran back to him and with my hands I grabbed the area around where I saw the most blood squirting out and squeezed as hard as I possibly could to slow the bleeding. All I was seeing was blood, bone, muscle, and veins. It's a gruesome image that has never left me.

My brother Willie took off his shirt and rolled it into a tourniquet. I yelled for people to bring us their tie-down straps, the cords we all used to tie the cars down to the trailers.

We wrapped them around his legs and cranked them down as much as we could. We still couldn't get the bleeding to stop. I was sure I was watching my friend die.

Fortunately, a couple of combat vets ran over to help. One guy put his knee right in Scott's groin, knowing that's where the artery was.

Scott wasn't sure why the guy was kneeing him in his crotch, and he said, "What the hell are you doing?" The guy looked Scott straight in the eye and said, "I'm saving your life, buddy. I'm saving your life."

Then it occurred to me, where the hell was the ambulance?

"We need an ambulance," I kept shouting. They were just moving too damn slow for my liking.

The safety protocols were atrocious. The accident should never have happened in the first place. It seemed like we were getting zero cooperation from the organizers, and I was getting pissed. Believe it or not, at one point, the guy in charge of the race that night was arguing with me. I was stunned by his lack of empathy. Then he actually started yelling at me. I was down on my knees, my left hand holding Scott's hand, but I still took a swing at him with my right. Luckily, I couldn't reach him because I was on the ground. If I would've hit him, they'd have needed another ambulance. Things were just completely out of control.

The guy driving the car that night wasn't qualified to drive it. He didn't know how to drive it, didn't even know how to shut it off. He panicked.

On top of it all, that dipshit driver never even bothered to come over to see how Scott was doing or offer an apology. Instead, he got out of his car, ran to his pit area, and immediately left the track.

Again, I thought we were just watching Scott die. He was bleeding on the ground for almost twenty minutes before the first EMT showed up. But he stayed conscious the whole time. Scott's one of the toughest guys I know. The pain must have been excruciating because he was squeezing my hand so hard it turned white and numb.

Experiences like that change you. The expression, "There but for the grace of God, go I" becomes all too real. Any one of us could have been standing where Scott was. Me, Erin, Willie, or Willie's son, Willie Jr., who normally was part of our crew but skipped that race to attend a friend's wedding. Scott was doing Willie Jr.'s job changing the tire that night. He was standing where Willie Jr. might have been standing.

Once the ambulance arrived, they quickly put Scott inside and headed to the nearest hospital. I turned and saw Scott's brother Doug holding a towel to his head. Doug's another big tough guy like Scott. Apparently, Doug was standing on the other side of my car and got hit by the wing, splitting his head open. He ended up having to get staples in his head to close the gash.

After Scott was on his way to the hospital, I called Ann, who was my assistant at that time, and arranged a flight for Scott's wife, Angie. I remember talking to Angie on the phone. She said, "Be honest with me, Ray, how is he?" I said, "He's hurt bad, but he's alive." I added, "His legs are in bad shape."

Scott was taken to this awful hospital in Camden, New Jersey. But it was the closest trauma center to the track, and for Scott's sake, that's all that mattered. The place was so bad, the police warned us we'd probably get robbed if we stepped outside.

Angie arrived around midnight. She walked in, stopped to see us briefly, then headed straight upstairs to meet with Scott's doctors.

About an hour or so later, she came back down to the waiting room. She looked at me and said, "His leg is gone." Then she started to cry.

Scott recovered. He had a long legal battle, which is a reminder of how critical it is to read and fully understand all the qualifying language of those pit sign-in sheets.

Eventually, he was fitted with a prosthetic leg, and in the spring of 2023, I had the pleasure of watching him walk his daughter down the aisle and dance with her at her wedding. It was an amazing and emotional sight.

September 10, 2011, is a night I will never forget. It's all part of the flow of the trophies and scars in life.

You get the trophies for accomplishments like winning a feature at Wall Stadium, or the Daytona 500, or a championship, or winning Pike's Peak. Victories change you. They affect your perspective on life.

Unfortunately, so do the traumatic things you go through. They can also have a lasting effect on your life. Bad things happen, but those scars prepare you for when the next bad thing occurs. They strengthen your tolerance for physical and emotional pain.

Half the time, it sends me into this whole frigging quandary where I try to figure out the universe and why things like that happen.

Emergencies can either bring out the best of humanity or really rock your faith in your fellow man. For me, nine-ten-eleven was a little bit of both.

I continued to race the 305-cubic-inch car and did well with it. We were having a lot of fun.

My sprint car career was another one of those things I wanted to do purely to see if I could get good at it. I actually won seven of the 305-class races, and I won the last time that I drove in 2012.

I felt like making the Knoxville Nationals and us running our own sprint cars on a part-time basis validated my driving and mechanical abilities. I was satisfied to walk away and move on to something else.

Bob Jenkins, Benny Parsons, and me broadcasting for ABC Sports at the Brickyard 2000. *Ray Evernham Enterprises Archives*

CHAPTER 28

BIG SCREEN DAYS

Television Appearances: 2000s

"Crew chief turned team owner turned TV personality?"

I've always thought of myself as a performer. Ask anyone who knows me, and they'll testify it's hard for me to resist an open mic and a great karaoke song.

So, when Jill Fredrickson, a sports producer working for ESPN, approached me about doing on-camera commentary for their NASCAR broadcasts in 2000 I jumped at the opportunity. I'm the Forrest Gump of motorsports, sometimes being at the right place at the right time is everything.

How else does a racer turned crew chief, turned team owner, with no real broadcasting background, end up in the booth with the Mount Rushmore of racing broadcasters: Bob Jenkins, Benny Parsons, Allen Bestwick, and Mike Joy? The greats.

Jill, who later became senior vice president, Production and Content Strategy for ESPN, said they'd love to have my viewpoint and I could do commentary for as many races as my schedule would permit.

"Let's do it!" was my answer.

I didn't even ask how much they'd pay me. I was sure it'd be something, but we'd work out the details later.

Money aside, I also knew having my face on TV could aid with getting sponsors for my team and help promote everything else I was doing.

I've always loved a team culture. That was one of the best things about working with ESPN. They had a great team of smart and dedicated people.

And I took the whole experience seriously. Like a coach who views game film, I'd watch back the shows I was on, studying them to find ways I could improve. I set a goal to get better every broadcast.

I also used to love watching former drivers like Sam Posey, Bobby Unser, and Jackie Stewart commentating and analyzing races. I thought Sam was especially eloquent in his word choice. They all made it look so fun and easy. Still, I knew there'd be a learning curve.

Back then, ESPN also broadcast NASCAR truck races. To provide me with more experience, Jill paired me with announcer Marty Reid for the Daytona race. A true pro, Marty guided me on how to stay out of trouble.

My first time doing live TV, Marty offered pointers. "Always assume the mic's on. Watch what you say, even when we're in a break. And don't stare at the racetrack. Look at your monitor. That's what the audience sees."

I managed to keep my nerves in check, and things were going well. Until Geoff Bodine, who I've raced with, against, and have been friends with for years, crashed on the front straightaway. His truck just disintegrated horribly.

Silent, I sat there thinking, "I just watched one of my friends die."

Luckily, Marty took over.

My eyes were glued to the monitor. Then I saw Geoff's hand move and brought that to Marty's attention.

Marty shot me a look and shook his head. He didn't want me to say something that may not be true. On live television, in a situation like that, facts matter.

We didn't know how badly Geoff was hurt. Naturally, I was preoccupied by the crash the whole time we were on-air. It wasn't until the end of the broadcast that we learned he was awake, a good sign. Thank God he recovered completely.

Once it was over, I was exhausted yet exhilarated. My adrenaline surged throughout it all. Take my word for it, there's much more that goes on in the booth than you see on TV.

Besides talking about what's happening on-track, you're hearing all the crosstalk and directions from the producer and director in your headset. You have to separate all that from the on-air conversation you're having with the play-by-play host.

All that said, I enjoyed the experience and the challenge of that first broadcast. I'm glad ESPN put me with great people like Marty Reid for my first event.

ESPN must've thought I did a good job because next they paired me with Bob Jenkins and Benny Parsons, top play-by-play guys in auto racing. Benny not only enjoys the distinction of being the 1973 NASCAR Winston Cup champion and Daytona 500 winner, he's also the dude who . . . taught me how to put on my TV makeup.

Yes, that's what I said, Benny Parsons gave me makeup lessons.

Seriously, though, I had a blast working with Benny. He was hilarious. Here I was constantly worried about my choice of words and grammar, and B. P. would just flat-out make up words.

I'd call him on it, too, if I caught him. I'd say, "That's not a word!"

He'd come right back, "Oh, it's absolutely a word and I'm using it."

On Saturdays as we were winding down our broadcast, Benny was already worrying about where we would eat. He always knew "the best place" in town for barbecue, steak, burgers, and fries—whatever he craved.

Then on Sundays, to beat folks to the airport, Benny had a "secret" way out of every racetrack. That might involve going the wrong way down a lane of traffic, with cops yelling at us, and other drivers giving us the finger.

Once at Talladega, we cut through a pasture. Cows just stared at us as we drove right past them. We might get to the airport only five minutes ahead of everybody, but it was vital to Benny we were there first.

My limited TV schedule in 2000 let me know doing TV was something I would really like to do in the future, but in 2001 I had a full-time job as a team owner waiting for me. TV would have to wait.

As the sale of my race teams was progressing, I restarted my conversations with ESPN about coming back to be part of their NASCAR broadcasts. My old friend Jill Fredrickson introduced me to Rich Feinberg, who was leading ESPN's NASCAR program. Turns out Rich was a Jersey boy, too, and we hit it off immediately.

Rich put me with first-class broadcaster Allen Bestwick, former NBA star and NASCAR Cup team co-owner Brad Daugherty, Cup racing champion Rusty Wallace, and Dr. Jerry Punch. We had a frickin' blast.

Allen is a longtime friend and a true professional. Rusty is a personality with little to no filter, armed with a wealth of racing knowledge from his storied career. Brad Daugherty is seven feet of the funniest guy I've ever worked with.

Most times we'd barely regain our composure coming back from commercial due to something Brad did or said during the break. Often, he'd wait until we were just about to return before he'd pull off some hilarious stunt or joke.

For example, I'd hear the floor manager counting down, "seven, six, five . . ." and Brad would just kick his seat back, throw his arms up, and in an exaggerated accent would say, "Oh my gahd, I'm starvin' to death! You not feedin' yo people. Cain't somebody feed me?!"

"two . . . one!"

I'd be trying not to lose it as we came back on camera.

Before the days of universal Zoom calls, he perfected the art of wearing a shirt, tie, and jacket on the top half of his body—with basketball shorts below. He never wore long pants in the studio. He was so much fun.

———

In the TV world, like most work environments, you must know your place. Play your role. For my part, I considered myself the team builder and motivator.

My method? Tequila.

We were in Phoenix for a race. I rented a limo to take us all to a cool cowboy steakhouse way up in the hills outside of town. We got the party started with champagne on the way there.

At the restaurant, I ordered tequila shots for everybody. We were all pouring it back, eating great steaks—I mean, we were having a blast.

After enough tequila and steak, we were headed for the exit and the band started playing a song I knew. I leapt on stage, grabbed the microphone, and started singing along. Next thing I knew, the rest of my crew jumped up there to sing with me.

We may or may not have had too much to drink, but, thankfully, we didn't have to be on air till 11:00 the next morning. When we rolled into the speedway, we were hurting. We all grabbed bottles of water. Our boss, Rich Feinberg, seeing how hungover we looked, just grinned, and said, "Good luck today."

The time I spent working with ESPN, both at-track and in-studio, were some of the most fun and educational times of my career, especially traveling to ESPN's headquarters in Bristol, Connecticut, for Sports Center. For my younger family members who weren't into racing, my being on Sports Center made me "somebody" to them.

Unfortunately, when the NASCAR television contract came up for renewal, ESPN opted out and the team was disbanded. I keep hoping every day when the phone rings that it's Rich or Jill calling to say, "Hey, we are putting the band back together. How soon can you be here?"

―――――

My next TV venture was a show I created called, *AmeriCarna*, a play on the word, "Americana," which mean things typical of America. I've always believed the automobile documents the timeline of American history as well as our own personal history.

I'll bet if you go back and look through your family photo album, you'll find at least one picture of someone standing by a car. In my family's album we have dozens of pictures with one of our cars in the background.

When I was growing up, cars meant freedom. They represented our social status, our personality, and our style. I have tons of memories linked to various cars. My first date, drive-in movies, racing with my friends. I don't know of many people that have an emotional attachment to their phone or their iPad, but there are plenty of people that have an emotional attachment to their car.

So as much as *AmeriCarna* was about cars, it was really more of a lifestyle show for car guys like me.

Back then, I was a big fan of an automotive-focused network owned by Discovery called, Velocity. When it came time to sell *AmeriCarna* to a network, my vice president Det Cullum and I pitched the show to Velocity's general manager Bob Scanlon.

Bob's a super sharp guy. He loved the concept and green-lit us. It didn't hurt that the founder and chairman of Discovery, a man named John Hendricks, happened to be related to Rick Hendrick. With Rick Hendrick being part of the show, it was kind of a slam dunk. Rick brought a wealth of knowledge, a hell of a car collection, and a star-studded list of friends we invited on as guests.

Rick knew being on TV could provide a boost to his car business.

Rick had a spot in every show. We set him up as our resident expert. At some point in a segment, I'd go, "Well, let's check in with Mr. H and see what he has to say about it."

I also counted on Pam Miller when getting the show together. I've known Pam for more than thirty years and she's an experienced producer. (Pam has been the producer on FOX's NASCAR race coverage for a number of years.) She was instrumental in creating and producing *AmeriCarna*.

―――――

Being a huge Elvis Presley fan, one of the most fun and memorable *AmeriCarna* episodes was one we did from the King's Memphis home, Graceland. You could say I was raised on Elvis. His music constantly played in our house.

To my mom, the man was a God.

The Elvis episode all started when a Charlotte, North Carolina, area car expert, Walt Hollifield, called to say, "Hey, I have a great idea for one of your *AmeriCarna* shows."

He then told me he was working on one of Elvis's cars and asked if I'd like to see it. "Hell, yes, I would!"

I drove down to Walt's place and, sure enough, he had one of Elvis's Stutz Blackhawks—rumored to be the last car Elvis ever drove.

(Elvis competed with Frank Sinatra to buy the first Blackhawk for sale on October 9, 1970, for $26,500, approximately $192,000 in 2023 dollars.) It was actually the second prototype built. Company founder James O'Donnell drove the first. Elvis would eventually own four Blackhawks.

After we shot footage of Walt with the Blackhawk, I thought to myself, "Let's go to Graceland to see Elvis's other vehicles."

The folks there couldn't have been nicer. I'd been to Graceland a couple times before, but not on this kind of a tour. While there, I met a groundskeeper who suggested we see the stuff in the warehouse.

I was like, "Excuse me? Warehouse?"

I asked Graceland archivist Angie Marchese about it.

To my surprise, she said, "Follow me."

It was amazing. Whatever wasn't on display in Graceland's various exhibits was carefully stored here: personal possessions like Elvis's clothes, costumes, jewelry, furniture, even years of Christmas cards from his manager, Colonel Tom Parker. Everything and anything you can imagine.

Apparently, he didn't throw anything away.

For our purposes, the coolest thing we discovered was Elvis's 1948 Chevy panel truck. It wasn't in the best shape. As it was explained to me, this truck was how Elvis managed to leave Graceland undetected.

Most fans expected him to exit from the ornate front gates in a Cadillac, Stutz, or on a motorcycle. But if he wanted to go incognito, he'd don a ball cap and a jacket and drive this truck out a back way. Etched into its dashboard, in his own handwriting, were dial numbers of radio stations he liked best.

Never in a million years would I have ever thought I'd be standing in a place surrounded by Elvis Presley's most personal possessions. Once again, I felt like Forrest Gump, wondering how in the hell I got there.

———

We had a lot of great guest appearances on *AmeriCarna*. Brad Paisley was one for sure. A real car guy and a friend of Mr. Hendrick, he came on to discuss cars and guitars, both topics near and dear to Mr. H.

I was thrilled to have Mike Love, Beach Boys lead singer and songwriter, as a guest. As we walked around a car show, Mike told me story after story of what inspired him to compose some of their car-themed classics like "409," "Little Deuce Coupe," or "Fun, Fun, Fun."

We also had the coolest man on the planet as a guest: Don Prudhomme. I love Don Prudhomme. He was an incredible drag racer. He was fast as hell coming off the starting line and that earned him the nickname "Snake." Don is such a diplomat he could probably end the wars in the Middle East if they all just hung out with him for a little while.

A smooth, caring person, he seems to know everybody. But I always warn guys: don't ever leave your wife or girlfriend around him. They don't call him the "Snake" just because of his driving. He's a charmer.

All kidding aside, Don's a fantastic guy, salt of the earth.

We also did memorable episodes with Dan Gurney and Mario Andretti. Dan and Mario are major celebrities to hardcore car guys like me. Being with Mario is like being with the Pope. A worldly person, he has a regal presence. Mario's a class act; he's the godfather of our sport and has earned that respect.

Dan Gurney was one of my lifelong heroes, an incredible race car designer, builder, and driver. One time while visiting his shop, after intellectually discussing racing for hours, Dan decided we were going to lunch. His son Justin was going with us and offered to drive. Dan said, "No, I'm drivin'!'"

We climbed into Dan's giant Ford Excursion with Dan in the driver's seat. Now, Dan's in his eighties, but you would've thought he was back on the racetrack the way he whipped that Excursion around the corners and sped down the highway.

I was like, "Holy shit! We're gonna die."

We did safely get to a Mexican restaurant where the hostess escorted us to a table set for twenty people filled with some of the most famous racers in California. I'm thinking, "My God, I'm sitting here with these legendary Indy mechanics, engineers, and car builders, and I'm just some freaking guy from New Jersey." For me, it was one of those days where you just sit, listen, and don't speak until you're spoken to. Even with all I'd accomplished by that point in my career, hearing their incredible stories firsthand was humbling.

Another favorite episode was one we did about Southern moonshiners with former bootlegger and NASCAR legend Junior Johnson. Junior and I drove around North Wilkesboro, North Carolina, in a 1940 Ford, and he pointed out where they used to keep moonshine stills hidden. He also explained the modifications they made to outsmart and outrun the revenuers.

Jeff Gordon and I did a special episode to help his Children's Foundation. He and I restored our 1999 Busch Grand National No. 24 Pepsi Chevrolet Monte Carlo to its former glory. This was the last car we ever worked on together as driver and crew chief. We raced it in the 1999 Phoenix Busch race, and in typical fairytale fashion we won. We took the car to the Barrett Jackson auction and sold it for over half a million dollars.

The popularity of the show helped me find one of the most significant Indy cars of all time, Mario Andretti's 1965 Brawner Hawk Ford. Mario drove the Brawner Hawk to both the 1965 USAC National Championship, as well as Rookie of the Year honors (finished third) at the Indianapolis 500 the same year.

One day I got a call from a viewer, which happened often, and he said he owned the car. I knew there was a replica of the Brawner Hawk out there, so I wasn't sure if this guy had the original or the copy.

As the story goes, after each racing season Clint Brawner, one of racing's most successful chief mechanics, would strip the car and put new parts on it. He would store all the parts he took off up in the attic of his garage.

After Clint passed away, his nephew, Tommy, knew he had all the parts from the 1965 car, but he was missing the chassis. So he built a copy of the chassis and then put on all the original parts.

Tommy sold the car, and it was resold a number of times after. The car showed up at an auction purported to be the original Brawner Hawk Ford, but knowledgeable collectors knew it was not the actual chassis, so it could not be the authentic car.

One day, I got a call from an art collector, of all people, in New Jersey saying he owned the original chassis of the Brawner Hawk Ford and wondered if I'd be interested in it. I went up to see him and took a lot of pictures. Then I called Mario and his former crew chief, Jim McGee, and I showed them the pictures. They said they'd built three chassis but raced only one of them. They told me it could be identified by the additional holes drilled in it to accommodate two different transmissions. They ran a two speed on the ovals and a four speed on the road courses.

Armed with this knowledge, I took another look and, sure enough, the chassis in New Jersey had the extra holes in it. So I bought it. Everybody thought I paid too much for it. Truth is, I did pay six figures for what some might see as a rusted old piece of junk. But I knew that if I could get it restored, it would prove to be a valuable and historic find.

I had read about the replica Clint's nephew, Tommy, had built, so I called him. "Hey, Tommy, I've got the real chassis. Do you have any idea who owns the copy with the real parts?" He said, "Let me make a few calls."

Fortunately, Tommy was able to trace the car to the current owner and gave me his number. I called him and offered to buy the car. He said, "No, I'll buy your chassis."

We went back and forth for six months.

"Let me buy yours."

"No, I'll buy yours."

He finally relented, turned out he was less stubborn than me. I made him a really good deal; I paid him fairly.

Then Hall of Fame Indy car crew chief Jim McGee, who had been a member on the crew that originally built the car, said, "Hey, I'd like to put that car together for you." So now I had the original car and the original car builder.

I sent the car to Jim's shop in Indianapolis. Steve Panaritis, a great fabricator, assisted Jim on the restoration. Jim, in his eighties, and Steve, in his sixties, put this car back together just in time for us to take it to Indy for the one hundredth anniversary of the Indianapolis 500.

The added bonus: Mario got behind the wheel of his rookie Indy car for the first time in a half century and drove a ceremonial pace lap. It was an incredible experience.

I just friggin' stumbled into one of the most significant Indy car finds in twenty years. Once again proving I'm the Forrest Gump of motorsports.

I ended up selling the car at auction in May 2022 for $2.2 million. It turns out my friends were wrong—six figures was chump change when you're talking about a priceless piece of racing history.

I loved doing *AmeriCarna*, but Velocity was going through changes, and we all decided to put it on pause for a while. I would definitely consider bringing it back, though, under the right circumstances.

———

When we put *AmeriCarna* on hiatus, my VP Det Cullum approached NBCSN to see what opportunities might exist. The next thing I knew, we were meeting with producer and program executive, Jeff Behnke.

Jeff's a smart programmer and a great guy. He had me do a NASCAR pre- and post-race show with Kyle Petty, Krista Voda, and Dale Jarrett. All solid folks.

But it wasn't long until traveling wore me down. I started to worry that I wasn't doing a good job—maybe I looked tired, unhappy. Those pre-race and post-race shows are tough because you're on before the race, then you wait four or five hours for the race to end, then you're back on again.

You're the first in and the last to leave the track.

I really wanted a chance at being in the broadcast booth full-time for the race itself. I knew if I could get it, I'd put up with the travel. But they already had a first-rate team in the booth. Steve Letarte, Dale Earnhardt Jr., Jeff Burton, and Rick Allen.

I was honest with Jeff Behnke. I told him how much I appreciated the chance, but it just wasn't in the cards for me then. We are good friends so we both decided to keep the door open.

———

You know the expression, when one door closes, another one opens? Another door did open: Disney's Pixar Animation Studio and the *Cars* movies. Pixar sent a group to Charlotte to do research about NASCAR for the third installment to the Cars franchise. Among them was Jay Ward, Pixar's Creative Director. Jay's a true car guy, so we really hit it off.

They wound up inviting Jeff Gordon and me to Pixar's LA office. A team interviewed us, and we shared tons of stories. We had a blast. Then they invited Erin and me to come back out. They wanted to hear about our experiences and get the perspective of a real female racer.

I collaborated with them on the script as a technical advisor.

Then Jay said, "Look, you've worked so hard on this thing. We need to make you a character and give you a couple of lines."

So, in *Cars 3* they made me Ray Reverham, Jackson Storm's crew chief. (Being kind of a smart-ass, I gave the character a New Jersey accent.)

Just before the movie opened, I participated in a few promo events. For one of them I was onstage at a huge Speedway Children's Charities benefit in Sonoma, California, with John Lasseter, chief creative officer for Pixar, talking about the movie.

For the second one, I hosted a panel purely by accident (again, just like Forrest Gump) with most of the stars, including Owen Wilson, Larry the Cable Guy, Kerry Washington, Nathan Fillion, Cristela Alonzo, Lea DeLaria, and Isiah Whitlock Jr.

Pixar had hired a local news anchor to moderate the panel of stars in front of the press, but the anchor was a no-show. I was already there to be part of the panel, so they asked me if I would fill in for the moderator. They gave me a piece of paper with topics and told me to have fun. I was nervous as hell, but excited. Larry broke the ice by making hilarious wisecrack responses to some of the press questions, but only loud enough for him and me to hear. We did two panels back-to-back, had a lot of fun, and, to this day, I don't think the press knew I was a last-minute fill in.

In 2018, using the door Jeff Behnke and I left open, I went back to NBCSN with a short-lived documentary series called *Glory Road*. In each episode I took viewers behind the scenes of some of motorsports' most historic moments, with the sport's biggest stars.

For example, we did an episode on the 2002 Indianapolis 500, which resulted in one of the most controversial finishes in racing. We got Hélio Castroneves and Paul Tracy to debate whether Hélio rightfully won the race.

We did an episode with Mario Andretti about two great American endurance races, the 24 Hours of Daytona and 12 Hours of Sebring.

Dale Earnhardt Jr. and Darrell Waltrip joined me for a look back at the International Race of Champions, or IROC.

I really love the history of motorsports, so I had a ball doing the show. Just as we were gaining momentum, *Glory Road* became another casualty of COVID. We weren't able to bring folks together to be interviewed, so we couldn't do the show. But I'd love to do it again at some point.

Looking back, I loved the whole experience with television. It was a lot of work, but it was rewarding. I got to do shows I would have watched—even if I wasn't the producer or host.

Though I never set out to be in the television or movie industry, I'm so grateful for the chance. If the right opportunity arose tomorrow, I'd do TV again in a heartbeat. It served as a reminder that I should always keep my options open and not be afraid to jump into things I may know nothing about.

You never know what you can do, until you do it.

Having Ray J. and Jeff presenting my NASCAR Hall of Fame ring together was incredibly special for me. *Jared C. Tilton / Getty Images Sport via Getty Images*

CHAPTER 29

THE HALL OF FAME

2017–2018

"Great news . . . great timing."

Just as I was grappling with my self-doubt and a desire for a new challenge, I received the gift of a lifetime.

I wanted to believe I was worthy of being inducted to the NASCAR Hall of Fame. But as the years rolled by, I began to think I would never be voted in for one reason or another.

Those thoughts entered my mind every time they revealed a new class of inductees and I wasn't on the list. It's not so much a sense of entitlement as much as it was needing the recognition of my efforts. Close friends and other NASCAR Hall of Fame members would always encourage me by saying, "It's not a matter of if, it's a matter of when, your time is coming."

In 2017, I was in Indianapolis for the Indy 500. I thought it would be a good way to take my mind off the anxiety of Hall of Fame announcement day. Erin and baby Cate were with me.

My buddy, Allen Bestwick, joined us for a burger and beer at one of the breweries right there by the Speedway.

As Allen and I sat talking, I could see Erin out of the corner of my eye on her phone, I suspected watching for the announcement. While I appreciated her curiosity, I refused to get caught up in it or worry about it. I was resigned to it being yet another year of questioning myself.

All of sudden, I saw Erin jolt in her seat. Then my phone started ringing. Allen said, "You better answer that!" It was an official from the NASCAR Hall of Fame calling to let me know I'd made it in.

At that instant, little Cate chose to celebrate Daddy's big moment with an incredible dump in her diaper. Whew! The aroma stunk up the whole booth. Everything started happening at once. All of our phones were ringing. We had to get this baby changed. Erin was rifling through the baby travel bag. Allen, being such a good friend, held Cate until Erin could take her back to the ladies' bathroom to get a diaper change.

In that instant, I experienced a fire hose of emotions. Every feeling you could imagine. Stunned. Humbled. Excited. Jubilant. Grateful.

I think the only people who would truly understand are people who have received the same phone call. It's an honor you can only dream about, but you really don't know how to describe it once it becomes reality.

You will not ever work with a finer or more organized team of people than those at the NASCAR Hall of Fame. They do an amazing job. They understand what the nomination means to you, they know what you're going through, and they keep the stress level low and the fun high. When you walk in, you feel like you're king of the world because they treat you that way.

They let me know what to expect and how to prepare for the ceremony. I wrote my speech myself. The toughest thing was fitting everything I wanted to say into eight minutes. Trying to thank everyone who's ever helped me, everyone who gave five bucks, a pat on the back, or an encouraging word, "Ray, you can do it."

I wanted to take the time to tell the world how much people like Jeff Gordon, Rick Hendrick, and my family meant to me. I did it, but it took me closer to nine minutes.

The experience is surreal. You're sitting there, dressed in your new Oxford custom-tailored blue jacket that is exclusive to inductees of the NASCAR Hall of Fame. They announce your name, play your career video, and then you walk up those stairs. The lights are blinding, the music is blaring, the entire audience is giving you a standing ovation.

Jeff and Ray J. met me on stage and handed me my ring as I made my way to the podium.

As I stood there, taking in the sights and sounds, I made eye contact with everyone in the front row. Competitors and family alike. They are there to honor you, and that rush of emotion makes it really hard to start your speech.

It was a once-in-a-lifetime experience that I'll remember for the rest of my days.

My involvement in Jeff's induction, and his involvement in mine, was the catalyst that brought us back together. Renewing our friendship was a bonus to my Hall of Fame induction. It made our relationship closer and stronger than it had ever been. That's so special to me.

PART IV

STILL GOT IT

2017 and On

In my opinion, The Ghost represents my best effort in race car design.
Ray Evernham Enterprises Archives

CHAPTER 30

THE GHOST

Building a Beast: 2017

"I'm going to build me a damn modified."

By 2017, I was out of NASCAR and had slowed down on my work as a TV analyst, host, and producer. I was doing a bunch of different things trying to figure out what made me happy.

I'd also been looking for another race series to get involved in that wasn't overregulated and that I could afford to enter. Vintage racing really appealed to me because you could take cars and run them as hard as you wanted.

Watching vintage races took me back to when I was a kid in the late 1960s going to Wall Stadium or Flemington Raceway at the Jersey Shore on Saturday nights and Sunday afternoons with my Uncle Nick. The cars that caught my eye the most were the modified 1936 Chevrolet sedans. There was something about those sedans I just loved. I thought they were beautiful. Big, rounded body with the powerful injector stacks poking through the hood.

Then one day it hit me. I was like, "You know what? I'm going to build me a damn modified."

I knew I wasn't going to have any fun driving a car that's built like it was in the 1960s. I wanted to build it really wild. A car that could be competitive on different types of tracks: ovals, road courses, and drag strips.

Truth is, I'd been building the car in my imagination since I was a kid. Sitting there in the stands thinking, "Man, if I ever race, this is going to be my car."

It ended up being a car I raced when I was sixty instead of sixteen. But now I'll be building it with the benefit of forty-plus years of know-how.

The car I envisioned would combine my love for old-school automotive styling with my knowledge and access to modern-day technology and performance. A modern-day modified stock car.

More than simply building a car, I wanted to see if my mechanical ability was still relevant. So, I built it the old-fashioned way: out of my head with the engineering that I knew. But it had to be a car we could race using new-school technology.

Luckily for me, I had two guys in my shop I knew could take what was in my head and make it a reality. Eddie Bohn, a longtime friend and gifted mechanic, and Dan Baker, a wizard with metalwork and shaping bodies. Dan can take a piece of metal and make it into something beautiful and then paint it as brilliantly as any artist.

I did very few drawings. We started with one of the 1936 Chevy bodies I'd picked up through the years. (I think I still have one or two sitting around.) I sat in the middle of it for hours, just looking around and thinking about where I wanted everything and how I wanted it to look and feel.

The 1936 Chevrolet body is about as aerodynamic as a brick. With the help of a local car designer, Robert McCarter, we produced a digitally rendered image of a tweaked, chopped, and trimmed version of the Chevy body. Then, like a sculptor with his hammer and chisel, Dan chopped, narrowed, and moved things around—and did all the work by eye.

We just started putting pieces together.

While I led the design, Eddie and Dan worked on the car every day and we built it pretty quickly, in about nine or ten months.

The final touch was the paint scheme. I love pearl white. I had Dan paint it all pearl white, and we later added some blue accenting decals.

One evening as I was turning out the lights, the car caught my eye. That garage had skylights and the glow of a full Carolina moon shone through and onto the car. The moonlight reflected on the pearl white encasing the rounded body, casting an eerie, radiant, soft-blue tint. I thought to myself, "That damn thing looks like Casper the ghost." And just like that, our new creation became The Ghost.

While it's a cool name for the car, it also served as a metaphor for that chapter of my life. The Ghost took me back to when I would watch those modifieds go around with Uncle Nick. It was like a time machine that reminded me I still had some unrealized dreams. The car became the manifestation of a lot of the things that I saw in my past and hoped for in my future.

The Ghost was everything I imagined it to be. It's a sweet car. It was not out to kill me, even though we were close to 900 horsepower in a 2,500-pound car that made 2,000 pounds of downforce.

I debuted The Ghost in the Valvoline booth at the 2017 Specialty Equipment Market Association (SEMA) Show and boy, did it turn heads. That's where I ran into Al Unser Jr. I've been a friend and fan of Al's for a long time; I admire and respect the Unser family, a motorsports dynasty.

One of the most storied chapters of the Unser history is their dominance at the Pikes Peak International Hill Climb. Since 1916, the Unser boys had been regular competitors in the "Race to the Clouds." An Unser claimed victory every year from 1958 to 1962. Louis, Bobby, and Al Sr. are all enshrined in the Pikes Peak Hall of Fame.

There's something about that hill climb that's always captured my imagination. While I had planned to enter The Ghost in a slate of 2018 vintage events at Road Atlanta, Daytona, and Indianapolis Motor Speedway, Pikes Peak wasn't really on my to-do list. Bumping into Al at SEMA started that conversation.

Al came by to look at The Ghost and fell in love with the car. I invited him to sit in it and he fit perfectly. As he sat comfortably in The Ghost, we talked about his dad, Al Sr., and his Uncle Bobby. We started talking about Bobby's wins at Pikes Peak and I said, "Al, you know what? We ought to run this son of a bitch up Pikes Peak." With no hesitation, Al replied, "Let's do it."

We both had personal services contracts with Valvoline, so I knew I had a sponsor to help pay for it, and an Unser in the car would make it a big deal. I told Al I'd get the car ready and shake it down by running Road Atlanta. Then to Indy for the Sportscar Vintage Racing Association (SVRA) race, and then out to Colorado for the run up Pikes Peak.

When we unloaded The Ghost at Road Atlanta, NASCAR Hall of Famer and friend, Bill Elliott, test drove it for me. I knew I could trust Bill to give me the straight scoop on the good and the bad in the ride. The Ghost was my baby, so it'd be really hard for me to pick it apart.

After running a few laps, Bill came in just shaking his head and said, "This thing is amazing. It has so much power and so much downforce that you can drive it way harder than you think."

Then I started learning to drive it. The first time out, I was just making sure everything worked. Steering. Braking. Shifting. But when I hit the damn backstretch and ran it up to the fourth gear, that thing raced to 170 miles per hour. I thought to myself, "Man, I'm not even on it yet." It just drove so incredibly nice.

That Sunday, I entered the SVRA race at Road Atlanta. Bill was in his own car. I started behind him, and I followed him for about five or six laps. On about lap seven, I started thinking, "Holy shit, I think I can pass him." So I did!

I wound up finishing third, and I think he finished fourth. After the race Bill put his arm around me and said, "Man, that thing's fast."

After the shakedown at Road Atlanta, about two months before we were supposed to go to Pikes Peak, I got a call I was none too happy to get. It was Al. He said, "Look, I've taken on a new job with the IndyCar folks, so I can't go to Pikes Peak this year."

Damn!

I called Bill, but Bill knew the unique challenges associated with driving Pikes Peak and said he didn't think he had enough time to prepare.

So that's when I decided, "Well, hell, I'll do it."

I'd become so numb between the years of being an owner, doing TV, and not really building anything, not really racing anything. I mean, even when I raced the sprint cars, somebody else built all those.

Building The Ghost from scratch and racing Pikes Peak seemed like the perfect one-two punch of a challenge I needed to reinvigorate myself at this stage of my life.

Now I had to face the biggest challenge of all. How do I break the news to Erin?

Above the clouds at Pikes Peak. *Larry Chen*

CHAPTER 31

BACK BEHIND THE WHEEL

Devil's Playground and More: 2017

"I don't want our little girl growing up without a father."

Since the Pikes Peak competition began more than a century ago, thousands of cars, trucks, and motorcycles have raced the once-dirt, now asphalt-paved, Pikes Peak International Hill Climb.

It's legendary for its beauty. And its danger.

The race to the 14,115-foot summit is one of the wildest and most dangerous in America. As you race past the clouds for nearly 5,000 feet, drivers don't race each other. It's everybody against the mountain. And no one wants to let the mountain win.

Many of the 156 turns in the 12.42-mile climb have a reputation or a name. Hansen's Corner. Gilly's Corner. Heltman's Hill. George's Corner. Others seem more like hazard signs threatening doom: Ragged Edge. Devil's Playground. The Bottomless Pit.

The race, named after a man who never made it to the summit (Zebulon Pike), is America's second-oldest auto race behind the Indy 500. Like the bricks at Indy, the narrow, winding, cliff-lined road of Pikes Peak dares you to test your driving skills.

While I knew there were those who thought I needed my head examined, to be racing Pikes Peak at this stage of my life, it was a dare I wanted, a dare I needed.

I'd known of the Pikes Peak Hill Climb since I was a young racer and how last names like Unser, Millen, Dunne, and Dumas had earned the title: "King of the Mountain."

Those guys were daredevils. Heroes. I thought it was amazing that men who raced all kinds of cars and motorcycles—at speeds of nearly 150 miles per hour—would race up a mountain (of all things) year after year.

At sixty years old I wasn't looking to be a hero or daredevil. I just wanted to wake my passion and purpose the hell up, and I believed a run up Pikes Peak in a car I built out of my head would do the trick.

We had nicknamed the car, The Ghost. I was just praying it wouldn't turn me into one.

———

When racing up Pikes Peak, preparation is crucial: mental, physical, and probably spiritual, too. Once I made my mind up that I'd be driving, I probably had only seven or eight weeks to cram it all in.

My right-hand guy, Det Cullum, started reaching out to Pikes Peak Hill Climb experts all over the world. He managed to get a pretty legit software program of the Pikes Peak course for my simulator. I also downloaded in-car videos off YouTube that other racers had recorded and posted of their runs. I probably watched Mike Skeen in his Nissan the most. I studied his shifting. I learned that timing is everything on the mountain, especially when it comes to shifting, and Mike's shifting seemed to be at the pace I thought I'd be running.

I'd spend at least an hour or more a day on my simulator, then I'd watch Mike's run over and over and over just to learn the road. I did that every day for days on end.

Then I would spend an hour a day on my Airdyne bike wearing an oxygen restrictive mask that allowed me to change my oxygen intake. The air gets a lot thinner the higher up the mountain you go. I rode the shit out of that bike until it would almost make me throw up.

That was my daily routine till we left for the mountain.

But meeting the physical, psychological, and mechanical demands to safely and successfully navigate the mountain all seemed like a cakewalk compared to the other challenge I was facing, getting Erin on board.

Erin knew all about the risks. And she didn't like them. No wilting flower, she was a good race car driver herself. She'd even raced at Pikes Peak International Raceway just down the road. She and her crew had driven the Pikes Peak International Hill Climb course as tourists, so she knew what I would be facing.

At the time our daughter, Cate, was two years old.

"I don't want our little girl growing up without a father," she told me. Erin had lost her own dad when she was young.

"I don't want that, either."

Weeks earlier I had tried to soften things. I don't want to say I lied to Erin, but I didn't tell her the whole truth. I just said, "Hey, you know, I might have to drive . . . but I'm still looking for somebody else to compete. I'm gonna ask so-and-so."

Privately, I knew I was readying myself. I don't know if I just didn't want to alarm her or if I didn't want to fight the battle. My mind was made up, if the right driver didn't show up, I was going to do this.

Still, I regret the tension it caused in our relationship.

Erin knows me well. She thinks I'm too fearless when I get in a race car, that I tend to overdrive. She saw me run the sprint car and watched me doing stuff that caused others to shake their heads. Worse, we'd recently lost a couple friends to racing accidents.

She only knew me as a crew chief and a team owner. I'm more than that. I just had to prove it. To who? Myself.

Looking at her in this moment, little Cate playing on the floor between us, it occurred to me: she also has to confront who I really am.

"I'm worried, Ray." She put her hand on mine. "I'm afraid you'll push yourself too hard with no margin for error."

I stared back at her waiting for her to say it. To finish her dark thought.

"What if you get hurt? Or worse? I have a bad feeling about all this."

Lowering to the floor, I scooped up Cate in my arms. She gave me a little kiss on the nose. I avoided looking at Erin as I gathered my thoughts.

"Look. This is me," I told her, rising. "You married me. This is who I am. This is what I do." Then I placed Cate in her arms. "I'm doing this. And if there are repercussions, then I'll deal with them."

Throughout my life I've faced some challenges that, for one reason or another, I felt made me a better person. That's how I felt about Pikes Peak. I was at a place in my life where I needed to know I could still rise to the challenge. It caused a rough patch in our marriage, for sure, but this was one of those things I wanted to do, moreover, I needed to do.

———

I had confidence in my abilities and in The Ghost. The guys that drove it, Bill Elliott and Boris Said, raved, "Wow! This thing is just incredible!"

We had one more test the week before Pikes Peak, the Indy Road Course. My guys, along with Erin and Cate, headed to Indianapolis.

Up to that point I had driven The Ghost on bias ply tires. The Goodyear guys at Indy said, "Hey, you put radial tires on, and it'll pick up speed."

We put the radials on it to shake it down, and holy shit, those guys were right. It was fast. But then coming through the S-curves on the backstretch, the car jumped sideways on me. I caught it, but it whipped around the other way, and spun at probably 130 or 140 mph.

I had never raced on radial tires, and I didn't think the hill climb course would be the safest place to learn. In addition to the 156 mostly blind curves, the mountain is notorious for its wildly changeable weather. You might start the race with the sun shining, but on the road to the top, it's not uncommon to encounter snow, rain, or hail. The road conditions are constantly changing. Radials are tricky to drive on because they generate more cornering force, but you lose that grip fast, too. You can get in big trouble. The grip loss of bias ply tires is more gradual, giving you time to correct mistakes. While I'd probably go faster on the radials, due to my lack of experience racing on them, I took the advice of my friends at Goodyear and switched back to the bias ply tires.

There was still the chance of mechanical failure. Even though I felt we had engineered the car really well, The Ghost had never experienced the type of forces it would when climbing that mountain. One unseen rock could take out a suspension part real quick.

As for the rest of it, I thought, "I got this."

———

I never felt more prepared for any race in my life. I was ready. My car was ready. My guys were ready. We packed The Ghost in the trailer, and Eddie, Dan, and Det headed for Pikes Peak.

Things were still frosty between Erin and me, but she knew this was a done deal. I kissed and hugged Erin and Cate and put them on a flight back to North Carolina. Then I got on my flight headed for Colorado.

Until then, I'd never been to Colorado Springs. It's some of the most breathtaking scenery our country has to offer, but I had little time to take it in or enjoy it. Seeing the jagged, snow-capped mountains as I was driving in only reminded me I had work to do.

Rookies were required to arrive on Monday before the race. My guys had staked out a portion of the designated inspection area and set up our makeshift garage. As we rolled The Ghost out of the trailer, I could hear the comments of the other drivers and crews, "What the hell is this?"

I've been in racing forty years, I am a NASCAR Hall of Famer, but I'm a rookie at Pikes Peak. So I had to attend the rookie meeting. There were about a dozen of us. Most were in the thirty-five- to forty-year-old range. Some were even younger, in their mid-twenties.

Sometimes the way officials in these drivers' meetings talk to you— even at the Cup level—makes you feel like you're back in kindergarten. Understandably, the Pikes Peak official wanted us to take things seriously. "Gentlemen, there are one hundred fifty-six corners you must negotiate to reach the top of this mountain," said the official. "Twelve of those can kill you."

I felt like I was in some movie. Being the smart-ass character that I am, I couldn't help myself, and I said, "Are those twelve clearly marked?"

The other drivers beside me laughed.

He didn't. "Very funny, Mr. NASCAR, but you need to pay attention."

At sixty years old, I didn't feel like a NASCAR champion. Or a former Cup level crew chief. Or a TV personality. Instead, I felt like I was starting all over again.

Then they split us into smaller groups and assigned each a coach. My group was assigned James Robinson. Formerly with Acura, he's smart. He's also a fellow driver and an engineer. Most importantly, at that time he'd raced the mountain seven times and knew how to negotiate corners and how to navigate the various terrains.

"Remember: guardrail to the left, you can dig through there. No guardrail to the right. Be careful, big drop off."

"How big?" someone asks.

"You die big."

You can almost hear gulps from the other rookies. Then he turns to me. "Look, this is your first race here. Don't try and memorize this place. You can't anyway because so many corners look alike. That's what gets people in trouble. When you're racing up that mountain and you're concentrating on so many things, it's easy to get lost." After the meeting we all got into two vans and headed up the course road. James would talk about a particular corner, and how best to take it and why. Everybody was taking notes. Then we'd stop, get out, and discuss the surroundings. That's also when they'd check our oxygen level. Levels had to be at a certain amount before you would be allowed to ascend to the next section of the mountain. If you couldn't pass the oxygen test, you weren't going up.

I had done a lot of research and discovered you could buy these little oxygen canisters to keep with you as you acclimate to the mountain. I bought a case of those things, and I had one with me that I kept hitting on the way up.

They discouraged us from talking because it burns up your oxygen. But sure enough, we had this one guy in the van who just wouldn't shut up.

I kept responding, "Mm-hmm, mm-hmm."

I said nothing because I knew if I didn't pass that oxygen test, I wasn't going to the next level. At sixty years old, they kept a closer eye on me than on the young guys. I wasn't about to blow this.

———

Once we got to the top, they gave us our practice schedule. It told us which day and on which section of the mountain we could practice run. Our schedule had us running the middle on Tuesday, the top on Wednesday, and the bottom on Thursday. Thursday was the qualifying day for my group. All entrants qualified on the bottom section because that's where the weather is the most consistent.

There were about eighty cars qualifying. The order that you qualify is the order you run up the mountain on race day. James had tipped me off that in order to avoid the risk of running into bad weather on the mountain, I needed to qualify in the top twenty-five. Historically, as it gets later in the day the weather gets worse. He gave me a target running time and I hit almost exactly to the second, qualifying twenty-fourth. While I know I could have gone faster, I followed James's advice and stuck to my commitment to race safe. Two things guaranteed to get you hurt up there are mechanical failure and ego. And I was doing a good job of keeping mine in check.

By then, we had been on the mountain for three days. I knew the challenges and the dangers, and I was still glad I made the decision to come.

Although we had the option to practice the top section again on Friday, I decided against it. I didn't want to risk wrecking or beating up the car. So, I got a haircut and a massage and spent two hours on the simulator with James's Acura team.

Later that evening, we all headed into Colorado Springs for Fan Fest. It's a chance for drivers, teams, and about thirty thousand fans from all over the world to get together and enjoy food and entertainment in a seven-block stretch of the downtown area.

On Saturday morning, I went over to Walmart and bought a sleeping bag, a bunch of snacks, and water. Then I went up the base of the mountain, parked my rental SUV, and camped with some of the other drivers and officials.

Det, Dan, and Eddie went back to the hotel for dinner and what amounted to a long nap. There's one way in and out of the mountain and we'd been warned about the paralyzing traffic jam that starts building early on race day morning. They set their alarm for 12:00 a.m. to be sure they'd be back on the mountain in time for final preparations.

Meanwhile, the breeze in the camping area was a sweet blend of mesquite and barbeque. I started wandering around talking to everybody hoping to get a bite. Luckily, I started hearing, "Hey Ray, have a hamburger." "Have a steak." "You sure you got enough?"

I was like Yogi Bear, bumming food out of everybody's picnic baskets.

The one thing I did not do the night before the race, and the two weeks leading up to it, was drink a drop of alcohol, not one. This is another kind of AA—alcohol and altitude—and they don't mix well. I did drink plenty of water, protein shakes, and stuff like that.

After dinner, I went to my SUV, folded the seats down, unrolled my sleeping bag, and laid there thinking about the race and how good I felt. I definitely felt good about The Ghost.

I also reminded myself I was racing on a mountain and I had to respect nature. Native Americans that live on and around the mountain have a saying that couldn't be more apt: "The mountain decides."

Tomorrow it would.

———

I don't usually sleep a lot. I have bad anxiety about getting up and getting somewhere on time; I've always felt the need to be early. I had zero anxiety sleeping on the mountain knowing I was already there. All I had to do was walk over to the pit area, which is what I did at precisely 6:00 a.m.

I walked through the camping area, breathing in the fresh, cool mountain air. Not being a big breakfast guy, all I ate that morning was an energy bar and a protein shake. I just needed a little boost.

As I chewed my food, I tried Erin again. I hadn't been able to reach her since Saturday afternoon. The reception was spotty on the mountain. "Call failed," my cell phone told me. I imagined her upset and felt bad about how things had ended between us.

Then I got into race mode.

My team: Det, Dan, and Ed had been on the mountain since 1:00 a.m. They plugged in the air jacks and fired up the space heaters and tire heaters. The latter were key to getting going quickly. Those tires needed to be warm because the first two or three corners are pretty high speed. We were scheduled to be "green" between noon and one o'clock. After that, you run the risk of bad weather at the top.

A couple of motorcycle crashes earlier that morning had already caused a delay, but I didn't let that shake me. I stayed focused, I said little, I had my plan, and I didn't want to consider anything else.

Getting dressed, I kept thinking about what I had to do.

I had my iPad with me, so I watched Mike Skeen's run, the same video I studied the night before until I fell asleep. Again, I paid special attention to his shifting. I watched it a few more times before getting in the car. I also played back in my mind the details James Robinson advised me about the guardrail placement.

"Aside from wrecking yourself, you pray the cars ahead of you don't crash either," James told us. "Nobody wants anyone hurt. But there are normally two or three cars on the mountain at the same time. Although they're kept far apart, the rule is, if a driver ahead wrecks or experiences mechanical failure, you have to stop, come all the way back down, and start again."

Starting over? I pushed down the thought. Focus.

————

At "go time" I drank water and tried once more to reach Erin.

No luck. I buckled in. Det put the window net up.

An official came over to check my safety equipment. "Ready to go?"

I gave him a thumbs-up. A second later, the guys pushed me toward the starting box.

The start line is at the Mile 7 marker on the Pikes Peak Highway, already at an altitude of 9,390 feet. Another 4,729 feet to the finish line and the summit. Once you're at the mountaintop—the good Lord willing—you must stay there until everyone's finished for the day.

So, I said to the guys, "Well, I'll see you around five o'clock. Catch me any sooner and you'll know it's been a bad day."

Just ahead was the LED starter clock, counting down the final seconds to the start. My motor revved. I set my switches.

Just me, The Ghost, and the mountain. Racing Pikes Peak is by far the coolest thing I have ever done in a race car. *Larry Chen*

CHAPTER 32

ALL OR NOTHING

On Pikes Peak

"The mountain decides."

This was it. All the planning, building, and training would come down to this.

Ten, nine, eight. . .

When it hit seven, I thought for a second maybe I ought to jam this bitch in reverse and get outta here.

Instead, I took a deep breath, I turned my oxygen up, and clicked into first gear.

One.

The light flashed green. I hit the gas, spinning tires. Just for fun I whipped the wheel to swing the back of the car sideways and fire up the spectators.

I blasted through the start line with my tires smoking, tripping the timer, and the race was on. Next stop: top of the mountain.

In that instant, all the training, everything I'd thought about in the simulator, all came back to me. It was all about "Okay, where are my spots? Where are my marks? Where am I on the hill?" And especially for me, "What gear am I in?" I wasn't the greatest shifter. It was one of the things I struggled with.

The rear suspension I'd designed used a torque arm that helped with acceleration and braking, but it broke while we were at Indy and we didn't have time to fix it for Pikes Peak. Now I was having difficulty keeping traction under acceleration and braking. I realized I'd underestimated how much force the engine would have. That engine had 760 pounds of torque in it. It had a ton of power. I wished I'd have had that torque arm, but I just had to run without it. That's just racing. When something like that happens, you just adapt. You change the way you work the throttle. You change the way you work the brake.

I do more shifting than I'd like. I tend to downshift too early. I had to keep telling myself, "Don't rush the shifts, don't rush the shifts." But I was trying to match the motor rpm with my shifts. It was all about sound for me going up the mountain. Without that torque arm to help braking, I was uncomfortable on corner entry.

The brake problem damn near caused me to crash twice. The car brake hops really bad, and I almost slammed into the guardrail. Moments later, I thought, "I have a flat tire."

I checked again. "No, it's just getting colder. I'm losing tire temperature." And I was in such thin air now that my downforce was gone.

I was losing time.

The view and terrain change quickly on the ascent.

Trees vanish, replaced by Volkswagen-sized boulders, and snow lines both sides of the road. Skid marks dot the pavement, reminders of what can happen if you're distracted for even a nanosecond.

To the left, the boulders, and to the right, blue sky and big drop-offs.

In the next stretch I went straight up like a rocket. All I could see was blue sky.

Okay, where do I make the turn?

I stayed far left, hugging the mountain. I don't want to slide too far right and drop off 1,500 feet.

Luckily, The Ghost has super quick steering—a necessity. As I steered and braked into one of the sharp switchbacks, the weight transferred to the front, causing the rear wheels to bounce under braking again. Damn! Nine times out of ten, bouncing like that causes wrecks.

Just as it jumped sideways again, I saved the car but caught a glimpse of dust in the rear-view mirror, meaning I was only inches away from going off.

Smirking to myself, I thought, "Damn good job there, boy. That could've been bad."

But I never thought about stopping. As soon as I made the save, it was eyes front.

When you're racing up this mountain, you have to focus on where you're going, not where you've been.

I knew I was getting close to the top. That's good. And bad. It meant

I had (at least) one more big challenge ahead of me. The last left turn before the finish line is treacherous. It's slightly banked so you can carry speed through it, but you can't see the exit because of the mountain so it's easy to make a mistake there and slide off. Hit it right and you gain time. Hit it wrong and you crash.

I did lose some time there. Not because of anything I did or didn't do. It was starting to snow, making the road even more treacherous. And remember, I was on Goodyear slicks, so no tread.

I'm not sure how I did it, but I made that final turn.

Seeing that checkered flag caused an overwhelming explosion of feelings: Exhilaration. Pride. Relief. I saw the other drivers who made it to the top standing by their cars waving and cheering. As I climb from The Ghost, several come up to congratulate me.

Then came the surprise of my life.

During all the chaos, the official informs me, "You didn't just make it to the summit in one piece. You just won the Exhibition Class!"

"What?" I was dumbfounded.

"You set the best time at ten minutes, eleven point three three seconds."

That was only made sweeter when I found out I stole some thunder from Bentley Motor Cars, who was trying to set the same class record in a race-prepped Turbo V-12 Bentayga SUV driven by racing legend Rhys Millen. You can be sure the Brits spent way more money than I did trying to get to the top faster. But the hot rod scored!

Like most of the other drivers who carried something with them to celebrate making it to the summit, I'd carried a Pabst Blue Ribbon tall boy. There I was, at the summit of "America's Mountain" proudly sippin' from my red, white, and blue PBR (same colors as The Ghost), and it never tasted better.

As I stood next to The Ghost in the falling snow and looked out over the mountain, all I could see for miles was cloud cover. Between that and the overwhelming feeling of peace I experienced after reaching the summit, it was almost spiritual. I thought about growing up. About having nothing but knowing I wanted more out of life. I thought about the people that shaped me into the person that became a champion crew chief. My dad, my mom, Jack Stoddard, Jay Signore, Rick Hendrick. I thought about the years of relentless hard work. I thought about all my teammates that were right there with me through it all. I thought about my family. My entire life flashed before my eyes.

It finally struck me that this journey to build The Ghost and race up Pikes Peak was more than just something cool to do. This was my life coming full circle. Something subconscious in me was pulling me back to my roots. Just build a car and go race it. That's all this was, but it meant so much more to me.

Then I thought to myself, "Shit. I still have to drive this thing back down the mountain through snow on slicks."

Obviously, you can't drive down the mountain while others are racing up, so you have to wait for everyone to finish before starting the trek back down. Unfortunately, two or three people crashed after I made the summit. Then, it started to snow so freaking hard they shut down the top part of the course and we were on hold for hours.

It wasn't the coffee or the free high-altitude donuts they gave us that made the wait tolerable. It was the camaraderie with other drivers who were stuck up there with me. I was shootin' the shit with guys like Travis Pastrana, James Robinson, J. R. Hildebrand, and Randy Pobst. These are all fantastic drivers, and we traded stories of our drive up.

We talked about Pikes Peak having its own identity, just like the 24 Hours of Le Mans, the Indy 500, or the Monaco Grand Prix. With over one hundred years of history, racing legends from around the world have gathered to challenge the mountain. We were proud to have our names on the list.

We were sitting at a table talking when somebody shouted, "Hey, Ray, they're talking about you."

Sure enough, the live stream commentators were discussing my run in The Ghost. It was odd for me to hear them talking about me as a driver. I knew, right then and there, this was my biggest win. While I might not have made it as a driver in NASCAR or IndyCar, I have a class win at Pikes Peak. As a rookie.

This was the greatest victory of my racing career.

––––––––––

The ride down was pretty wild. We were escorted down the mountain by two snowplows clearing the road for us. Snowplows only move the heavy stuff, so it was still pretty slippery. My biggest fears were sliding off the road with all four wheels locked up or banging into the back of one of the million-dollar Porsches in front of me. I didn't feel the cold on the way up, but I was freezing on the way down. I couldn't stop thinking, "Damn it, I didn't put a dent in the car the whole way up. We won our class, and now I'm gonna fly off the mountain and never get the chance to tell anybody about it."

It was a white-knuckle adventure for sure, and I did some of my best driving on the way down. As soon as we broke the clouds, the sun was shining again, and the road was dry.

As I neared the bottom, almost to the pit area, there were thousands of fans lined up along the temporary fence cheering while I held my class winners' flag proudly out the window. They had their hands outstretched and wanted to give all of us a high-five. It was an incredible sight.

I made it down without a scratch, my second victory of the day. Det, Dan, and Eddie were fist-pumping and grinning as I pulled up. They were elated and relieved. Everybody had worked so hard. I don't know of a better way to reward someone with race car passion than to bring them a "W."

I got out of the car and immediately thought of Erin. I still had zero service on my phone, but I noticed someone using theirs. They were nice enough to let me borrow it.

"Hello, Ray."

I could tell by her tone that she was upset. I couldn't imagine why, because I knew she had watched my successful run on the livestream, so she knew I was okay and that I had won. Then she told me why.

"I've been trying to call you. Jason Johnson died. He crashed at Beaver Dam [Wisconsin] Raceway last night."

That was a gut punch. Jason was a friend of ours. Just forty-one years old and a hell of a sprint car racer.

This book is called *Trophies and Scars* for a reason. You just don't expect them to come an hour apart.

In a split second I went from celebration to shock.

I understood why Erin was so upset. She did not want me to do this for fear of something bad happening to me. Jason's death intensified those feelings even further, and with no way of reaching me, she didn't get to talk to me before I got in the car to race up the mountain. I can't imagine how hard it must have been for Erin.

I told her I loved her, and I'd call her later.

———

When I clicked The Ghost into gear to start the run, everything that I've ever felt, believed in, worked for, or thought I was, came down to running that mountain. I know that sounds crazy. People said I didn't have to do this. I didn't have to prove anything to anybody.

But I know the following to be a fact: people who are truly competitive go through their entire life trying to prove something to themselves, period. Your biggest competitor is you. Sure, in sports or business, there are outside competitors you may want to beat. But anybody who is really competitive or who's been really successful, understands competition comes from within. From your soul.

If I could go back and offer advice to that small boy on the plastic go-kart, I'd say this: believe in yourself, work hard, and stay true to who you are and not who people think you should be.

AFTERWORD

Well there it is, my best shot at summing up the last sixty years or so of my life into 100,000 words or less. At least that's what the contract said.

We covered all the things I said we would talk about, plus some. I have been open and honest about the things that happened and how I was feeling at the time. Whether you loved it or hated it I'm sure by reading it you now know something about me that surprised you.

I sincerely thank you for taking the time to allow me to share what I feel has been a memorable journey. From the early moments of riding around in a go-kart to the pinnacles of success in NASCAR racing, it's been a hell of a ride.

I hope the book has both educated and entertained you. I also hope that telling you about the highs and lows, the triumphs and setbacks, the trophies and scars of my life will be a source of inspiration for yours.

This book was never meant to be a list of my achievements, but rather a portrait of the experiences, relationships, and moments in my life that define who I am.

If you take one thing away, it should be this: life is filled with challenges and opportunities. There is no difference between the two. You will never face one without the other. Your skills, commitment, and attitude will determine the outcome of either.

I know my story will continue to evolve just like the ever-changing world that we live in. As I face those changes and my inevitable evolution, I will carry with me the lessons I have learned and the memories of the people who taught them.

I will look at my trophies and recognize my scars, knowing that I am better prepared for the next chapter of my life.

Jeff and me before the start of the Porsche Carrera Cup race at Indy in 2022. *Ray Evernham Enterprises Archives*

ONE MORE RUN

Timeless Chemistry: 2015

"Hey Ray, let's go race!"

In 2015, Jeff and I did a project together. We united to restore our 1999 Busch Series No. 24 Pepsi Chevrolet Monte Carlo and auction it off to benefit the Jeff Gordon Children's Foundation. It was a big success. We felt like, man, we still got the magic.

When he and I get together, good stuff happens.

We've gotten even closer since our Hall of Fame inductions. He was such a huge part of mine. And he literally went out of his way to ensure I was a big part of his, too. He took me with him to every press event and had me sit at his table. He treated me like family.

So gradually, we just started doing things together again.

———

In 2022, Jeff called out of the blue one day. "Hey, I got this Porsche GT3 race car. These are really special, and I had to pull a lot of strings to get mine. But part of the deal is, I've gotta race it."

I was like, "What?"

"Yeah. One of the conditions of owning it, is racing it."

I just said, "Holy crap, what're you gonna do?"

"I'd really like you to help me."

"Hell, yeah, man. I don't know anything about Porsches, but we'll figure it out."

Then Jeff said, "But. . . I don't want you to be you."

Okay . . . Sounds harsh, right?

But I knew just what he meant. Like Jekyll and Hyde, he knew my instinct was to switch into "crew chief mode." Map out every tiny detail. Have us start working out. Eating right. Getting to bed by nine o'clock. Blah, blah.

When I was leading the No. 24 team, I guess I could be a bit of a tyrant. Although I saw myself as Vince Lombardi, others saw me as kind of overbearing.

Jeff continued, "Look. We're gonna do this. And we're gonna enjoy it."

While I appreciated the sentiment, I still felt the pressure.

Sort of the same feeling I'd have when we raced the No. 24. I just wanted to do a good job for him. There's always been something about working with Jeff that makes me want to perform at my very best.

There are certain people you work with who always seem to operate at the top of their game. When that happens, you want to make sure you are, too.

It's always been that way with Jeff. I had a slight insecurity when it came to working with him. I always wanted him to be able to say, "Nobody could have done a better job than Ray."

That's important to me.

So, I thought to myself, "Shit, I'd better find out what to do with this Porsche." I started with my automotive "brain trust." I called on everyone I knew with expertise in all racing formats, including Porsche.

The fact is, Jeff could have taken his car to a regular Porsche racing shop to get it ready to race without a hiccup. But I think it was important to him we did it together. It was just a matter of doing our homework, getting expert help, gaining a little experience, and getting it done.

———

The first time I actually saw the car was when Jeff asked me to meet him at Carolina Motorsports Park, in Kershaw, South Carolina. He wanted to run some laps and get a feel for it. I put my radio headset on, then Jeff headed out onto the track. When I pushed the button to talk, it was the first time we'd been on the radio together since October 1999.

And it wasn't like we were starting a new conversation. It felt more like a continuation of our previous in-car chats. In that moment, it was as if all the time had faded away.

The team of Gordon and Evernham picked up right where we'd left off. Jeff pushed that Porsche as fast as he could. We had a blast.

Throughout the course of the day, he ran thirty to forty laps and kept getting faster with each one.

After the test, the car was delivered to my shop.

The next thing I knew, Jeff scheduled us for a Porsche Carrera Cup race at Indianapolis Motor Speedway over Labor Day weekend 2022.

It had been years since I'd been a crew chief or team manager, and Porsche Carrera Cup and NASCAR Cup are in two different universes, like football and hockey. Yes, I may have been in unfamiliar territory and more than a little rusty as a crew chief, but I was, as always, up for a new challenge.

Task one? Build a solid team around us.

I called all my friends who were in vintage Porsche racing. We subcontracted a data person from one team, a maintenance dude from another. We poached a Porsche mechanic right out of Rick Hendrick's Porsche dealership. We took Graham Smith, son of Speedway Motorsports Inc. CEO Marcus Smith, as our tire guy. Steve Barkdoll, who helped Jeff begin his stock car career in 1990, was our spotter. We bought and borrowed equipment, got some uniforms, and put together a great crew.

Two weeks before Indy, I went to see a Porsche race for myself at the Road America course, near Elkhart Lake, Wisconsin. I was a sponge. I talked with anybody and everybody, taking in the whole Porsche racing experience.

Feeling my crew chief instincts kick in, I also spent time talking with officials, getting to know them, understanding the inspection process. I watched how closely they scrutinized those cars. I saw them disqualify five.

That's when I thought, "Oh shit. These guys are sharp."

The last thing I wanted to do was screw around and get us disqualified. Coming to that unusual decision for a guy like me was a relief. It meant I didn't have to spend half my time thinking about how to break the rules.

Or I should say, bend the rules?

Plus, Porsche is very particular about every aspect of their race series, right down to decal placement.

———

When we were racing at Indy back in the Cup days, it was serious business—wrapped in a ton of pressure. But when Jeff and I rolled in for the Porsche race, there was a lot of laughing. We still worked hard, but we were there to enjoy ourselves . . . and to ensure Jeff could keep his car.

Indianapolis Motor Speedway is now like an old friend.

Once upon a time the place intimidated the hell out of me. I literally sensed the ghosts of all the greats from bygone eras watching me, judging whether I was worthy to be there. Thank God, it's also been home to some of my greatest successes.

I climbed in my motor coach Wednesday morning before the race at 4:00 a.m. I was driving to Indy by myself, so I wanted to get an early start. Erin and Cate were flying in on Friday in time for the races.

I love driving my motor coach. It's kind of therapeutic. As I sipped on coffee, I began the nine-and-a-half-hour drive thinking about all the details, the unknowns, and logistics for the weekend, and how much I didn't want to look like a total rookie.

Fortunately, my satellite radio provided just the right soundtrack for all those concerns playing out in my mind. As my thoughts shifted, so did the channels, bouncing from fifties and sixties music to Outlaw Country.

More than anything, I kept thinking how incredible it was that Jeff and I were going racing. It had been twenty-three years—a long time.

I arrived in Indianapolis Wednesday night. Early Thursday morning I unloaded all our stuff, got our team acclimated, and took the car through inspection. It was awesome seeing it stickered with the number No. 24, graciously loaned to us by Porsche Carrera Cup driver Adam Adelson, who normally has No. 24 in the Porsche Carrera Cup race series. A picture with Jeff was all he wanted in exchange.

Jeff arrived later on Thursday, in time for us to have dinner together. Those are always so much fun. Laughing over stories only he and I know about.

Friday saw an endless parade of people pouring through the garage area to see us. Other drivers would introduce themselves, get a picture with Jeff, and talk about what an honor it was to race with him.

One of the cooler guys who stopped in to hang for a bit was John Oates of Hall & Oates. That caused quite a stir for a while.

Unlike the grueling, hectic, and pressure-filled days when we raced NASCAR at Indy, we were more relaxed. In many ways, Jeff saw this as a way to say "Thank you" to the fans who turned out to see him. He was very Richard Petty–like with everyone. He was talkative, took pictures, signed every autograph.

We started practicing Friday. I thought the car performed well. There aren't many adjustments you can make with those cars, so he kept driving and we kept learning.

We were on the road course and one basic thing we had to learn was how to get on and off the track without collecting rubber on the tires. We just couldn't get it off the Porsche tires the way you can with a NASCAR Cup car.

Based on the way it felt, Jeff thought there was something wrong with the car initially. At one point he thought he had a flat. But it was just the rubber build up on the tires. Like threading a needle, he had to carefully find a clear path for getting on and off the racetrack while avoiding what we call marbles, which are small pieces of rubber that come off the tires while racing. We missed part of the first practice just trying to figure all that out.

Jeff asked one of the younger Porsche drivers, Parker Thompson, to work with us, to provide him needed advice. Can you imagine being some twenty-one-year-old Porsche guy—you're the hot dog in the class—and *the* Jeff Gordon asks for help. I'll never forget watching Jeff sitting there like a student while this kid's critiquing his laps.

We started the second practice, but we weren't performing well. We were trying to properly analyze computer data and dial in the optimum tire pressure balance. We didn't totally figure it out for qualifying.

Consequently, we didn't qualify as well as we would have liked to.

But again, for us, this was more about enjoying the experience.

The weekend was split into two separate races, one on Saturday and one on Sunday. On Saturday, we finished twentieth. Not a great day but still productive.

We learned so much from that first race. At one point in the race, we were getting faster and Jeff radioed me, "I know you've been working hard on the car, buddy. But I'm telling you, a lot of this speed is just me figuring out the braking."

Unfortunately, it didn't pay off with a strong finish, but we knew we'd be better on Sunday.

In preparation for Sunday's race, Jeff' watched the in-car video from Saturday and analyzed the data from the onboard computer with his new driving coach, Porsche Carrera Cup champion driver Parker Thompson. Parker won the first race on Saturday, then crashed Sunday. Regardless, he went on to win the Carrera Cup North America 2022 season championship.

My role wasn't that of the typical Cup crew chief. There was no pit box for me to climb up on. I purposely kept the radio talk to a minimum. There was no need, really. When Jeff slowed down, I asked him about the car or reminded him about keeping the tires clean.

I used to talk to him about all kinds of things during a four-hour Cup race. But this race was only forty to forty-five minutes, and we had a great spotter in Steve Barkdoll, who'd learned all the rules.

Jeff's always been good at explaining the feel of a car, telling me just what he needed at certain track positions. At one point, he struggled a bit coming off the last right-hander to get on the straightaway.

"You know, I'm just not confident enough," he said. "I don't know if it's me or the car. I just know if I gamble and lose, I'm gonna take a big hit."

As I was listening, I couldn't help but feel nostalgic.

Hearing the precision in his description reminded me of how good Jeff was, and still is. Mentally, he was as sharp with his feedback as ever. Jeff hadn't had enough time in the car to trust how far he could push it.

But he was still talking to me as calm as if he were in the TV booth—while whipping the Porsche around the course at 150 miles per hour. Even though I couldn't do anything to help him with this car, I always enjoyed hearing the way he described the things he was feeling in the car. When we were winning races and championships together, it was his explicit descriptions that helped us dial in the exact remedy to make our cars perform better.

Yeah, he's still got it.

Race number two on Sunday proved to be a more successful run.

Jeff just missed a top-ten class finish and placed sixteenth overall. Not bad given his lack of experience in the Porsche Carrera Cup series, going against a field of thirty-five other competitors, and not racing competitively for seven years.

I've often tried to explain just how extraordinary Jeff was to work with. Roger Penske said it well. "The best drivers look out a much bigger windshield."

Like Jeff, that metaphor applies to the greats in other sports. Michael Jordon. Tom Brady. Tiger Woods. I could go on. Their sense of vision—their sense of timing—is different than ours. They just seem to see so much more.

It was exciting to experience that again after all these years. I'm not saying I'd want to return to doing it forty times a year, but I wouldn't mind it occasionally. I'm embarrassed to admit it, but in the back of my mind, I went into this thinking we stood a chance of winning.

I can't help it. I just thought somehow, we'd find a way to pull it off.

I know it wasn't realistic. Those cars are all so equal. Plus, we were racing against younger superstar guys from all over the world.

Maybe our chances would have improved if it had been an endurance race, but this was a sprint race with no pit stops. No real strategy. Still, in my imagination, there's forever this little guy in a rainbow fire suit who's going to somehow, some way, figure out how to win.

Maybe if we could have raced one more day, we'd have run top ten.

I didn't know how long it would take but I just knew we would get better every time we raced. There's no doubt in my mind. If Jeff and I halted everything else going on and just ran that series, we'd be winning some of those races. I might be eighty and Jeff sixty-five by then, but we'd still be victorious.

———

In some respects, racing that weekend reminded me of the start of our careers. Having no experience. Borrowing stuff.

After Sunday's race we went back to the bus. Jeff and the guys had a beer or two. I packed up my stuff in my motor coach and headed out.

As I started to go, Jeff said, "Man, I'm so impressed with you." I waited for him to say something about how I did a great job with the Porsche.

Instead, with a hint of genuine amazement in his voice, he added, "You pack up all your own stuff and now you're gonna drive it back yourself? That's impressive."

I thought, "Dude, I built you race cars that went two hundred miles an hour and you're impressed I can handle this bus?" To this day, he can crack me up. We shook hands, and after the standard "bro hug" and "I love you, man," I got in the motor coach and hit the highway.

As I was driving home, I thought about what an awesome experience it was for Jeff and me to do what we love and have fun doing together. While we know we'll do something like it again, neither of us wants to do it more than a few times a year. We don't want to spoil the magic.

In the end, that weekend at Indy was about being back together with people we really enjoyed, doing something we really enjoyed.

INDEX